We Gambled Everything

We Gambled Everything
The Life and Times of an Oilman

Arne Nielsen

Foreword by *Peter C. Newman*

 THE UNIVERSITY
of ALBERTA PRESS

Published by

The University of Alberta Press
Ring House 2
Edmonton, Alberta, Canada T6G 2E1
www.uap.ualberta.ca

Copyright © 2012 Arne Nielsen
Foreword copyright © 2012 Peter C. Newman

Library and Archives Canada Cataloguing in Publication

Nielsen, Arne, 1925-
    We gambled everything : the life and times
of an oilman / Arne Nielsen ; foreword by Peter C. Newman.

Includes index.
Issued also in electronic formats.
ISBN 978-0-88864-598-2

    1. Nielsen, Arne, 1925–. 2. Petroleum industry and trade—
Employees—Canada—Biography. 3. Gas industry—Employees—
Canada—Biography. 4. Businesspeople—Canada—Biography.
5. Petroleum industry and trade—Canada—History. 6. Gas
industry—Canada—History. 7. Canada—Economic conditions—
20th century. I. Title.

HD9574.C32N54 2012   338.092   C2012-902672-7

First edition, first printing, 2012.
Printed and bound in Canada by Houghton Boston Printers, Saskatoon, Saskatchewan.
Copyediting by Meaghan Craven.
Proofreading by Kirsten Craven.
Maps by Wendy Johnson.
Indexing by Adrian Mather.

The University of Alberta Press is committed to protecting our natural environment. As part of our efforts, this book is printed on Enviro Paper: it contains 100% post-consumer recycled fibres and is acid- and chlorine-free.

The University of Alberta Press gratefully acknowledges the support received for its publishing program from The Canada Council for the Arts. The University of Alberta Press also gratefully acknowledges the financial support of the Government of Canada through the Canada Book Fund (CBF) and the Government of Alberta through the Alberta Multimedia Development Fund (AMDF) for its publishing activities.

Canada Council   Conseil des Arts
for the Arts   du Canada

**Government
of Alberta** ■

To my wife Valerie, who instigated this book.
Without her help and encouragement, this
book would never have become a reality.

CONTENTS

Foreword

How Arne Nielsen Made His Own Luck

Peter C. Newman

THERE ARE NUMEROUS BIOGRAPHIES, memoirs and autobiographies of senior Canadian oil and gas personalities and one or two more are published each year. They form part of the broader Canadian business literature that has recorded and preserved a plane of our common life that is as much a part of our lifeblood as politics. If, however, you are expecting just another corporate life story when you pick up this book, you will be disappointed. Arne Nielsen's memoir on his life of geological, corporate and personal discovery is not a conventional business biography. It contains no plea bargaining or self-justification. This is not a hymn of self-praise. The Arne Nielsen in this book is the modest unassuming man who scores of Canadians know without knowing the full extent of his rich life and astonishing accomplishments.

In a career of six decades, Arne mastered an impressive list of skills in geology, corporate management, corporate governance and politics, but he never learned to be self-serving. One of his final achievements in a long and fruitful life is to have learned to write a book. Drafting this manuscript by hand and in many hours of reflection and dictation, Arne achieved the degree of detachment and perspective necessary for the story of the man and his times to override the litany of bragging rights that another in his position might have produced.

Arne and I are just four years apart in age. I met him for the first time a quarter of a century ago. His remarkable career was reaching its zenith as the president of Canadian Superior Oil, the Canadian Petroleum Association's point man on the National Energy Program and a much-sought-after corporate director, and I was preparing the second volume of my series of studies on the anatomy of the Canadian establishment (published in 1980).

I believe I did a good day's work in that book when I described Arne at what it turns out was just past the midpoint of his working life. The Canadian oil patch had just reached its apogee as the new powerhouse in the Canadian economy. It was also in the fight of its life over the debilitating provisions of the National Energy Program. It was a creative turbulent time in Calgary, and Arne was at the pinnacle of his influence. Here is some of what I wrote of him:

> If Calgary cleaves to any faith, it is to the notion that each individual should live by the illumination of his own inner light. Nothing much is sacrosanct here. There is no place to hide under the bright mid-day sun, shining almost at right angles on the mirrored walls of the new office towers...
>
> An establishment certainly exists in the Oil Patch but its members exercise their authority with the laid-back wisdom of big-league play-ers who are beginning to feel the burgeoning self-confidence of being lords of the technology of the hour and owners of the natural resour-ces that will determine the country's economic well-being...
>
> Alone among the interchangeable honchos who head the multi-national oil companies, Arne Nielsen is universally accepted as a big hitter off his own bat. It's partly because he discovered a major oil field (Pembina No. 1), partly because he has extended his personal authority through influential directorships (TD Bank, Excelsior Life, Rockwell International), and partly because his brain was officially certified as brimming with oil secret (in a famous lawsuit described in the present book)...
>
> But the main reasons for Nielsen's recognition and acceptance are his background and his manner. He represents grassroots Alberta-on-the-hoof...
>
> Nielsen is a self-confessed work addict who relaxes by reading history and always has time to help soothe his peers' psyches...he is something of a father figure to young geologists just entering the game...

Thirty years on from writing my cameo of Arne Nielsen, I wouldn't change a word of it, except to add—having read the pages of his beguiling memoir that follow—that the defining hallmark of his personal and professional life was that he always made his own luck. This made for a fortunate man who led a fortunate life.

His luck was inaugurated by the fact that his Danish father immigrated with his family to Standard, Alberta, so that he was in a position to follow his career in country less explored than the US, where the Nielsens had originally landed. He grew up so isolated on his father's farm that young Arne didn't visit Calgary until he was fourteen, when his mother bought him his first suit for his confirmation in the Lutheran Church. He joined the Canadian Army's Tank Corps during the Second World War, and when he was demobilized was lucky again. His service qualified him for free tuition for two degrees in geology from the University of Alberta, a BSc and an MSc. His great sense of timing held because he came to maturity just as the oil patch was moving into its most exciting phase: the years before most of the major discoveries that followed Imperial Oil's dramatic strike at Leduc in 1947. He was equally fortunate in his choice of summer jobs, joining a Geological Survey of Canada crew on the subarctic Barren Lands and in the Rocky Mountain foothills, north of the Athabasca River. Invited back as the unit's second-in-command, he opted instead to join Imperial Oil for the summer of 1949 to follow up the fabled Leduc oil discovery, which stood him in good stead when he switched to one of its global rivals, Socony-Vacuum, later (and more sensibly) rebranded as Mobil Oil Canada, whose parent Mobil Oil Corp. qualified as one of the Seven Sisters.

"It was more than a job; more than a career; it was a way of life," he recalled, stressing the point that his ambition was never measured in dollars. He is not boasting, when he writes, "My generation discovered not only abundant petrol-eum wealth in the rocks of western Canada, but something about our identity as a nation and a people, and something about the greatness of our future because of the quality of our past."

His next stroke of good fortune was being asked to set up a new Mobil branch office in Edmonton, where he had the freedom to follow his instincts from a place much closer to most of the exploration action, especially around the area's Devonian reef structures. His discovery well (Pembina No. 1) was drilled in the spring of 1953 near the tiny hamlet of Drayton Valley (population 75) in the wild country southwest of Edmonton. Mobil executives in Calgary had initially objected to Arne's request for $30,000 for building a forest road to bring in heavy-duty well-testing equipment for the drilling site.

But his luck held. Nielsen's head office mentor, Dr. Joe Spivak, overruled them, the well was fracked and tested. Just like Arne had predicted, oil flowed to the surface. It wasn't a gusher and its initial modest flow of oil masked its significance. Although he didn't know its magnitude at the time, Arne's discovery turned out to be the key to the biggest conventional oilfield in Canadian history and one of the three largest in North America measured by the size of its production and reserves. In terms of its aerial extent, it proved to be one of the largest in the world.

Petroleum geologists live to strike oil, but only a few find elephants. Having found an elephant at the age of twenty-seven, Nielsen moved up through Mobil's hierarchy until he was appointed to head its Canadian operation, a position he held for thirteen years. More luck followed: he led the Mobil team that discovered natural gas at Sable Island offshore Nova Scotia. However, his career path had taken him where he didn't really want to be: his company's chief bureaucrat continually ensnarled in disputes with head office in New York.

He switched incarnations to become chairman and CEO of Canadian Superior Oil, which he built from a modest Canadian player into a major one. Immediately, his luck seemed to turn: Mobil sued him for walking off with their secrets in his head. However, in a trial that humiliated the big multinational, Nielsen won vindication plus legal costs.

Canadian Superior became his base for the counter-attack he led on behalf of the Canadian Petroleum Association against the National Energy Program. His luck held because the politician he persuaded to accept his Alternative Energy Program was British Columbia MP Pat Carney, who became Brian Mulroney's first energy minister when the Progressive Conservative Party was elected to form the government in 1984.

Then the first really bad news of his career broke. Mobil Oil acquired Superior Oil and Arne figured his luck had run out. Surely the company that had sued him for quitting would never rehire him. He was wrong: he became the dual head of Canadian Superior and Mobil Oil Canada. He arrived back at Mobil just in time to participate in the development of the offshore Hibernia field and natural gas discoveries in the Mackenzie River Delta.

Nielsen "retired" four times, but Lady Luck never left his side. He was snapped up each time to be the active chief executive of four successive, emerging, mid-size, independent exploration and production firms, extending his run. He still goes into the office five days a week when he's in Calgary.

The senior players of Alberta's oil patch rightly pride themselves in being the best equipped technologically for the twenty-first century, but their political power base remains far from secure. They have always acted more like pioneers than pilgrims, tentative in their claims to their province's future, because too often at strategic moments Ottawa—or some other alien power—has moved in and imposed its own priorities. The sudden confiscatory National Energy Program (NEP) of October 1980 ought to have faded into bitter memory by now. But for Nielsen and most of the oil patch big hitters, it might have happened only yesterday. As he reiterates, "Oil in Canada was then selling for $14 a barrel but on the global market, it fetched $28." An enormous reservoir of anger and resentment is captured in that chronology of price changes that penalized oil companies and producing provinces without a commensurate benefit to the Canadian economy. Thousands of jobs were put at risk, and the drilling rigs started to head south to find work in the United States.

"Ironically, the NEP was more damaging to smaller Canadian independents than the big American-owned subsidiaries. It didn't escape the notice of the oil industry that the Liberals never attempted to 'Canadianize' any other sector— for instance, the big American automobile makers in southern Ontario. It takes a high level of political maturity to not become bitter about that kind of hypocrisy and regional prejudice, and frankly I'm not sure we in the oil and gas industry have that maturity. It is one more reason why Albertans—at least for another generation or two—are unlikely ever to trust either the Liberal Party or a Liberal government."

Arne is a good Canadian, but he's a better Albertan. He would agree that it's not really fair to accuse central Canadians of having forgotten the history of the western plains, since they never knew it in the first place. Which, by the way, will be the most important legacy of this book: it's nothing less than a lively history of the twentieth-century oil patch, as shrewdly observed by one of its most successful and colourful animators.

Nielsen, and the other serious oil patch players over the past half-dozen decades, started with the proposition that the Canadian West was never a child of Canada's eastern provinces—and thus ought not to be patronized. The westward immigration that populated the plains was directly related, first to the expansion of the Hudson's Bay Company and later to construction of the Canadian Pacific Railway. Those corporate dynamics were independent of the political pressures that gave birth to Quebec and Ontario as offspring of the Empire of the St. Lawrence.

Such historical conjecture may seem irrelevant in the present digital world, but Albertans like Arne Nielsen want one thing understood, plain and simple: they are not—and have never been—anybody's country cousins. That's partly what this book is about: the quest by one man, arguably the most successful among his peers, to persuade those Canadians unfortunate enough to live outside Wild Rose Country that Alberta is our most valuable entry point into the twenty-first century.

There remains in the province a ferocious craving to be heard—and to be understood.

Most members of central Canada's political elite have yet to accept the notion that westerners are anything more than bubbas from the boondocks, whose lives are consumed in envy of the privileged few plugged into Actions Central in the downtowns of Toronto, Ottawa and Montreal. That brand of elitism has never appealed to Albertans of Arne's generation, but gaining official recognition of their distinctiveness does. What they want—and what they deserve—is greater control over their own destiny. At the moment, they still feel abandoned by a country that continues to mobilize its best and brightest to satisfy Quebec's demands without ever realizing that another larger chunk of valuable geography has aspirations that are just as urgent and equally valid.

Arne Nielsen says it best, when he returns to the mysteries of Mother Nature to sum up his life. "When I made the Pembina discovery," he vividly recalls, "I probed a stratigraphic trap built by the forces of Earth a hundred million years before the present day. Perhaps that's why at this stage in my life, I can look into the future, long after the end of my lifespan, with a certain degree of equanimity. My lifetime of discovery, founded as it has been on the fundamental principles of geology, reassures me that Earth and all that is on it have a future—not quite the future that environmentalists seem to fear, and a future that is in a separate category from the one mapped out by theologians—but a future that can be counted on."

I was assisted in completing this book by the editorial guidance of Frank Dabbs, whose experience enabled me to judge what should be included and how to tell my story effectively.

This book is built around the handful of major events in the oil industry in which I have been involved, and which turned out to be pivotal moments in Canada's economic history. The story of my career cuts across six decades and stretches from the Atlantic to the Pacific to the Arctic Ocean and Beaufort Sea.. In pursuit of the discoveries of my lifetime, I have huddled miserably in a rain-soaked tent on the Barren Lands, walked the sands of Sable Island, worked at a desk in the well-appointed New York offices of a multinational oil company, and dined with politicians from Ottawa to Peking. This is the sixtieth uninter-rupted year in which I go to the office every morning, still drawn by the promise of discovery.

Many of the young men and women in the oil industry today, including those in senior management, have had little contact with the events that shaped the framework in which they work. Except for a hazy outline, more myth than history, they know nothing about how the discoveries and decisions were made in the years after the Second World War, and how those discoveries and decisions brought about the great outpouring of wealth and resources in Canada that we continue to enjoy now. What they do know is shrouded in exag-geration and lacks the detail and the perspective needed for understanding. Yet they have a hunger to know the past of the Canadian oil and gas industry. They face the challenges we did, seek the same rewards and find the same satisfac-tions. They understand as we understood that the life of discovery to be found in the oil patch is more than a job and more than a career; it is a way of life.

The Canadian oil and gas industry owes an incalculable debt to the genera-tion of Canadian geologists, geophysicists, engineers, roughnecks, cat skinners, executives and managers, who were raised on the farms, in the mining camps, logging and railway towns, and emerging cities of the first half of the twenti-eth century. Scarcely a week goes by without my reading the obituary of some-one who I worked with and respected. Already the twentieth century is slipping away from memory, with it the colleagues and friends of a lifetime in oil and gas exploration and development during its golden decades. It is not a moment too soon for me to set down the record of one life lived during those years.

Most important for me is to tell this story to my now eight children. From time to time, several of them have said it would be a good idea if I told them more of my experiences. They want to know more about my roots and theirs. They know something of the events of my life but not enough, especially about the early part of it. They knew very little about their grandfather and about the life of their grandfather's family who grew up on that farm on the rolling prairies near the Danish Lutheran community of Standard, Alberta. Reading this story will tell them something of their roots and will help them understand the part of their inheritance that is not measured in dollars.

Now I have the opportunity and the insistence of my family to write this memoir, I can look across my own lifetime with the sense of perspective and, hopefully, the wisdom, that comes only in the harvest years of a career. This is, I hope, a record—more important for the significance of the events and milestones it describes than for the life of one man who was privileged to be a player in these great years and great events. My generation discovered not only the abundant petroleum wealth of western Canada but also something about our identity as a nation and of the greatness of our future because of the quality of our past.

Acknowledgements

I BEGIN THESE ACKNOWLEDGEMENTS by remembering, with gratitude, the start in life I received as a son in the home of Aksel and Marie Nielsen. The things my parents valued and encouraged—reading, education, hard work, the importance of family and community—contributed indelibly to my success.

Books, like geological discoveries, are a gamble and a team effort. My wife Valerie, to whom I have dedicated this book, not only persuaded me to tell my story, she also introduced me to Frank Dabbs, who in turn introduced me to the writing of a book. Valerie organized the countless details involved in completing the manuscript, and cared for many personal details of life as the writing progressed.

Judy Britton transcribed my oral recollections. Doug Cass and the staff at the Glenbow Archives provided facilities that allowed for fact checking. The Calgary Public Library's collection of newspapers on microfilm was also an invaluable resource in the project's early stages.

Linda Cameron and her team at the University of Alberta Press did a fine job preparing this manuscript for publication and were very enjoyable to work with. Dave Fitzpatrick endorsed this project at the outset and encouraged its development. Peter C. Newman contributed a very gracious foreword. Shirley Phillips assisted in organizing and reproducing the photography. I would also like to thank Mary Blue for her help in editing the book.

I relied on the writing of others to supplement my memory. Among these was Jens Rasmussen's book, *From Danaview to Standard* (1979). I benefitted from corporate accounts of Mobil Oil and Socony-Vacuum history, including *The Flying Red Horse* magazine. I consulted Imperial Oil's records of the famous 1947 Leduc discovery. Media accounts of the Pembina discovery and its impact were very helpful, particularly those published in the *Daily Oil Bulletin*, the *Calgary Herald* and the *Toronto Star*.

The 1968 Watkins Report on *Foreign Ownership and the Structure of Canadian Industry*, which marked my initiation into oil and gas politics, is still unpleasant but enlightening reading. Chinese government publications on their oil industry, such as *Taching: Red Banner on China's Industrial Front* (1972), are idealist propaganda but were also very helpful. Corporate publications from Superior Oil and Canadian Superior supplied important details, especially concerning the story of the Keck family. I relied on the Canadian Petroleum Association's files for information on the National Energy Program, as well as our Alternative Energy Program. Regarding my legal battles with Mobil Oil in 1978, I referred to articles published in *Time* and *Oilweek* magazines, as well as Peter Foster's accounts.

Abbreviations

AAPG	American Association of Petroleum Geologists
AOSTRA	Alberta Oil Sands Technology Research Authority
API	American Petroleum Institute
APMC	Alberta Petroleum Marketing Commission
CAODC	Canadian Association of Oilwell Drilling Contractors
CAPP	Canadian Association of Petroleum Producers
CAUC	Canadian Army University Course
CCF	Co-operative Commonwealth Federation
CIDA	Canadian International Development Agency
CPA	Canadian Petroleum Association
FIRA	Foreign Investment Review Agency
GSC	Geological Survey of Canada
IPAC	Independent Petroleum Association of Canada
NACOP	National Advisory Committee on Petroleum
NEP	National Energy Program
NFA	Northern Foothills Agreement
NRMA	*National Resources Mobilization Act*
OPEC	Organization of Petroleum Exporting Countries
PGRT	Petroleum and Gas Revenue Tax
PIP	Petroleum Incentive Program

PART ONE

Early Years

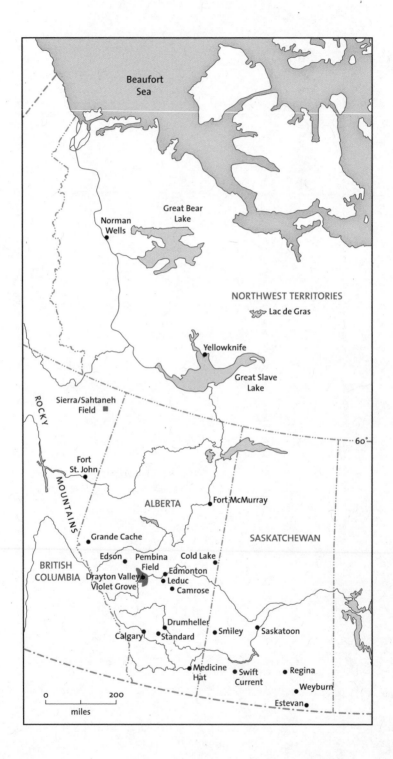

1

My Parents

I WAS BORN on July 7, 1925, on my parents' farm in the immigrant Danish community of Standard, Alberta, approximately eighty kilometres east of Calgary. I was the youngest son of Aksel Harold and Marie Catherine Nielsen and the second-youngest of their seven children—three boys and four girls. My father and mother were childhood sweethearts who had grown up in an agrarian community on the island of Funen, which lies in the middle of Denmark between the Jutland Peninsula and the larger island of Zealand on which is the capital, Copenhagen. The people of Funen were basically dairy farmers. They also raised cattle, pigs and a certain amount of corn to feed the stock. On the whole, however, Funen was a dairy-farm community.

Other Danes looked down their noses at Funen and its people because they were humble rural folk. They called the residents of the island "the Fynsk"— which was not a complimentary designation. The manner in which other Danes treated the people of Funen always bothered my parents because the great Hans Christian Andersen was born in Odense, the capital of Funen, and the people of the island were very proud of him. Andersen's most famous work *Eventyr* (*Fairy Tales*), first published in 1835, was translated into many languages, distributed around the world and had become popular in Canada by the time my parents immigrated to Alberta.

My father, born in 1890, was raised by his grandparents and never knew his father or mother. Aksel and Marie Catherine, as well as their families, were members of the devout Danish Lutheran Church community in Funen, and their faith placed a great deal of emphasis on Bible-reading, prayer and the history of the Protestant and Lutheran Church in Europe since the Reformation. Funen gave my parents two very important legacies that they took with them to North America: first, the strong religious faith that they practiced and shared with the other devout Lutherans in Funen and subsequently in Standard, Alberta; and second, a desire for a good education for their children as they had been deprived of one.

My parents went to school together in the small town of Kjong. They could not afford to continue their studies for long because they had to get out and work to support themselves. When he left school, my father became a farm labourer. He saw no future for himself in Denmark, but his original immigration dream didn't involve Canada. At that time the United States was the great country over the water, and everyone aspired to go there. All Europeans dreamed of going to the United States, and the Danes were no different.

He knew some people from Kjong who had established farms at a place called Elk Horn in Iowa, raising corn. In time, Elk Horn became the largest Danish community in the United States and still commemorates its traditional Danish settler culture. When he had the opportunity, that's where my father went. In Iowa, he resumed work as a hired farm hand, preparing himself for the opportunity to improve his prospects. From the time he left Funen, he and my mother stayed in touch by writing letters regularly to one another.

A leader of that Danish community in Elk Horn, Jens Rasmussen, wrote a brief history (*From Danaview to Standard*) about the origins of Standard, Alberta, which was established at about the same time Aksel Nielsen arrived in Iowa. Rasmussen noted, "Canada had begun to attract attention as a land of promise for ambitious farmers." The reason for this was a publicity campaign by the Canadian Pacific Railway (CPR). It had received a 25-million-acre land grant in western Canada from the federal government as part of the compensation for building Canada's first transcontinental railway. It wanted to dispose of the land to farmers who would then become a major customer group for its railway freight services, shipping their grain east and receiving farm equipment and supplies shipped west. In 1881 the CPR began a program of selling land to immigrants for farm development, which would eventually serve to establish eight hundred prairie towns with groups of farmers. The railway's land disposition was given a boost by federal national policy for the development of the northwest hinterland, and by Ottawa's own campaign to recruit immigrants from Europe after the turn of the century.

The CPR particularly liked the Scandinavians because this hardworking people had proven their worth as farmers across the American West from the Dakota States to Washington. "The Danish people," Rasmussen recalled, came to North America seeking "how to live a richer, fuller life." While they had prospered in Iowa, some were still restless and felt drawn to Canada. The Danes were interested in the CPR's promotion of opportunities in the new country. They hoped to find there, "a sufficient area of fertile virgin soil available not only to build our own homes and rear our own families, but where there would be ample room for later comers in numbers sufficient to establish and maintain a Lutheran church and secure for our children and youth the benefits of a Christian education." It was Rasmussen's plan to be the leader of an enterprise to establish a large Danish colony in Alberta and make some money as a land broker, purchasing tracts of land and reselling them to his fellow immigrants.

In 1908 Rasmussen travelled to Alberta for the first time and put a deposit on land there near the province's founding Danish colony at Dickson. He made a second trip to Canada in March 1909 accompanied by other Danes from Elk Horn interested in relocation. On the train from Iowa, they met a CPR land agent who told the Rasmussen party about "a tract of land some twenty miles [thirty-three kilometres] north of Blackfoot Crossing [now Gleichen] in Alberta which he recommended" for a Danish colony. The group disembarked at the Blackfoot Crossing CPR railway stop and travelled north by wagon to inspect the land. They visited with farmers in the area who spoke glowingly of the prospects for agriculture in the region. They next went to CPR headquarters in Calgary and arranged a 17,000-acre reservation—26.5 sections, or nearly a full township. The CPR agreed to put a rail spur into the new colony by 1911.

The CPR's terms for purchasing land made it possible for a settler to set up a farm with only a small amount of money, so long as he was willing to work. The price of land ranged from $11 to $15 per acre, less expensive than in the United States. The railway gave settlers twenty years to pay for the land and charged an interest rate of 6 per cent per year, which was very reasonable for the time. As well, they loaned up to $1,000 to purchase sheep and livestock, also at a reasonable interest rate. The railway also arranged for the drilling of water wells—which were of depths from 20 to 120 feet—on each farm if no surface springs were to be found. It provided plans and construction supplies for barns and houses: small homes of twenty-eight by thirty-two feet, with four or five rooms.

The Danish men from Elk Horn were especially impressed with the taxation system. There was a land tax of $2.25 per quarter section, considered modest by the prospective settlers. The most expensive levy was the school tax of about $10 per hundred acres. Paying a school tax was not thought to be onerous because these men valued school as the most precious institution next to the Church. In return for the school tax, they found that the government organized school administration and provided teachers that were certified and regularly inspected. The government provided books and some supplies; the families of young students were only responsible for small expenses, such as scribblers, pens and pencils.

And that was it. No other taxes were imposed. In the United States, farmers paid taxes on property improvements. They paid taxes on machinery and live-stock. They paid taxes on their personal effects. Not in Canada. Not in Alberta.

Other expenses in Canada were also considered to be affordable. Fence posts were twelve cents apiece; lumber cost from $18 to $30 per one thousand board feet. Coal for the winter was plentiful in the area at a cost of $2.50 to $3.00 per ton. The newly created province of Alberta, as we might say today, was very competitive as it bid for settlers.

In a promotional booklet on the Standard Colony circulated in 1915, one set-tler testified that, "a man with $2,000 of capital who will exercise the same care and economy that all successful early settlers of another country have to exercise is bound to progress here."

After acquiring the CPR reservation of land at what would become Standard, Jens Rasmussen returned to Elk Horn, formed a three-member colonization committee and advertised for people to join train excursions to visit Alberta. The first, composed of thirty people accommodated in a sleeper car, went in the autumn of 1909. A total of 5,000 acres were taken up by these men. The railway excursions continued on a monthly basis. Aksel joined one in the spring of 1910. He was twenty years old. "You'd better not go up there, the mosquitoes and flies are as big as horses' heads," an American farmer back in Iowa said. However, the reports that Aksel had heard indicated something much different.

In Iowa, Aksel Nielsen was strictly a labourer for other farmers. He had been just that in Funen and wanted to have his own land and develop his own farm. He would have had to work for many more years in Iowa to buy a farm, and might never have been able to afford one. He might have spent his life as a labourer or been forced to move to a city for an industrial job. Alberta was a different story.

The area the Danes were planning to settle boasted good land and ideal climate for both health and agriculture. In the summer it had sunny warm days, cool evenings and only eighteen or nineteen inches of rain, which was considered moderate and therefore adequate. The winters were not as severe as they were in Iowa. Most winters had only a few days with temperatures below zero on the Fahrenheit scale. There were light snowfalls and weeks of warm weather during which the snow disappeared. In winter, regular chinook winds occurred. The soil was a productive loam with good clay subsoil. They could grow crops of wheat, oats, barley and flax, gardens of potatoes and vegetables. There would be forage crops for cattle, grazing land for the summer.

When the excursion train arrived at Blackfoot Crossing, Aksel climbed into a buggy and set off for the emerging town site, which was being cleared at the same time the rail line from Blackfoot Crossing was under construction. He stayed for the summer to help with the work. He lived in a ten-by-twelve-foot sidewall tent with six other men. There were no women in the party, and the men weren't very skilled in the kitchen. They subsisted mainly on coffee and potatoes. The highlight of the diet was the game they hunted on the prairie. The drudgery of work was relieved on alternate Sundays when the men scattered across the district gathered at the town site in the afternoon to hear a reading from a Danish book of sermons, sing hymns, pray and socialize over coffee.

During that summer, the small crew built a barn for the horses, with a room for the men to live in during the coming winter. They hauled two tons of coal per day to stockpile for the winter. Water also had to be hauled daily to supply the crew with its needs. The land was to be cleared with steam plows. In addition to those provided by two contractors, Jens Rasmussen had a steam plow shipped to Blackfoot Crossing. It took two weeks to drive it across the muddy prairie to the town site because it bogged down continually and had to be hauled out by the horses. When the plow arrived, the men used it to break 1,100 acres of prairie before the end of the season.

There were dangers and setbacks. A horrendous prairie fire that burned across thousands of acres and threatened the town site that summer also destroyed feed that was being gathered and stocked for the winter. This was followed by an early frost that hit the community's first gardens. By the end of the autumn, however, the tiny community was ready for the first migration of families from Iowa, which took place in the spring of 1911, the year the railway spur was completed.

Aksel Nielsen, circa 1910.

Marie Catherine Nielsen, taken in Denmark circa 1910.

A CPR map of the area made in 1910 clearly shows that the community was originally called Danaview. However, that name was not to last because a town northeast of Saskatoon bore the same name. With the stroke of a pen, a CPR official in far-away Montreal renamed the settlement Standard, for the Royal Danish Standard, the flag bearing the coat of arms of the Danish royalty.

At the end of the work season in 1910, Aksel returned to Iowa where he worked for nearly two years to save the money he needed to buy his own farm in Alberta. He returned to Danaview, now Standard, in 1912 and acquired a half section of land and had a CPR house built on his property. A barn and a chicken house soon followed. The summers of 1912 and 1913 were years of good crops and good earnings. In the winter of 1913–14 Aksel travelled to Denmark to bring Marie Catherine back to Canada.

My mother had a terrible voyage because she got horrendously seasick on the boat coming over. It was about a five- or six-day trip and she was deathly ill the whole time. She believed she was going to die. When they arrived in Halifax, they disembarked and continued across Canada by train. They were married at Blackfoot Crossing on April 3, 1914, and went by horse and wagon to Standard. My mother was the eldest child in her family, and after she was established in Standard, her two younger brothers, Ejvind and Peter, followed her to Canada. Peter became a farmer near Standard and Ejvind obtained employment in Calgary; they both lived the rest of their lives in Alberta.

Aksel and Marie established themselves on the new farm in their four-room clapboard house. They had only basic furniture and ate their first meals on a wooden trunk. My father grew wheat and established a cattle-feeding operation in which he cared for other men's cattle in the winter, a hard physical job that raised cash. He kept chickens and raised pigs. He had his own dairy cattle for the family's milk, cream, butter and yogurt. My mother began what would become the best garden in the district. It became a life's work for her, laid out very neatly and attractively. It featured plums, cherries and apples, as well as vegetables, potatoes and flowers.

The community also thrived. In less than ten years it outgrew the original 17,000-acre reservation, taking up another twenty sections. My parents and their friends built the colony around the congregation of the Nazareth Danish Evangelical Church, founded on May 14, 1911, with fifty-one charter members. The church was the community centre, but the community members built the school first. They built a wooden schoolhouse in 1912, then, when they had enough money saved, they built Standard's first church in 1917. Prior to the church, they met on Sunday in homes and barns.

My parents and their friends were peaceful Danish farmers creating a new community on land with an ancient history that included legendary battles between the Blackfoot and the Cree. It was land not explored by Europeans until Captain John Palliser passed through in 1859, two centuries after Europeans began to settle on Canada's Atlantic coast. It was a land made habitable for modern settlement only in 1883 by the coming of the Canadian Pacific Railway. Prior to that, it had been open-range cattle country. The market for beef was local and in the United States, and there were legendary cattle drives each year, first to Texas, then to the rail head in Montana. The cowboy era lasted barely two decades and was cut short by terrible winters of cattle-killing blizzards at about the time my father paid the area his first visit.

By the time my parents had established their farm, the town site had two stores, a rail line, a grain elevator, a doctor of limited ability, two coal mines, a school, a church and even a little park beside a pond that the CPR created by damming up a little creek to supply water for their steam engines.

The population of the little Danish colony that became Standard was about 250 souls when I was born. Today, more than eight decades later, it is about the same.

My parents lived their entire lives on the farm. My mother died prematurely in 1954. My father was still working on the farm when he died in 1971 of old age, although by that time my brother, Gerhardt, had taken over running the operation. However, my father still wanted the final say. It amused me sometimes to listen to them argue. Gerhardt was younger and he had other ideas on lots of things, but my father said, "This is the way it's going to be," and that's the way it was.

He was eighty-two years old when he died, and I have outlived him. As I write this story, I am eighty-five.

2

Life on the Farm

MY FIRST MEMORIES of my home on my parents' farm were in the decade from 1925 to 1935. This was during the Dirty Thirties, the era of drought, dust storms and poverty on the Canadian prairies. As the years passed, the wind-blown sand slowly piled up in the caragana hedges that protected our home place. Farming was a major struggle in those years. The biggest problem was the lack of rain resulting in drought, which didn't let up from year to year. On top of the drought, there were invasions of grasshoppers, saw flies, army worms and gophers, all of which were a curse for the farmers. My brothers and I spent a good deal of time trapping gophers by various means in order to try and remove this pestilence from the farm. Vicious hailstorms, which could wipe out the crop in a matter of minutes, were also prevalent. It was difficult for the farmers to produce a living for the family.

In order of their birth, my older siblings were Ejvind, Esther, Ruth, Lillian and Gerhardt. Ejvind was born in 1915: three years after my father purchased our farm from the CPR and the year following his trip to Denmark to bring my mother to Canada. I was the second-youngest child in the family. My younger sister, Miriam, was a late child, born seven years after me. As of this writing, two girls—Ruth and Miriam—and one boy, me, remain.

Our farm at Standard, which was a mile-and-a-half south of the town, consisted of a four-room house, a chicken coup and a barn. The house had a

My parents with my eldest siblings, Ejvind and Esther, circa 1918.

kitchen, two bedrooms and a family room with a dinner table. It has always puzzled me how a house with two bedrooms could handle a family of nine. During the summer, the boys slept in the barn loft or a granary. The granaries were always painted red and looked just like small square houses, but there was nothing in them except wheat after harvest and sleeping boys before.

A family picture from 1936: me (far left), Esther, Mama, Miriam the "baby" (in front), Gerhardt and Papa.

During the winter, we boys could no longer sleep out; we all had to sleep in the house. The children shared two beds, and we slept in rows, alternating head and feet. In the evenings, my mother heated irons on the stove and wrapped them in flannel to warm the beds. We heated our home with a round coal stove that had an exhaust pipe that ensured the poisonous fumes didn't remain in the house. We put the coal in and used paper and wood to get it going, and we kept the fire going by shovelling more coal in. It was all very well for the founders of our little colony to boast in their recruitment literature that winters in Standard were relatively moderate due to chinooks, but we had blizzards and hard cold frosts, as well. When it was very cold outside, it was warm around the stove but miserably cold against the walls. The CPR farm houses didn't have insulation, and the cold came in through the windows and cracks.

My mother cooked on a coal range in the kitchen. We obtained our fuel from a coal mine just north of town, which had a seam about twelve feet thick of bituminous coal. Two families mined that coal and sold it to neighbours in the area. Years went by and the coal seam ran out. Then my dad had to get coal in Drumheller, a mining town some thirty-five miles northeast of our farm. He'd take a wagon and a team of horses and come back with a big load of coal and put it into a corner of the barn.

A painting of my childhood home in Standard, Alberta.

We had little money. My father struggled to make a living for us. Everything was hard work, but he was disciplined and he taught us discipline. Although my mother was a more laid-back person, she worked from before dawn until after dark to care for us. Nonetheless, my mother and father were contented and happy on the farm, in spite of all the trials and tribulations. We children shared that happiness and contentment and didn't think of how much better it might be if we were doing something else.

I believe my parents were the best parents in the community of Standard. My mother was short and stocky and an extremely hard-working woman. She took care of the house. She cooked. She worked in the garden; she planted most of the vegetables that we needed for our meals. She hoed the weeds. She picked her produce. She did the chores around the garden and chicken house. But she never did farm labour, such as pitching hay, because my father would not allow her to do that. As was the custom in North America at the time, my father did not want his wife to have to do field work, even though many European women would get out there and share that kind of work with their husbands.

My father ran the business end of the farm. It was not that he was a sharp businessman by any means, but he was the head of the family. My mother was much more articulate than he was when it came to writing and reading. She

My sister Ruth holds me on her lap in our garden in Standard, around 1926.

could write beautifully, fast and clearly. My dad was a very slow and precise
reader. They each had their pluses and minuses and had a good partnership.

In those days, cars and tractors were unknown to our family. My father was
an expert with horses and could handle them in great fashion. We used horses
for transportation and heavy farm work. When it came to machinery, he was
somewhat lacking in mechanical skills. He once owned a Model T, but it eventually disappeared from the scene, after it broke down, I think. After that, it was
horses and "lumber wagons" wherever we went. Unfortunately, my father's in-
ability to handle machinery was passed on to me. I have never been able to do
anything mechanical or build anything worthwhile—maybe just a birdhouse!

My father and mother told us many stories about their early years on the
farm. I remember stories of danger: of prairie wild fires and wild cattle on
the open range that were dangerous and had to be avoided; of blizzards when
my father tied himself to the house so he wouldn't get lost while going to
feed the cattle. We relived some of those moments. I remember going the mile-
and-a-half to school in the blizzards. Our sisters wrapped their faces in scarves
and we, their brothers, led them along.

Our parents were very proud of their Danish background and traditions. We
spoke only Danish in our home. Church services were conducted in Danish, and
we celebrated Christmas in the Danish tradition: with the big dinner and gifts
on Christmas Eve. My first family and I still celebrate in this manner; with my
second family, celebrations focus on Christmas Day.

When I started school, I could not speak a word of English. The schools had English teachers and all communication was in that language. In order to promote the English language, our teachers prohibited any Danish from being spoken on the school grounds. I still speak Danish today.

A central part of our community, and our home and lives, was the Danish Lutheran Church. The founders of our community, including my father, thought of our little colony as a congregation. My father and mother were devout Lutherans and we children were raised as Lutherans; strong Lutheran principles governed every area of our lives, and we were all christened and confirmed in the Lutheran Church. I still have my christening gown made head to toe of crocheted lace. Although we were poor, each of us had such a gown.

No member of our family was allowed to be involved in such sinful pursuits as smoking, drinking alcohol, dancing, going to the movies or playing cards. The only books we read were of a religious nature, although, as time progressed, I was permitted to read a few books by the western author Zane Grey. The church was the centre of our life, and we attended every Sunday unless someone was sick. My father did extra chores through the week so he wouldn't have to work on Sunday and could keep it as the Sabbath according to the commandment, "Remember the Sabbath Day, to keep it holy." So, we weren't allowed to do much on Sunday for a long time except go to church.

Not only did we go to the Sunday service but we also had to go to Sunday School. In fact my father was the Sunday-school superintendent for a long time. We also participated in church-organized young peoples' groups. There wasn't much to do for fun on those farms, and the church groups organized social events. One of the great events of the year was the Annual Sunday School Picnic, an event at which I tasted ice cream for the first time (at five cents a cone).

One of the things I liked about Sunday is that my mother always cooked a large, very special, Sunday dinner, and right after we got home from church we sat down to eat. The farmers had got into the custom of sharing Sunday dinner. On occasion, we would go to our different neighbours' houses for dinner, and they would come to our place. I found the church services in the Danish language most boring, and I would often go to sleep and wake up in time to go home for Sunday dinner.

At every meal that I remember at my parents' table, my father read from the Bible before we ate. My mother never read: that was the duty of the head of the household. I remember one time he read through the whole Book of Corinthians, a long "letter" in the New Testament written by St. Paul. I have

My favourite cow at the farm, circa 1940. She was a beauty!

never heard anything drier, although I know it is highly regarded by religious people.

I much preferred Exodus and Kings in the Old Testament, back when they were doing some fighting. They were rough guys and they killed each other off. You wonder how they got away with putting all that stuff in the Bible; I certainly found it most interesting to read. However, my father would never read that; it was always Paul's letter to the Colossians or some other group of people. It was stuff that was hard to understand, particularly when I was young. When I got older, I didn't really care if I understood it or not. My eldest brother, Ejvind, became a Lutheran pastor, a career he continued until his death. My eldest sister, Esther, was married to a Lutheran pastor of Danish background and resettled to Wisconsin.

The main product of our farm was wheat, but we also grew oats and hay to feed the horses and other livestock. We raised chickens and pigs for personal consumption. We also had beef cattle for our own use and my father and his neighbour handled the butchering, a skill they had learned in Denmark.

My father continued feeding other people's cattle over the winter to earn much-needed cash. Hay for the operation was cut and stacked in the summer and a shed built against the barn for our calves.

There were no fancy milking machines in those days with which to milk the few dairy cows we had; we had to do it the hard way. I would be out in the morning before breakfast, before I went to school, to milk several cows. We had our own manual separator to separate out the milk and the cream; my mother would make butter out of the cream. We were able to make all the cottage cheese and yogurt we needed.

Every year I'd take four days off school to dig potatoes. We dug them all out by hand and then they would go into a root cellar where, in the dark, they could last through the winter. We lived pretty well off the potatoes and peas and corn that we grew.

I was an avid baseball fan from a very early age, and the New York Yankees was my team. I was lucky I picked the right team because they won consistently year after year. I was able to time the potato-digging operation with my father so that it came at the same time as the World Series. I really only dug potatoes half the time, because the rest of the time I was attached by earphones to the crystal radio set listening to the Yankees' games. I am still an ardent Yankees fan, but for some reason they aren't doing as well these days.

When I was old enough to help in the fields, combines weren't yet available so we were still taking the crop off with harvesting machines. The wheat was cut and left in bundles in the field, and we had to stook it. That was work for the boys. My brother and I spent hours and hours putting up dozens and dozens of stooks—shaped like tipis or tripods—in the fields. Eventually the stooks were put into a big threshing machine and the wheat was removed. Frequently, however, there would be early winters and sometimes it wasn't possible to get them off the land before the snow came. But stooks left in the fields were okay; their shape allowed them to shed moisture. You could leave stooks in the field all the winter, and when you got around to threshing them in the spring, the wheat was still good.

There were a limited number of families that had belt-driven threshing machines. Families who owned one not only did their own work but also for their neighbours, and their neighbours paid them accordingly. We never had our own threshing machine. My father had a hard time accumulating the money to buy one. However, when the time came that people started using combines, which allowed you to cut and thresh in one fell swoop, he was able to get a combine. Then my father, brother and I did all our own work, combining and getting the wheat into the granaries. The wheat was brought in from the combines by truck. We used two systems to load the wheat into the granaries. The first was the hard way: shovelling it by hand. The second was to build a hole in the roof and run the wheat into the granary via the opening on a conveyor.

All told, my father was a better naturalist than a farmer. He would move a nest of eggs rather than run over it with a piece of machinery. He refused to allow hunting on his property. He was also curious about rocks. His land was extremely rocky. Every year after the lands were plowed and cultivated and prior to seeding, we had to go out and pick rocks. We piled them on a flatboat drawn by two horses and laid them along the fence line. My father took the particularly interesting rocks into carefully arranged piles in our yard and garden. He pondered rocks with marine fossils in them: how did they end up on his farm, hundreds of miles from the ocean?

My father was the dominating force in my life when I was growing up, and one of a circle of people who permanently influenced my life; a quiet, simple, humble man, disciplined in his work, deeply religious and deeply devoted to his family. It was his interest in the rocks on our farm that caused me to elect geology as my career. I wanted to be able to explain to my father how these rocks were formed, where they came from and why they were all so different.

After my first year at university, I was able to go to the farm and tell my father about the rocks: the reason we had so many rocks was because the continental ice sheets had paused in our area and dumped their load of rocks on our land, the geological term of such a deposit being a "terminal moraine." Most of the rocks came from northern Canada—the area known as the Canadian Shield and were of Pre-Cambrian age. Geologically, they were called igneous or metamorphic in contrast to sedimentary, which were formed by erosion and subsequent deposition in lakes, rivers and on coastlines to form stratified layers.

3

The Larger World

ALBERTA BEFORE THE WAR included many islands of small, rural, immigrant communities like our Danish-speaking one at Standard. The wave of immigration before the Great War that brought my parents also brought thousands of Germans, Ukrainians, Rumanians, Italians, Polish, Dutch, Norwegian and other European ethnic, linguistic and cultural groups. The coal mines, the wheat farms, the timber crews and the primitive drilling rigs of the province were populated by many peoples isolated by language and religion. When William Aberhart was elected premier of Alberta in his 1935 Social Credit political landslide, he translated his campaign material into the seven languages of the major immigrant groups.

The community of Standard, in which we Danes were linked by language, religion and the common struggle to survive the Depression, was just one of several hundred other villages and towns across the prairies. The records show that as many as thirty-five nations were represented in the population of Alberta by the time I went to primary school, in 1931 at the outset of the Great Depression. This was a portent of the multicultural Canada that has developed in my lifetime. But I was a child who spoke only Danish in my formative years, and my first horizons did not extend past farm, school, church and the baseball field.

Nazareth Lutheran Church in Standard was the centre of my family's universe. Here is the Danish congregation of the town. Jens Rasmussen, the founder of Standard, is in the front row wearing a hat.

Our family was a unique and special place for us children, and we were part of a social network that revolved exclusively around the Lutheran Church; looking back I can see that we were sheltered and really knew little of the larger world. My sheltered upbringing led to challenges in later years, when I joined the army and ran into rougher, more worldly men. Looking back, I can see a picture of myself as a boy slowly becoming aware of and familiar with the world beyond the fence line of our farm.

Although we could see the far-distant Rocky Mountains from the heights of our farm on a clear day—mountains coated in snow in winter and the colour of exposed greyish rock on a summer day; pink at sunrise and dark blue during sunset—my parents infrequently visited the mountains and Banff National Park, and even then not until we children had grown up.

We did not own an automobile and our family travelled by foot, horseback or lumber wagon. My father went to Drumheller for coal but that was an annual expedition requiring some planning and time. When we went to Lake Chestermere for swimming parties or to neighbouring towns to play baseball, we travelled in other people's vehicles. The road to Calgary was unpaved in the 1920s and 1930s when I was growing up, but going there was nearly always out of the question anyway. I did not see Calgary until I was fourteen years old, when my mother took me there to buy my first suit for my confirmation

Our neighbour's combine at Standard in 1935. We couldn't afford one.

into the Danish Lutheran Church. We were given a ride there by a friendly local tradesman. Before then, I had dressed in coveralls, which were as common then among young people as blue jeans are today.

The town of Standard was only a mile-and-a-half from our home, but before I went to school, going there, except to attend church, was an event. We needed some things for our meals that we couldn't grow, things like sugar, flour and coffee. There were two grocery stores in Standard—competitors in a small town where everyone knew everyone else very well. We had a swap arrangement with one of the grocers. They were happy to take trade from us, especially eggs. For a certain amount of eggs the grocer would give you a certain amount of groceries back in exchange. The grocer had connections in Calgary and sold the eggs there, too. This barter system was advantageous for a family like ours with little ready money.

When I was a little guy, the grocer had one other thing: he had jellybeans in a jar behind the counter. Every time my father went in there to get groceries and I was with him, the grocer would put his hand into the jellybean jar and I would leave with about ten jellybeans. I still do like jellybeans, but I never thought much about them as an adult until Ronald Reagan was president of the United States, and it became public that he liked jellybeans. Well, you know my opinion about Ronald Reagan went sky high when I heard he liked jellybeans just as much as I did.

Baseball provided the only opportunity for me to visit other towns around us; it was the only sport my brothers and I played in those years. All the small communities had a baseball team, and Standard had both an adult and a junior team. The local doctor was coach of the junior baseball team. My brother Gerhardt and I were both avid ball players. I was a catcher and Gerhardt played first base. Our competitors came from adjoining small towns, such as Rockyford, Rosebud, Hussar and Gleichen. The competition was fierce among us, particularly on the big July 1 Sports Day.

Many of our games took place on Sundays and also one night a week during the summer when we could make the arrangements with some other town to play and line up cars to drive the team. For a while my father was concerned. He thought that maybe playing ball on Sunday was breaking that commandment: "Remember the Sabbath Day to keep it holy." And my father and mother lived by the Ten Commandments completely. So he wondered, "Playing ball: was that remembering the Sabbath day to keep it holy?"

Well, it was a matter of judgement. Fortunately, my brother and I persuaded Dad that we were keeping it holy doing everything else that he asked—going to church, going to Sunday School—and this was the one fun thing we could do on Sunday that didn't really break the Good Lord's law.

Of course, our lives were not entirely just going to church and Sunday School. We belonged to the Boy Scout troop in Standard. There were about thirty of us in the troop. We scraped together the money for a uniform and our scarves had the Danish flag on them to show that we came from a Danish community. The Boy Scout master, however, was not Danish. He was the local CPR freight agent, F.D. Knowlton. He handled the few trains that came through Standard, all of which were freight trains usually holding wheat. There were six wheat elevators in Standard to which the farmers brought the wheat after the harvest season. They were another point of contact with the larger world: the railroad was the lifeline for our agrarian economy. Mr. Knowlton's son, Gerald, who was a few years younger than me, became a well-known Calgary real estate man (Knowlton's Real Estate) and a familiar face from "home" for me on the occasions I ran into him when my migrant early career brought me to Calgary.

The two-storey red-brick schoolhouse we attended was in Standard, a mile-and-a-half walk for us. Long since replaced by a modern edifice, it had four rooms, two on the first level and two above. Here the classes ran from Grades 1 through 12, so each room accommodated three grades. The government recruited teachers from elsewhere and posted them to towns all over Alberta. They lived in Standard for nine months of the year, boarded in individual homes.

There was a huge variety in the quality of teachers—some good and some bad. The one thing that is so different now from then is discipline. When I was in Grades 1 through 9, the teachers were allowed to give corporal punishment with a strap. You would hold out your hand and depending upon how bad you had been, you'd get strapped, and hard, and your hand would be absolutely sore. The strap never drew blood, but you'd get a mighty sore hand.

The real trouble, however, came when you got home. You had to confess to your parents what had happened to you, and what you'd done to deserve it. Maybe you had lied or cheated, or perhaps you were playing on the fire escape. (Different teachers had different levels of tolerance for "bad" behaviour.) Once you had confessed to your parents, well, then came the big licking. The parents had total confidence in those teachers. If they strapped you in school, you deserved it and had done something you should not have, and therefore the parents were responsible and they took it out on you. I only rarely got the strap because I was nearly always well-behaved. Gerhardt, however, once got it four times in one day, and then again from Dad when he got home that night.

One of the fun things to do for the more daring kids was to find the teachers' straps in their desks and to hide them. When the time came for a strapping, the teacher couldn't find the strap. That was big fun while it lasted, but eventually the strap turned up and then the guilty ones really got wonked.

I can remember once when the teacher lined us all up on the sidewalk outside the school on a hot day. We were there to confess. Somebody had stolen the strap, and the teacher said that we would stand there until someone pointed out the evil one who had done the deed. Those were hectic times for a young boy, I can tell you, but it is funny thinking back on it now.

Our parents weren't just involved in any punishment that came along. They oversaw our homework. And boy, did we ever do homework. We shared the space around the kitchen and dining room tables while we completed our assignments. There was no distinction of gender with regard to homework. The boys and the girls alike were expected to perform in school and to show our parents that we were working to the best of our abilities.

For many years, the only light we had at night in our home was a little, old-fashioned, kerosene lamp with a small flame. After dark it only provided half-light, semi-light. The day came when we took one step forward. My father got a gas lamp with mantles and it gave a lot better light, improving our lighting and homework situation. In all the years I was on the farm we never had electricity. There were only a collection of lamps that would now be considered antiques. They did finally get electricity many years after I left.

Most of our school supplies were provided for us. However, we had to buy our own scribblers, those little paper blue-line books, to write in. They cost ten

Portrait of my parents, Aksel and Marie Catherine Nielsen, September 22, 1938, at my sister Esther's wedding.

cents apiece. Frequently we didn't have the money to get a new one and after one was full, I'd end up going back to the start of the book and writing in all the margins and across the top and down the side in order to have something to write on until Dad could afford ten cents to get another scribbler. That's a pretty good indicator of how tough things really were during the Depression years. Still, we were more fortunate than others during those years; we had plenty to eat and didn't have to go to school hungry.

And we did have books, some bought by my father. My brothers and I also acquired some books as prizes. In our home there were enough books to fill a small case. About half of them were religious. The others included a cheap set of *World Book Encyclopedia*, and a couple of atlases. My mother's youngest brother, Klaus, was a sailor who sailed all his life, mostly on European and Asiatic seas. He survived his vessel being torpedoed in each war. Although we kids were stuck on the farm, we could use our atlases to track our uncle's progress around the world and look up the places where we someday hoped to go.

There were two libraries in Standard, one in the school with a limited number of books, and the other one in the church. It also had a limited number of books, such as the history of the Lutheran Church, inspirational books and religious instruction. I can tell you that before I left the farm when I was eighteen, I had read all the books in those libraries.

These happy memories aside, I knew that my doorway to the larger world beyond Standard would come by attending school until the completion of Grade 12, doing well in my studies and going to university. At least that was the plan until the war broke out in 1939.

Farm children of that era left school at an early age, as their parents preferred their sons and daughters to help out full-time on the farm. Most farmers kept their sons at home to work on the farm and their daughters were expected to get married at an early age. My father, however, knew that he had paid the price for having only the equivalent to, probably, a Grade-4 education. He knew that this was hurting his career because he was stuck on that farm whether he wanted to be there or not because he had no education. So he determined that his seven children were going to complete high school.

Dad was a little more lax on this idea with his daughters than he was with his sons. In those days, daughters got married early, and all my sisters did so. They didn't marry rich people but they married good people. However, they all continued their education until they married, and some completed their education to Grade 12.

Two of the three of us boys went on beyond Grade 12. My elder brother, Ejvind, was a religious man and became a preacher. He attended university in Edmonton to accomplish that. My second brother, Gerhardt, completed his Grade 12 and decided he was going to stay on the farm and hopefully inherit it, so he stayed at home. I graduated during the Second World War, and took a roundabout route to university.

I graduated from Standard High School in April 1943. A career decision at that time in Canada was simple. Everyone who was medically fit joined the Canadian Forces: the army, air force or navy. However, an unusual opportunity became available to me. The federal government was not pleased with the

A hayrack with my dad and Miriam, 1942. All the hay stooks were loaded by hand.

education level of many of the officers in the army. It therefore set up an organ-ization known as the Canadian Army University Course (CAUC). Graduates from high school who had a good academic standing were offered first-year engi-neering at any one of a selected group of universities, one of which was the University of Alberta in Edmonton. It was necessary for an individual to join the Canadian Army and remain in the army, not only during the year at university but also for the duration of the war. With agreement from my parents, I decided to proceed in this direction. I was on the path that would ultimately lead to my university education and my life of discovery as an exploration geologist.

4

The Army

AT THE BEGINNING of summer in 1943, after I had completed high school,
I hitchhiked from Standard to Calgary. I had just turned eighteen. I reported
to army headquarters in Calgary where I took a medical examination, which
I passed with ease. I then proceeded to Mewata Armoury and was sworn in
as a soldier in the Canadian Army. On that first day I met Ray Phillips and we
were sworn in on the same Bible. We were together for the remainder of the
war and became the best of friends, and to this day he is still my best friend.
I disliked farming, and the army was not only a good way to get out of farming
but also a great way to pay for my education with the credits I would earn from
service, if I survived the war.

After the swearing in, we were assigned to Mewata, an impressive brick
structure built in 1917 as a training facility for soldiers fighting the Great War
of 1914–18. An encampment to accommodate recruits had been erected behind
the structure, and this is where we stayed for a month. We took military drill
inside the armoury. We were taught to know our right foot from our left. What
I remember clearly about those first days is the language of the older soldiers
who had been in the army for a while was just awful. The first night in the
encampment was a terrible shock. I found myself in a world of obscenity. I had
come from a home where any kind of swearing was not permitted. I came
from the shelter of a farm, a small Lutheran community and a religious family.

In military uniform in Edmonton, at the beginning of the Second World War.

I listened to the older men, to their crude profanity and obscenity as they boasted of their escapades with women. Their language and apparent behaviour were contrary to everything I had been brought up to believe in! I wondered, "How am I ever going to get through this?"

Soon we were transferred to a camp at Camrose, Alberta, travelling by train. We moved into barracks and started two months of basic training. The work was extremely strenuous with a very high level of discipline enforced by our officers. We learned a lot about being soldiers in a very short time. We were issued rifles, and I can still remember my rifle number: 27L6358. The officers in the training camps were demanding, profane and completely ruthless. They were assigned to train recruits. Then the recruits were sent off to fight overseas where many would be killed. Training camp was neither a place for weakness among the men nor tolerance by the officers.

Following the basic training, sixty of us who were in the Canadian Army University Course program went by train to Edmonton to start studies in the Faculty of Engineering at the University of Alberta. Soldiers from British

The Canadian Army University Course at the University of Alberta, Edmonton, 1943.

Columbia and Saskatchewan who were in the CAUC attended their courses at University of British Columbia and the University of Saskatchewan. My year in the CAUC was one of the highlights of my army career because of the strong friendships and esprit de corps that developed among the soldiers and the amount we learned, both academically and militarily, in a short period of time. I was a good student, so I did well. I came to know my fellow student-soldiers, some of whom are still my friends today. All of us were Albertans between the ages of eighteen and nineteen and most of us were farm boys. Unfortunately, several of our number would be killed in action on overseas assignments.

We completed one academic year, attending classes for nine months from September to May. We took the regular engineering course with the civilian students. We were students but we were also soldiers, so we were billeted together in an old residence at St. Stephen's College, which had been taken over by the army. Military discipline was enforced, so we wore uniforms and marched to and from class. On weekends we continued military training, learning more military skills. We ate in the college refectory. In memory, the staple of our diet was bologna. I like bologna now, but when it was served then, we'd all yell, "Oh, no. Bologna again!"

At the end of the school year, we were given a choice as to which military service we wished to join: infantry, artillery or tank corps. The majority of men elected the infantry and were transported to the Currie Barracks on the southwest edge of Calgary for their training on the Sarcee weapons range. It takes less time to prepare an infantry man for war than an artillery or tank soldier, so they were ready for active combat first. Most saw active service and many died or were wounded. Those who chose the artillery went to Camp Petawawa in Northern Ontario for training on the big guns.

Ray Phillips and I chose the armoured tank corps. We wanted to stick together and we agreed that fighting in the armoured corps would be a great and daring adventure, a life quite unlike the quiet rural existence of my sheltered childhood. Two other men in our group, Dick Percifield and Bill Mills, also chose the tank corps. The four of us embarked on a long train ride to the wartime training centre at Camp Borden, forty miles north of Toronto.

The camp had been an empty scrubland of sand and stunted pines, known locally as Pine Plains, when it was selected as a military base in 1917. Positioned atop a great glacial moraine that lies across south-central Ontario, it was an excellent location for a military airfield and is considered the birthplace of the Royal Canadian Air Force. It had been the headquarters of the Canadian Tank School since 1938. The tank was invented during the Great War to break the bloody war of attrition that consumed hundreds of thousands of lives on the Western Front. Tanks first saw action in September 1916. Within a year, tank battles were a part of modern land fighting. Under a great Canadian named Major General F.F. Worthington, known as the father of the armoured corps, the Canadian Army became expert in tank warfare. By the time we arrived there in 1943, the combination of the air force and armoured fighting vehicle forces meant Camp Borden was the largest and most important Canadian military base of the war. I was one of more than 200,000 men who trained there during the Second World War. I was based there, as it turned out, for the better part of three years.

I became a trooper in Armoured Corps No. 3. That meant I held the lowest rank in the tank corps. That was a sore point for me as I was in the CAUC, which was an officer training program. My status could be accounted for by my age. I had just turned eighteen when I enlisted, and I was in the echelon of the youngest soldiers, not eligible to join the army until nearly four years after the war started. We were attached to the famous Lord Strathcona's Horse, which had first been formed as a cavalry unit made up of mostly western cowboys and farmers to fight in the Boer War.

For months we took intensive armoured corps training. We spent a lot of time in Sherman tanks, day and night. We learned all aspects of tank warfare, including driving the machines and operating the wireless set, as well as gunnery with the tanks' 75 mm guns and Browning machine guns. I was trained as

Dick Percifield and me on a Sherman tank at Camp Borden, just before the end of the war, 1945.

a gunner operator in a Sherman tank, firing a 75 mm cannon capable of hitting targets half a mile away.

I learned teamwork, which was especially important in the confines of a tank. I learned to follow orders. I traded the freedom of the farm for the lowly rank of trooper and a gunner's seat. I was not in a position to be giving orders, but I sure had to follow a bunch of them.

Our field training in the tanks took place on a 17,000-acre tract of farm and orchard land, a half-day's drive from Camp Borden, informally called the armour fighting vehicles camp, and later the Meaford Tank Range. It was located in an area of farms and orchards on Cape Rich north of Meaford, a small town near Owen Sound on the shores of Georgian Bay. The land had been expropriated in 1942 from 101 farm and fisher families in a whirlwind operation that included the evacuation of the area in truck convoys that resembled the stream of refugees fleeing Paris a year previously. The cape was ideal for tank and artillery training because it was surrounded on three sides by water into which spent ammunition fired from the big guns fell. Many of the farmers left their land believing they would return after the war ended. But I was a member of one of the tank crews which destroyed those homes during our training, and it remains a military site called Land Force Central Area Training Centre.

A typical abandoned house near Meaford, Ontario, on land expropriated by the army during the Second World War.

Upon completing our training, we returned to Camp Borden. We then waited to be advised when we would be going overseas to England and, as it was after D-Day and the invasion of France, to participate in the drive for Berlin. My friends gradually left Camp Borden on assignment overseas or elsewhere in Canada. But I was kept at Camp Borden for longer than I cared.

Ever since elementary school, I have been comfortable speaking to groups of people about any number of subjects. At Camp Borden, I showed an ability to teach men to utilize maps for strategic purposes, as well as how to operate the light submachine guns—Sten and Bren guns—that were basic arms for the tank corps. Because of my ability to teach, I was kept in Canada to train new recruits. My position, teaching the use of weaponry, was ironic because we didn't have so much as one gun on our farm, only rifles. It was also ironic because I wasn't at all mechanical and the men needed to learn how to strip, clean and reassemble these guns quickly so that in battlefield conditions they could maintain their weapons while fighting. However, I was a good teacher, able to explain things clearly. I also taught basic field first aid. The soldiers would have to care for the wounded in battle when there was no medic available.

The Sten was a British-invented light submachine gun named for its inventors Sheppard and Turpin. The Bren gun was Czechoslovakian in origin, from the city of Brno, manufactured during the war by Enfield in England. The Bren

At the barracks in Camp Borden, Ontario, during the Second World War.

fired a .303-calibre round and was gas-operated and air-cooled. It was a matter of great pride to many Canadians that, by the time I joined the tank corps, the Bren gun was a centrepiece of Canadian small arms manufacturing, alongside a weapon known as the Number Four Rifle. We were making Bren guns quickly and at a cost of less than $195 per weapon. We troopers in the tank corps also took pride in the success of Canadian tank manufacturing, producing Ram and Valentine tanks in factories that had built railway locomotives in peacetime.

An unfortunate side effect of the Canadian weapons-manufacture accomplishment is that the Bren gun kept me in Camp Borden as a weapons instructor when I wanted to be sent to Europe to fight.

My friends were fighting, and I was stuck in the safe haven of Camp Borden. I hated it. I continued to teach weaponry and first aid, but I pleaded with those in command to send me to Europe to fight. Finally, they agreed. I was slated to go to officers' school in Kingston after D-Day, but when they agreed to send me into action, the officers' school closed. I was on embarkation leave for a last visit with my parents when the war in Europe ended.

I was very disappointed at not having had the opportunity to fight in Europe, and I immediately joined the Pacific Volunteers, which was a Canadian contingent slated to join an American armoured group in Fort Knox, Kentucky. The intention was that the Canadians would join the Americans for armoured action in the Pacific Theater of Operations. On my tunic, I wore a small badge with the initials "GS" on it: General Service. When I joined the Pacific Volunteers, we were given a new badge to wear on our tunics—the "PV" badge.

My friend Ray Phillips, who had also joined the Pacific Volunteers, went to Fort Knox—he didn't end up going overseas—but before I could join him I came down with the mumps, a serious thing for a young man my age, and I was hospitalized for three weeks. While I was in the hospital, I had another experience with the realities of Canadian society, military and political. It all began when I became friends with a man next to me from Quebec; we played endless games of hearts.

With the war already begun, in June 1940, the Mackenzie King Liberal government approved the *National Resources Mobilization Act* (NRMA)—a kind of conscription for home defence. This act allowed the government to register people in the Canadian Forces but keep them in jobs related to wartime production. None of these conscripts were meant for overseas service. This act was considered expedient, politically—Mackenzie King did not want to force conscription on the population, especially given how conscription had resulted in a French Canadian–English Canadian crisis during the First World War, in 1917 and 1918. Until 1942, the Liberal government maintained the policy that no one should be sent overseas against his will.

A registered person who chose not to go overseas was, in government parlance, an "R" man—a member of the Reserve. We men in General Service would not talk to them. Men who volunteered or were drafted and volunteered for overseas service were "A" men, members of the active force. The "A" men initially nicknamed the "R" men Mother's Boys or, contemptuously, Maple Leaf Boys. Then the term "Zombies" was coined, and it stuck. Farley Mowat, in his books *The Regiment* and *My Father's Son*, recalls feeling much the same I did: he disliked those who wore a uniform but refused to make the same sacrifices as those who volunteered to go overseas.

As the war progressed, the government realized that it would eventually run out of troops. A plebiscite in 1942 introduced Canadians to the possibility of future conscription. Mackenzie King's immortal words were: "conscription if necessary, but not necessarily conscription." English Canadians voted 83 per cent in favour of the plebiscite. Anti-conscription voters in French Canadian Quebec, however, voted 72.9 per cent against. With 63 per cent of Canadians in favour, the plebiscite passed. The government was thus allowed to repeal parts of the NRMA that did not allow for overseas conscription. But the government didn't act on conscription until much later in the war.

In the meantime, reservists had become a serious impediment to reinforcing Canadian battalions in battle. After the invasion of Europe, because there were 70,000 "Zombies" in the land forces whose fighting strength was 450,000, 15 per cent of the army refused to serve in battle. The attempt to persuade reservists to switch to active service was pathetic. Of the 70,000 reservists, only an average of twenty-five per day switched to the active force after the invasion of Normandy, D-Day in 1944, a tragic fraction of the Canadian boys dying each day in Europe. The army urgently needed 15,000 replacements to take the place of men fallen in the vicious fighting. On November 23, 1944, the government finally did what was necessary, sending a so-called partial draft bill through Parliament that conscripted 16,000 NRMA-registered reservists—some 23 per cent of them—to active service. When 10,000 were given notice of overseas posting, 7,800 deserted or went AWOL. Of the 14,500 given embarkation orders, 4,000 remained unaccounted for. Eventually, although 16,000 reinforcements were needed, only 13,000 were dispatched to Europe, of which 9,500 were moved into the theatre of war before Germany surrendered.

As I recovered from the mumps and played hearts with my neighbour in the hospital, I didn't think about who was an "A" man and who was an "R" man. None of us wore tunics, of course; we wore hospital garb. So there was nothing to indicate who was a reservist and who was an "A" man. The "Zombie" issue had come to a head by the time I was hospitalized. The sorry record of desertions and absences-without-leave was known among the men. You can imagine my eagerness to be posted overseas for active service because, in spite of the honourable General Services badge on my arm, I wanted no doubt in anyone's mind that I was willing to serve and sacrifice. For the time being, however, I was stuck in the hospital playing hearts. Then, someone took me aside and said, "That man you are playing hearts with all the time is a Zombie." That labelled him for me, and from that very moment on, I did not speak to him again, play hearts with him or even acknowledge his existence.

It was around this time that the event took place that changed the Second World War and the "peacetime" world that followed. The US dropped the atomic bomb on Hiroshima. Following a second atomic bomb dropped a few days later on Nagasaki, the Japanese called it quits and the war was over. The Japanese surrendered just as the doctors declared my complete recovery from mumps and I was ready to return to active duty.

I was disappointed and have been all my life that I did not have the opportunity to see action. From that time on, my only objective was to get an honourable discharge so that I could go to university. As armoured troops were no longer needed in Europe or the Pacific, I received a discharge in the autumn of 1945 and went home to Standard.

In our little Danish community, most of the young men I knew had joined one of the branches of the service, and many of the young women had, as well. At the same time, a number of neighbour boys spent the war on the farm with their parents. It was considered to be in the national interest to have farms produce their crops to feed soldiers fighting for their country. In order to contribute to this effort, the sons of many farmers were given "farm leave." This allowed them to stay out of the military while they were helping their parents maintain farm production. This was a sore point with many farm soldiers, who felt that some of their buddies were avoiding combat by taking advantage of farm leave.

My two brothers and I all joined up. Ejvind and I were in the army and Gerhardt enlisted in the Royal Canadian Air Force. My sister, Ruth, was a nurse in a military hospital in Canada. Among our Standard school mates and buddies, five were killed in action overseas. Although one of my cousins was also killed on active duty, thankfully, all my siblings came back home.

5

University

AT THE BEGINNING of 1946, I was back at the University of Alberta in Edmonton, studying for my career of choice: geology. I was among thousands of young Canadian men returning to civilian life through the classroom in the winter after the war. Our education was paid for by credits we earned through our military service. The army had inaugurated this arrangement because it needed an educated officer corps; now the country was getting an educated professional class. It was one of the few good things that came from that terrible conflict that cost so many young Canadian lives.

Edmonton seemed to be the most promising city in western Canada that winter, and therefore I was especially fortunate to be studying there. The city was the gateway to the Arctic, with airplanes lifting off for the vast Barren Lands every day. My generation believed that the North was destined to be the treasure house of a nation that had proven itself in war and would prove itself in peacetime. Located in the centre of the rich Alberta hinterland, Edmonton was also surrounded by abundant wheat fields, lucrative coal mines and rolling pastures thick with cattle. To the west, timber crews and homesteaders were beginning to penetrate the solitude of forest and muskeg. To the south stretched hundreds of thousands of fertile acres, a storehouse of wheat, grain and beef.

Hitting the books during my first year at the University of Alberta.

At the University of Alberta, they called my group the "January class" because we began that academic year four months after the rest of the student body. The university organized things so that we went to class from January 1946 to the end of July and took one full year of courses during that time. Then we started again in September with all the regular students and completed the second academic year by June 1947. We went to classes for seventeen months out of eighteen, and by the spring of 1947 had completed the first two years of undergraduate work.

The University of Alberta was conducting its thirty-seventh year of classes when I began my studies. Geology had been one of the natural sciences that the founding president, Dr. Henry Marshall Tory, included in the arts and sciences curriculum. The department was small but outstanding. The first professor of geology appointed was Dr. John A. Allen. Very shortly after, Dr. R.G. Rutherford and Dr. P.S. Warren joined him. Dr. Warren was expert in sedimentary rock and palaeontology, a fossil scientist. This area of study would be important for me when I embarked on graduate studies. Dr. Charlie Stelck and Dr. Robert Folinsbee, however, became my mentors. They were not only outstanding scientists but also great people who had a major influence on my future years.

The study of petroleum geology was not as sophisticated then as it is now. The sedimentary soft rocks of erosion and deposition—sandstone, shales and slates—were not of much interest to us yet. Our courses were more focused on "hard-rock" geology, and we studied the igneous and metamorphic rocks found in places like the Canadian Shield. The economic value critical to the postwar economy was in the minerals they contained—gold, silver, radium, nickel, lead. Mining of Canadian natural resources had been critical to wartime national defence, and we expected peacetime careers in the mining industry, probably in northern Canada where mineral exploration was taking place.

The faculty was reasonably balanced and could teach both hard-rock and sedimentary geology, but in those first couple of years the emphasis was on the hard rocks and the opportunities available to young geologists who were willing to explore for them in Canada. We started out with basic geology courses. I was particularly pleased when I could apply my knowledge directly on home visits by identifying the rocks on my father's farm and explaining their origins to him.

I stayed in residence at Assiniboia Hall and, as there were two students in each room, I had a roommate: Harris Kroon. Coincidentally, Harris, who was the same age as me, also came from Standard and was taking geology. His father was the town barber and had given me many haircuts. In spite of the confined quarters we shared, Harris and I got along famously. We became good friends and remain so to this day. Harris was quite a character. He liked to visit the bar on Saturday nights, and I frequently had to put him to bed. After completing his geology degree, he joined Texaco Exploration Company and spent his entire career with that organization.

In the summer of 1947, I became part of a great Canadian tradition in the training and development of geologists and other natural scientists. I joined a field party of the Geological Survey of Canada (GSC) as a summer student exploring for gold on the Barren Lands north of the 60th parallel. We were following in the footsteps of a century of explorers. Every summer since 1848, the GSC had hired university and college teachers and students from all natural

My roommate at the University of Alberta, Harris Kroon (left), 1946.

sciences to make a systematic and comprehensive inventory of Canada's natural resources: minerals, flora, fauna, soil, water and climate. They wrote reports on everything of potential economic significance that had a bearing on the settlement of the country. It was one of the greatest ventures in the history of natural science. The explorers of the GSC travelled from Atlantic to Pacific to Arctic coasts on foot or by canoe and York boat so that the nation could measure its wealth of natural resources.

These journeys of frontier exploration hundreds of kilometres from civilization were demanding and dangerous, often involving privation—hunger, illness, flies and mosquitoes, blizzards, floods, capsized boats and broken equipment. They were carried out between the end of one winter and the beginning of the next. GSC field parties traversed every area of the country. Sometimes the

During my summers with the Geological Survey of Canada, I saw so many archetypical Canadian landscapes. Here, an iceberg floats on a lake in the Barren Lands.

explorers travelled alone, but usually they went in teams of two or three, accompanied by seasoned guides who knew the waterways, portages and trails, the places to hunt game for fresh meat, or fish, not to mention the best campsites. Today the GSC still conducts field work, but now they have helicopters, radios, more comfortable accommodation and better food.

These seasonal explorers completed the most thorough national inventory of natural resources of any country in the world, and they did it for one of the largest land areas on the globe. In western Canada from 1871 to 1905, GSC geologists found evidence of coal, oil and gas deposits from the tar sands and the shallow gas of southern Alberta to the coal of the British Columbia Rockies. Before there was an oil and gas exploration and production industry, the GSC correctly forecast how big it would become and the impact it would have.

By the time I came along in 1947, the GSC had moved its reconnaissance north. When I applied and was accepted for work in my first summer, I was assigned to a field party on the Barren Lands near the Coppermine River. Our field party chief was Dr. Bob Folinsbee, then a young professor at the University of Alberta.

In 1952, a few years after my first foray into the North, Farley Mowat made the Barren Lands of the Canadian subarctic famous to Canadians in his book, *People of the Deer*. The Barrens are a vast landscape with many small lakes and streams lying between Great Slave Lake and Hudson Bay. Its waters are

Fording a stream in the Barren Lands during my first summer with the Geological Survey of Canada.

plentiful with fish, but the land is rocky with just a few stands of scrubby trees. Animals such as Arctic hare, wolves and migrating caribou populate the Barrens, along with a variety of migrating birds and smaller mammals. There was a sparse population of a few hundred Dene and Inuit, but the Dene stuck to the interior rivers and the Inuit to the Arctic coastline, and we saw none of them for the entire summer. We were alone on the endless expanse of rock, small lakes and streams.

Dr. Folinsbee's party consisted of four young geologists and three older men. As I was from the University of Alberta, I knew Dr. Folinsbee and had a good relationship with him. The others had been engaged from the University of British Columbia, the University of Manitoba and the University of Toronto.

We met in Edmonton and flew in a Twin Otter aircraft to Yellowknife where we spent a week getting ourselves ready for the summer. The Barren Lands had a huge reputation as a place for people to get lost. It was a wild and woolly country we were going into.

After we had become acquainted with each other and oriented to the Barrens, our team boarded a single-engine Norseman bush plane and flew out to Providence Lake. We were dropped off with our basic equipment: tents, food and gear. This gear included rifles and fishing gear for hunting and fishing, as we were expected to provide for ourselves to supplement the basics of our summer kitchen. We relied on the canned food for a while, until we knew we would be able to hunt for some of our daily nutrition. We had no radio or any other form of communication with the outside world. We were given a rendez-vous point and a date in August when we were expected to be there.

The plane dropped us off on the shore of the lake in June, and we were told not to expect to see it again until the end of the summer. We could expect no mail unless an airplane had some other reason to fly into the area we were working. We had two, seventeen-foot, bright orange canoes for transportation.

As we paddled from lake to lake and up and down rivers, there were lots of waterfalls and we had to take everything out of the canoes and portage to the other side. It was hard repetitive work, particularly when we were traversing extremely rocky terrain. In this manner, we went from Providence Lake farther inland to Lac de Gras.

At this point, Dr. Folinsbee had been going out on these parties for about twenty years. The GSC would be a lifetime vocation for him. There were five of us working the area, and our encampment had two tents. Dr. Folinsbee had his own tent. He was the boss and there weren't many benefits, but one was his own tent. The rest of us had one tent between the four of us. We had a lot of ground to cover that summer, and we'd started behind schedule, so we had to split up. A party chief named C.S. Lord was operating a second crew in an adjacent territory.

When I headed north that summer, I had never been in a canoe in my life. Being in a canoe for the first time isn't as easy as you might think because they tip very easily. We were going into some uncharted quarters and deep lakes. Somehow I escaped drowning, but it was as much due to good fortune as to skill.

We had a cook who was really just another geology student from the University of Alberta. His name was Hugo Greiner and he had been a cook in the army so he got stuck cooking. He didn't get paid any extra money for it, but his cooking didn't amount to much so I guess that was okay. Hugo selected what we were going to eat, opened the cans and cooked the food on a Coleman stove. We ate out of cans unless we got fresh meat: an occasional Arctic hare or, toward the end of summer, a caribou. Some of the men fished and sometimes lit a fire on the lakeshore to cook and eat their catch. I wasn't fond of fish, so I didn't much enjoy those fish fry-ups.

I was paired off with a geologist named Walter Fehrig. Dr. Folinsbee frequently sent Walter and me to map a certain area while the other two guys mapped the area adjoining it. Walter was from the University of Manitoba. He had been on the Barren Lands with the GSC the summer previously and he was

Laundry day in the Barrens. I'm in pyjamas because all my clothes are being washed.

next to the party chief in the pecking order and as a result had some benefits. When we were separated from the other fellows, for example, we had a tent between us.

I enjoyed his company, not because we had similar views but the opposite. Walter and I shared a tent together during the days when socialism was making strides in Canada under the umbrella of the Co-operative Commonwealth Federation (CCF). The founder and head of the party was an elderly gentleman named J.W. Woodsworth, a Winnipeg Methodist clergyman. Walter, it turned out, was a strong believer in Woodsworth's ideas. I was a right-winger to the core and always have been. So, Walter and I had violent disagreements and, because we were isolated, out there on the Barrens in our tent, all of our conversations took on an importance that they wouldn't have if we'd been discussing the same ideas in Edmonton or Winnipeg.

We should not have discussed politics. One of the things that should be put in the GSC instruction manual for students is not to discuss politics and religion if you want to get along with other people. Long nights stretched out in front of us at the end of long working days, and we often had nothing to read. After a long day of hiking, we would argue politics—right versus left. Fortunately, we liked each other, so the disagreements, though heated, were forgotten in the morning.

Walter Fehrig readies the canoe on Lac de Gras during my first GSC summer.

Every day we would hike for roughly twenty miles on a pattern called a traverse, mapped out the night before by the party chief. Each day we took a different route and recorded the surface rocks and features that we crossed. The purpose was to record the surface geology and make a geological map of the area. Throughout the brief summer, we covered about fifty miles of barren land on foot, or in canoes. The map that came out of that event was called the "Lac de Gras" sheet. The government published maps based on our recordings two years after the summer in which we gathered the data. We were one small part of a long-term operation whose purpose was to gradually map the entire Northwest Territories.

The primary commodity for which we explored was gold. There were already several gold mines to the west of Yellowknife. The gold in the Northwest Territories was found in quartz veins, which we could map in the rocks on the surface. Unfortunately, we found no quartz veins that summer, no matter how hard we tried. More unfortunately, we also missed the diamonds that were discovered in the area many years later.

There is a good reason we missed finding those diamonds. We were unable to detect the diamond-bearing kimberlite structures because they lay under Lac de Gras—the only large lake on the Barrens that we explored—not visible to field geologists! Kimberlites are intrusive volcanic-type rocks that have come from the magma in the centre of Earth. The kimberlites push their way up fractures and solidify into giant rock plugs. During that process, a lot of the minerals in the kimberlites crystallize, and that's how diamonds are formed.

A Barren Lands lake, 1949. Many years later, diamonds were discovered near this area.

On an esker overlying ancient streambeds in the Barrens.

Even if we had thought to look for kimberlites around Lac de Gras, we didn't have the geophysical or geological technology to search below the surface of the water. Years later a prospector named Chuck Fipke believed that the kimberlites were under the lakes, and he was able to determine, on the basis of other minerals on the shore, that there should be diamonds in them—and so there were! There are now two giant mines related to the kimberlites of the Barren

Lands, and Canada has joined South Africa and Russia as the largest diamond producers in the world. But when I was up in the North, unaware of the treasure beneath my feet, I slugged along through June, July and the early part of August.

With August came the tremendous migration of the caribou. The caribou—unusual deer with slender bodies and big antlers—have been migrating ceaselessly across the Barren Lands for centuries. Twice a year they migrate from the Arctic Coast all the way down to the southern part of the Northwest Territories and into the northern parts of Alberta, Saskatchewan and Manitoba. When winter arrives, they don't relish the Far North, so they migrate south together. In the spring, the weather gets warmer in the North, and then they travel back, toward the twenty-four-hour daylight. Young caribou are born on the Arctic Coast.

When the caribou arrived in our vicinity, we on the GSC could harvest some fresh meat. The caribou were so tame that you could walk up and pet them. We were careful to take only what we needed and not waste anything. The migration of the caribou was also great for the wolves. Almost every night in August we heard wolves because they were out catching young caribou.

The wolves, which we saw during the day, howled loudly every night. If you want to hear a lonesome sound, go up to the Barrens and listen for wolves, particularly if you are nineteen or twenty years old and you are alone in a vast unpeopled area. The rifles we carried afforded us not only some fresh meat but also a sense that we were protected, though the wolves never approached our camps.

The biggest challenges to our physical comfort were the weather and the insects. In July it rained constantly. We would get soaked, as would our clothes and tents. When the rain stopped, the sun was warm, even hot sometimes, and we'd spread out our gear to dry. Often we worked in our pajamas while our clothes dried.

We couldn't avoid the pint-sized curses of the North—mosquitoes and black flies. There were absolutely hordes of them twenty-four hours a day and their stings and bites were uncomfortable. I got black fly bites the size of my thumbnail all over my legs. We had two forms of protection: face nets and insect repellent. When we traversed the country wearing the netting, we sweated because it didn't allow air to circulate. I kept on lifting the netting up, risking mosquitoes, in order to get fresh air.

But, you must wonder, why not just use insect repellant? If you think that repellent in 1947 was anything like the repellants we have today, you are making

Posing in my mother's beautiful garden in Standard the summer after my first year at the University of Alberta, all dressed up to go out.

a huge mistake. It was gooey guck and it stunk. If you put it on you would have some protection from the mosquitoes, but the feel and smell of the stuff were almost unbearable.

Toward the end of the trip, we experienced nights of frost. After the first frost, the mosquitoes and black flies were gone. It was as though a heavy weight had been lifted; for the rest of the summer, I didn't experience another mosquito bite. Of course, something had to rush in to take the place of the horrible insects. With frost came the blizzards. I grew up with blizzards on the bald prairie, but nothing prepared me for the Barren Lands blizzards of August. That year was perhaps particularly cold. We had snow in June, and again in August as winter began to show its face on the Barrens while it was still summer back in Alberta. The storms would come down from the North Pole and would sweep across the plains. Storms could last three days, during which we were stranded. The four of us crowded into our tent and listened to the wind howl.

It was lonely work, for the most part. We did have one unexpected social event that summer. Dr. Folinsbee and Dr. Lord arranged for us to meet at a designated spot when we were due to be working not too far from one another. We had one big happy night together, some good food, and the chance to visit with the other young geologists. Perhaps it doesn't seem like much, but it is as memorable to me as a great gala or night out in New York or New Orleans.

Earlier that year I had become engaged, and I was looking forward to getting married in September before starting my second year of university. While I was up in the Barrens, my future wife Evelyn was living at the family farm in Standard. Our only communication was through the few letters we exchanged.

When we finally returned to Yellowknife at the end of that memorable summer, my team and I were scheduled to spend four or five days wrapping up the work and making sure all the maps were done. However, Dr. Folinsbee, knowing I had worked hard and that I was due to be married, told me that I should go back to Calgary.

Evelyn and I married in the Danish Lutheran Church in Standard on September 21, 1947. All of my family attended the event. My mother held a very small reception in the home in which I had been born and raised. After our honeymoon at the York Hotel in downtown Calgary, we returned to Edmonton so I could go back to university. Unfortuantely I had somehow managed to spend all my money, but Evelyn's father gave us a sum so that we could buy the first groceries of our married life in Edmonton.

Dr. Folinsbee's practical help with the pre-wedding arrangements was the beginning of a lifelong friendship. As time went on after we were married, Evelyn and I were invited to visit with Dr. Folinsbee socially. His first wife died of cancer, but he married a second time and moved to Ontario with his second wife until his death in 2008, as I was finishing the first draft of this book.

My summer with the GSC determined my future. I learned more about geology in this hard-rock country than I ever did in school, and I acquired a taste for the challenge of geological exploration. I had my mind made up: I would earn my living by exploring the remote places of the North as a hard-rock exploration geologist. This aspiration brought with it a personal problem. I would be exploring in the North most of the time, and Evelyn would be living in the South.

This would not have been a happy arrangement.

6

From the Tower to the Field

THEN CAME LEDUC.

On a frigid afternoon in February 1947, in front of a crowd of several hundred oil, government and newspaper people, a drilling crew from Imperial Oil brought the first discovery of Alberta's modern oil era onto production at the famous Leduc No. 1 well site. Leduc was an oil deposit found in a deep Devonian carbonate reef, geographically outside that little farming community south of Edmonton. It was detected with a relatively new exploration tool for the time: the geophysical survey. Premier Ernest C. Manning had often said, "The oilmen always told us that there was oil in Alberta if only they could find it." At Leduc, the promise became a reality.

Until that discovery, geology undergraduates at the University of Alberta like me concentrated our studies on the igneous and metamorphic rocks of the Canadian Shield, preparing for a career exploring Canada's remote north for minerals, such as gold, uranium, copper, silver and zinc.

By the time I returned for classes in the autumn of 1947, the major oil companies—Amoco, Mobil, Chevron and Imperial—really wanted to get into western Canada. These were companies with plenty of money and plenty of exploration expertise. However, these were companies headed by executives who knew, from worldwide experience, that they could become very unpopular if they didn't handle things properly. They had plenty of very talented geologists on staff, but they knew that one way to become popular would be to hire and train Canadians.

Imperial Oil, of course, led the way. By this time, it had already been exploring for oil in the Western Canadian Sedimentary Basin for a number of years. The Western Canadian Sedimentary Basin is a term used to broadly describe the subsurface geology extending from the Rocky Mountains to Hudson Bay, across the western plains. The basin is deepest in Alberta, adjacent to the foothills. Imperial, the Canadian subsidiary of what was then Standard Oil of New Jersey (later, Exxon), was already a major refinery and marketing oil company, with head offices in Toronto but major facilities headquartered in Calgary. At the time, Imperial imported its supply of crude from oil-reserve-rich Middle Eastern countries, such as Saudi Arabia.

Overnight, young Canadian men like me wanted to become petroleum exploration geologists.

The geology professors at the University of Alberta quickly noted that sedimentary and petroleum geology was the geology of the future for students in the Western Canadian Sedimentary Basin. The professors understood the potential of the Devonian reefs in Alberta, and the prospect of many more oilfields.

I remember Professor Rutherford saying: "This is a great moment for you young people. You are no longer going to have to go to the Barren Lands for a career; the opportunity will be right here near Edmonton!" Immediately, the emphasis shifted, the faculty adjusted, and the study of sedimentary rocks took up a dominant position in our courses.

This shift in focus required investment in new labs, more professors and more classroom space. Enrolment in geology courses exploded, and class size jumped from a dozen or so to twenty, then thirty, then forty. Meanwhile, the university was coping with the same escalating demand for petroleum engineers and other professionals needed in the rapidly expanding oil industry. Those in charge did a good job and the graduating classes for the next few years produced the first generation of western Canadian oil professionals who would go on to discover new fields and become the executives and presidents of major and junior companies.

In the summer of 1948, I had my first taste of the changes that the dynamic decade of Alberta's first oil boom was bringing to my profession when I joined a GSC field party in the foothills mapping sedimentary deposits. My party chief that year was another university professor named Win Irish. Like Dr. Folinsbee, he ran such operations every summer. Not only did the GSC provide Drs. Irish and Folinsbee extra income in the summer months but it also made them better teachers. Dr. Folinsbee had given me a positive evaluation after my first summer with the GSC in the Barrens. When I applied again for another summer's work with the GSC, Dr. Irish checked my record then invited me to join his party. He told his team that we would go to Entrance, Alberta, to map an area of the foothills north of the Athabasca River called Grande Cache.

I spent that summer on horseback. A rancher who operated north of the village of Entrance provided horses to the field parties that were going into the foothills. I grew up with horses on the farm, so I had little problem with them, nevertheless, early in the summer I got bucked off twice! The horses carried us and our gear through some pretty rugged country. Learning how to pack them was something new to me, and it took time to get the hang of it.

This time with the GSC, my party had a full-time cook, a matronly lady whose husband was the packer. There were four student geologists under Dr. Irish: Tom Parry, Dick Hughes, Hugo Greiner and me. Dick became a very good friend of mine, and we socialized together after that summer in the foothills until he sadly died of cancer in his twenties.

Initially, we mapped rocks on the Muskeg River. To do so, we had to cross the fast-moving Smoky River. As we were fording the river, my horse decided to rid himself of me and bucked me off. I couldn't swim well—we didn't learn that skill on our farm—but on the Smoky, swimming was essential. Thankfully, the other party members helped me out.

Our map sheet for the year was called "A la Peche." We were covering an area in the high foothills country near the Rockies, and every day was a struggle. The rugged country necessitated many days of climbing and hiking—hard work. We were doing the same geological surface mapping as I had done the previous summer in the Barrens, but the camp life was different. Win Irish was easygoing and approachable. We would sit and talk at night before we went to bed. The tents were bigger than the pup tents we had in the North, and we had room to play hearts and rummy. When I grew up it was a "sin" to play cards in my parents' house, but I was happy to play cards away from home in the foothills.

Another big difference between foothills and Barrens camps was that Win Irish allowed us to take Sundays off. We slept in, had a Sunday dinner prepared by our cook, and then we played horseshoes. I had played horseshoes on the farm in Standard and was a tough competitor. We played a lot of horseshoes that summer, but I have not played the game since. I remember the time I spent in that camp fondly.

When we were working, we mapped the rocks that covered most of the geological section all the way from the Belly River formation down to the Mississippian strata, including the Cardium sand, which is a Cretaceous formation. The Cardium in the foothills was a sandstone formation from thirty to fifty feet thick, and we could walk across it and map it on the "A la Peche" map sheet. I did not yet know my future but, as it turned out, studying and mapping the Cardium in the foothills had a major impact on my life.

During my first summer with the GSC, I was planning to get married. During the second field season, Evelyn was pregnant and my first child was due to arrive. Because of this, Dr. Irish released me three days early. I made it back to Edmonton for the birth of my first son, Allan, on September 25, 1948.

Evelyn and I had a small apartment in Edmonton, not very far from the Misericordia Hospital. We lived with an old lady who owned the suite that we rented. I didn't own a car, so when Evelyn and I realized "things were happening," I started getting Evelyn and myself ready to walk the four blocks to the hospital. Our landlady was shocked. She said, "Arne, she's in labour—you had better not walk." I called a taxi. It was a good thing I did because it was not too long after we arrived at the hospital that Allan came into the world.

I graduated with a BSc in Geology in the spring of 1949. Instead of striking out into the workforce straight away, I decided to pursue graduate studies. I had earned a scholarship at Northwestern University but opted to stay in Edmonton and take an MSc beginning in the autumn semester. That summer, while I waited for my graduate work to begin, I had the good fortune of having two choices for summer employment.

The first was in the field with Imperial Oil. I was interviewed at the University of Alberta by Dr. Ernie Shaw, one of Imperial's senior geologists. Shaw offered me a position as a well-site geologist on several of the company's wells being drilled in the rapidly developing Leduc oilfield. Leduc was a very new and significant discovery, and many wells were being drilled south of Edmonton, resulting in many opportunities for young geologists.

The second employment opportunity came when I received an offer from Dr. Irish to become his leader on that summer's field party, and he specifically wrote me a letter of invitation. I had a major choice to make.

I could do something I loved with a man for whom I had a lot of respect, versus going to work for a huge corporation. I came very close to accepting Irish's offer, but my better judgement told me that having experience with the big company would serve me well in the long run. I made one of the major decisions of my life and took employment with Imperial Oil.

I became a well-site geologist in the Leduc oilfield and lived in Edmonton with my family, which soon would include two sons, Allan and Brian (not yet with us in that summer of 1949, as he was born March 27, 1950). I was able to go home with great regularity. The company had barracks in Devon for any of the staff working in the field, so I would stay there some of the time. Many times, however, I hitchhiked to Edmonton to be with my family in the evening, and then hitchhiked back to work in the morning. I still had my Tank Corps battle dress because the army had given us our uniforms when we were demobilized. We had to dye them if we wanted to wear them; we couldn't pretend we were still active soldiers. Nevertheless, when I wore my dyed battle dress, people could see that I was a veteran, which helped immensely in getting rides.

When I was working with Imperial, it was actively developing the Leduc field. There were two key geological points that had to be identified during the drilling of each well. One was the top of the Nisku reef, or D2, and the second was the top of the D3—the Leduc reef. The reason these points were critical was that they were the two producing horizons in the field. A producing horizon is a reservoir bed from which hydrocarbons can be obtained; in this case both Leduc and Nisku horizons were limestone reefs. As soon as oil in the D2 horizon was encountered, it would be put on production. If it was both a D2 and D3 well, we would have a dual completion, or the well would draw from both horizons. These important horizons had to be identified by a geologist based on drill cuttings, which would enable geologists to determine what formation the rock coming to the surface was from. The roughnecks took samples of the drill cuttings every ten feet and then brought them to the geologist, who identified the critical geological markers.

There were four well-site geologists who covered the Leduc field. One was a classmate of mine, Don Stewart, a University of Alberta graduate who is now retired and still lives in Calgary. He showed me how to pick these D2 and D3 tops during the drilling of a well. Learning how to do this wasn't as interesting as the field work I had done in the previous summers but I knew I needed to know well-site geology in order to be an exploration geologist in the oil and gas business.

My Leduc summer would prove to be indispensible training. I learned all about drilling and completion techniques, as well as the detailed aspects of operating the drilling rig. I also absorbed some of the lore of the great Leduc discovery. It was invaluable to me as a young geologist starting my career to understand geological teamwork, to grasp that every great discovery—no matter whose idea spurred it on—is completed through the efforts of several, sometimes many, individuals.

During the war, Imperial's thirty-two geologists had drilled a lot of wells and found nothing but natural gas, which had very little market value at the time. In 1946 Imperial was at a crossroads. It could build a plant to manufacture synthetic liquid fuel from its natural gas reserves, or it could make one more attempt at finding oil. The chief geologist, Ted Link, believed that the Devonian-era limestone reefs, deposited more than four hundred million years ago and now buried deep in the Western Canadian Sedimentary Basin, could be large oil traps. He had discovered one such Devonian reef at Norman Wells on the Mackenzie River in 1920.

However, in 1946, rather than teaching his exploration geologists what to look for, Link assigned a senior man, Jack Webb, to conduct a survey of all thirty-two people on the team. Where did they think Imperial should drill next in western Canada? The overwhelming opinion was to explore in a broad area of central Alberta, south of Edmonton. A geologist named Hank Kunst was assigned to work with a geophysicist named Ray Waters, an American from a very prominent geophysical firm called the Heiland Research Corporation. Heiland conducted a regional seismic survey across a swath of the province.

On the data of that survey, near the farming village of Devon, Heiland spotted an anomaly in the Devonian horizon that looked promising. Kunst wrote a report to Webb recommending the location. Webb agreed and took the proposal to Link. Approval came and another geologist, Steve Cosburn, was assigned to supervise the drilling of Leduc No. 1. Drilling commenced in the late autumn of 1946. Meanwhile, a young geologist on a drilling rig working in Saskatchewan, Aubrey Kerr, received instructions to move his rig at once to Alberta and start the drilling of Leduc No. 2. In February of 1947, Imperial struck oil at Leduc No. 1 and a few weeks later made a second—and actually better, with more pay—discovery at Leduc No. 2.

Aubrey Kerr, the geologist at Leduc No. 2, became the chronicler of the great oil discoveries of Alberta and of the geologists who made them. Aubrey died while I was writing this book. A few weeks before his death, we discussed my project and he told me about the book he was working on. The Leduc discovery had happened sixty years previously, and the bonds that tie exploration geologists still meant something to us.

The three summers of field work were of tremendous help to me as I embarked on my graduate studies, and then my career. A student geologist should pick jobs that will contribute to his or her future career, and I did that in all my summers.

In contrast to my field work, my master's degree thesis work was done indoors, with one eye looking through a microscope. My thesis involved the study of a Cretaceous-era family of fossils called the Foraminifera, a shelled amoeba with an anatomy that could only be seen through a microscope lens in a laboratory. There are many members of this fossil family, and by 1949 not much work had yet been done to identify the members of the family and give them names. Only one geologist before me, a man named R.T.D. Wickenden, had begun to classify the Foraminifera.

The first step in my thesis preparation was the familiar task of going into the field and collecting samples. I collected mine from the Upper Cretaceous shale from the Shaftsbury formation located on the Peace River. This formation was the product of millions of years of deposits in the floor of a temperate sea that once covered present-day western North America. Dr. Stelck was a great help to me in this effort.

I returned to the lab at the university and painstakingly collected the Foraminfera fossils. I soaked the samples in water for a time. After a while, the tiny fossils floated to the surface, and I could pick them up using a small artist's paint brush, place them on a slide and prepare the slide for inspection under the microscope. I wrote up descriptions of their anatomy and gave names to many of the genera I found in the shale. My thesis had to be approved by senior university academics. I was also subjected to an intense oral examination by a committee of two geologists from the department, Drs. Stelck and Warren, and a third university professor who was a scientist from the zoology department. I graduated with an MSc in Geology in the spring of 1950.

What did I contribute to mankind with my work with the Foraminifera? Not much, or so it seemed. However, fossil identification skills are essential to identifying rock and dating the geological era it comes from. In oil and gas exploration, dating and classifying the rock on the mud screens or in the drill core is one of the fundamental operations of drilling and completing every well. Behind the study of every drill core lies countless hours of lab work, such as the work I did on my thesis. Sooner or later, the kind of work I did that year pays off for another geologist.

In the early 1980s there was a geological controversy over the mass extinction of life on Earth, including large dinosaurs. It was proposed that a large comet had hit the globe on the geological time boundary between the Cretaceous and Tertiary eras (the K-T boundary), 65 million years ago. The theory stated that within a few decades, much prehistoric life became extinct.

Then, a palaeontologist named Keller conducted an intensive study of Cretaceous fossils on the K-T boundary using samples he collected in Tunisia. Sure enough, on the K-T boundary, eight species of Foraminifera disappeared in a major geological event. But he kept looking and found that there had been an earlier extinction of six species, and after those two geological incidents, additional extinctions of twenty-two species of Foraminifera. In other words, the extinction on the K-T boundary was not a single event triggered by a catastrophe but instead had taken a much longer period of time of several millennia.

The surface and subsurface of our planet and every planet are endlessly changing. Knowing the immense amount of research that has been done on the changes in our planet, and having participated in the kind of lab work it takes to accumulate the scientific knowledge necessary to making statements about Earth, I am skeptical about any rush to publish hasty judgements on geological events.

7

Professional Life

WHEN I ENTERED the "January class" at the University of Alberta in 1946 to study geology, oil and gas wildcatters and speculators ranked with cowboys and whisky runners in the romantic legends of western Canada. There were a hundred companies looking for oil and gas in the sedimentary basins of the prairies that year. Many who lacked formal geological training made some of the early discoveries, but because of the presence of the GSC from the outset of exploration, well-trained geological exploration spearheaded the effort to find the hidden riches that lay beneath the expanding fields of wheat and pasture.

Nearly a thousand wells had been drilled during the previous half-century and 17 fields had been discovered consisting of 37 oil and 101 natural gas wells. Between 1917 and 1945, the tally of investment in drilling was $200 million. It was a risky business. Approximately 850 dry holes had been drilled with the cumbersome cable tool rigs, which were just sophisticated rock chisels that bashed away at the ground for months and a depth of 1650 feet was considered an achievement. The experts believed they had identified 250 million barrels of oil reserves in the ground and 6 trillion cubic feet of gas, but the 20 refineries in the West processed oil imported from Wyoming and Montana.

The first discoveries had been made by accident, or because oil and gas seeped to the surface from shallow reservoirs. Construction crews of the Canadian Pacific Railway drilling for water near Medicine Hat in 1883 struck natural gas that blew up their drilling rig. John George "Kootenai" Brown, a scout for the Geological Survey of Canada, found oil seeps at Cameron Creek in present-day Waterton National Park by having the Blackfoot people of south- ern Alberta taste a mixture of kerosene and molasses, and asking them about places in their ancient lands with water that tasted the same. Of course, the Aboriginal people of the area—the Blackfoot and the Kutenai—knew about the oil, and its medicinal value, long before Brown arrived on the scene. On a canoe trek through the interior of the North-West Territories in 1875, John Macoun, an Ontario college biology teacher on a summer field trip for the GSC, identi- fied the enormous potential of the tar sands after he first smelled the exposed bitumen deposits on the bank of the Clearwater River near the Hudson's Bay Company trading post of Fort MacKay.

William Stewart Herron made the first big oil discovery at Turner Valley in 1914 because he taught himself the science of surface geology by reading wide- ly on geology and touring the earliest oilfields in Ontario and Pennsylvania. Herron correlated the gas seep on Sheep Creek with nearby surface structures indicating the presence of an oil-trapping anticline. Sedimentary rocks can be flat-lying or curve upward like a rainbow or downward like an upside-down rainbow. Rock that curves upward is called an anticline; rock that curves down- ward is called a syncline. In oil and gas history, there have been many finds in anticlines. Herron collected and sent samples from surface gas seeps on the structure to universities in Pennsylvania and California, and when they tested positive for petroleum traces he drilled his discovery well on the location where he had collected the samples.

Imperial Oil geologist Ted Link was a superb geologist who also used science to discover the Norman Wells oilfield on the Mackenzie River in August 1920. This oilfield is located in a Devonian reef. Link's find made Devonian reefs the prized target for oil exploration in Alberta, and led to the Leduc discovery in 1947.

The two world wars of the twentieth century inadvertently perfected a new tool for oil exploration: the geophysical or seismic survey. For two hun- dred years, researchers had developed seismic theory to measure earthquakes and locate icebergs at sea. Rival British and German scientists used geophysi- cal recorders for military intelligence during the First World War to measure the locations of enemy artillery and provide target co-ordinates for their own guns. In 1924 seismic surveys identified oil-bearing salt domes and discovered the Orchard Park field in Fort Bend County, Texas. Further advances in military intelligence during the Second World War, combined with more oil-industry research in the interwar period, resulted in the geophysical survey technology used by Imperial Oil to find the Leduc field in 1947. So, when I finished school in 1950 and set out to work in the industry, geologists and geophysicists were working together to combine their scientific expertise in the search for western Canadian oil.

When I completed graduate work, the oil industry was booming in western Canada as a result of the Devonian reef oil discoveries in the three years following Leduc. New oilfields were found around Edmonton, such as Redwater—a town northeast of Edmonton (the second-largest find next to Leduc)—and Golden Spike—west of Edmonton, so named because the reef in which oil was found was shaped like a spike—which are now legendary in the oil patch, were fresh and exciting. American companies were flooding into the country with the objective of finding more oilfields. These companies were looking for good Canadian geologists, and I received five job offers because of my academic record.

My supervisor during my summer at Imperial, Ernie Shaw, offered me a permanent job, fully expecting that I would accept it because Imperial was the biggest of the exploration companies at the time. He couldn't imagine that I would want to work anywhere else, especially now that I had a young family. Amoco and Gulf also made me firm offers, which meant that three of the top five companies in the country had made overtures. All of these companies were subsidiaries of multinational giants, and their offers promised a well-paid, secure, lifetime career. A smaller company, Rio Bravo, also offered me a job. Rio Bravo subsequently became Canadian Superior and hired me many years later.

Oddly, the Geological Survey of Canada did not offer me a job, although I would have considered it seriously had an offer been extended because I had enjoyed the field work. But the GSC tended to pick guys for permanent jobs who had been around for a while, working on the summer field parties and proving themselves loyal and reliable. I, on the other hand, had taken the first opportunity to work for Imperial Oil instead of the GSC.

My fifth offer came from an oil company called Socony-Vacuum, later renamed Mobil Oil. The person who interviewed me at Socony and made me that offer was Dr. Joe Spivak, a Canadian geologist and chief of Socony's geological group in Canada.

What should I do? In my own head, I boiled the offers down to Socony and Imperial Oil. Some of my best friends went to work at Amoco but the president at Amoco was such a "smoothie" that I knew I would be taking a big chance working for him. I'm never comfortable with people who seem to need to get along in life with a smooth-talking line; I always wonder why they can't be more straightforward. It was hard for me to take Rio Bravo out of the picture, but I reasoned that its parent, Superior Oil, wasn't as big in the US as Socony-Vacuum was. I also had a bad first impression of the person who ran the exploration and production side of the company, and who was doing the hiring of young geologists. Ironically, many years later, when Rio Bravo changed its name to Canadian Superior Oil, I accepted an offer to become its president for an extended period of time.

They both came to me with final job offers, and then I went to see my two geology professors, Charlie Stelck and Bob Folinsbee. They told me that both were great companies. Then they reasoned that since Imperial already had a big geological staff, if I went with Imperial I might end up doing a lot of well-site work, not so much exploration. They figured I would be better off going to work for a company that was not nearly as big in Canada as Imperial was, one that could use guys with my background as a field explorer. In short, they thought I should accept Socony's offer because that company would give me more opportunities for pure exploration work than Imperial, which already had a large number of geologists working in the Western Canadian Sedimentary Basin. They were particularly keen on Dr. Joe Spivak, Socony's chief geologist, who was an accomplished explorationist.

It was a tough call, especially because I liked Ernie Shaw so much and appreciated the break he'd given me by giving me my first job in the oil exploration business. However, I took Imperial out of the picture because of the advice of my university professors and I accepted the job with Socony. Dr. Spivak, whom I had liked right from our first meeting, became my mentor for the rest of my career. I started work on May 1, 1950, and, with only a seven-year interlude when I was with Canadian Superior Oil, I worked at Socony, later renamed Mobil Oil, for the next forty years. Throughout my career, however, I retained a great respect for Imperial, that great company that did so much to develop Canada's oil and gas resources, particularly during the early years, and for whom I enjoyed working during my first summer as a professional geologist.

When I started my full-time job with Socony-Vacuum in Edmonton, I felt that I needed to meet face to face with those executives from other companies who had extended job offers. I hitchhiked to Calgary and met with each of them personally to thank them for their offers. I came away from the brief calls on the men whose offers I had turned down knowing that my best decision was going to Socony-Vacuum. How true that turned out to be!

Socony-Vacuum's rather odd name dated back a century to the invention by a man named Matthew Ewing, in 1859, of a method of distilling kerosene from crude oil in a vacuum. An oily residue from the process turned out to be an excellent lubricant, and in 1865 the Vacuum Oil Co. was created to produce and market it. In 1879 John D. Rockefeller and the Standard Oil Company bought a 75 per cent interest in Vacuum. In 1882, when the oil billionaire organized the Standard Oil Trust, one of the pieces was the Standard Oil Company of New York, or Socony for short. In 1911, when the United States Supreme Court ordered Standard Oil Trust broken up—the company was too large for the current anti-combines law—Socony and Vacuum were among the nearly three dozen companies created. They merged in 1931 as Socony-Vacuum.

In 1940 Socony-Vacuum looked north for opportunities in Canada. It opened an office in Windsor, Ontario, to market its lubricants to Canada's burgeoning wartime industrial complex. Three years later, Socony-Vacuum moved a small exploration team—a manager, two field geologists and a secretary—to Calgary. Throughout the remainder of the war, this team did basic geology in the foothills of Alberta, and in British Columbia and the Northwest Territories. It also drilled Canada's first offshore Atlantic well—on a manmade island in Hillsborough Bay, Prince Edward Island.

Before the Leduc discovery, Socony-Vacuum acquired a 169,000-acre block of oil and gas rights south of the long-established Turner Valley fields and signed a 2-million-acre farm-in agreement to drill on a CPR-owned freehold in southern Alberta. These deals established the company as a significant player in the basin.

When I went to work for Socony in Calgary, that city had been a rancher's town for most of its history but was in the process of becoming the financial and executive centre of western Canadian oil and gas exploration. It was an exciting time to be a geologist. Immediately after the war, there had been few geologists in western Canada, except for the handful working in the big companies. Socony had just five geologists in western Canada in 1947. Immediately after the Leduc discovery, that number expanded to about fifteen. By 1950 Socony employed between twenty and twenty-five geologists.

When I joined Socony-Vacuum, the pace of drilling rights acquisition was picking up and had extended into Saskatchewan. There were now more than forty employees on the payroll in western Canada, and the only cloud on the horizon was that our first seven post-Leduc wildcats were dry holes. It was common in those years to drill a few dry holes before the exploration team found its feet and significant geological plays were identified. However, Socony-Vacuum's luck was about to change for the better.

My initial work with the company involved logging wells, which consisted of describing drill cuttings from wells in which Socony had an interest. Although maintaining this meticulous record was essential in mapping and understanding a geological basin, the work involved was extremely tedious. It was particularly demanding when the work was continuous from 8:00 a.m. to 4:30 p.m. It was in many ways similar to the unglamorous work of describing and naming those microscopic Foraminifera when I was preparing my thesis.

The company's executives were located in offices in the Lancaster Building on 8 Avenue SW—in 1950 theirs was a pretty fancy address. Many prestigious young companies and law firms had offices in the Lancaster. It had a history of housing successful businesses even before the Leduc oil boom. Thankfully it still survives today, one of several buildings in Calgary's city core that are appreciated for both architectural grace and historical connection, which haven't been torn down to be replaced by the towers of marble, steel and glass that later oil booms created.

The working conditions for the geologists were not exactly the best. Our offices were located in a garage-like structure, a former warehouse that had no ventilation and no natural light. The tomb-like conditions were made worse by the amount of smoking that went on in the "offices"; I never have smoked, but many of my colleagues certainly did! We took our breaks by going out into the back lane, where we could get some sunshine and fresh air. All over Calgary—now a boomtown—buildings like this one were being converted from previous uses to meet the incessant demand of a fast-moving, competitive, exploration rush. As a result, the accommodations in which the day-to-day work of discovery was taking place were not fancy or pleasant.

There were about six of us working in that dilapidated structure, all young geologists doing the same thing day after day, week in and week out, to pay our dues in the profession and earn our place in the company. We were laying the groundwork for what would prove to be many great oil and gas discoveries in Canada over the next fifty years, but of course we didn't know it at the time. Hollywood had begun to make dramatic movies about life in the oil patch, featuring oil-soaked gushers and wild well blowouts, but none of them was about a young geologist logging wells. Nonetheless, we were young and keen, glad to have reasonably paid jobs and confident that, when we got our break, we would do great things.

I now worked for an outfit whose roots lead back to the founding of the modern multinational oil industry and was in a position to prosper in western Canada's emerging oil patch. Since Socony-Vacuum in its various guises was to be my employer for most of my career, and eventually I was to become its leader, I was fortunate to have chosen to work for it in 1950. However, I didn't appreciate my good luck as I bent over those well cuttings, hour after hour, in the dingy warehouse lab.

After a couple of years, I finally caught what seemed to be a break. Socony was drilling a rank wildcat only three miles from my former home in Standard. Dr. Spivak, the chief geologist, knowing that I grew up in the area, assigned me to the job of being well-site geologist at this location. The well took about three months to drill. Although there was a geological shack on the rig floor, I spent a lot of time at home with my parents. It was the first well to be drilled any-where in the area, and it attracted a lot of community interest. For a short time, I became a local celebrity. Every Sunday afternoon, and frequently during the week, inhabitants of Standard, who had known me since my childhood, showed up at the drilling rig to get a tour of the facility. My father was particularly proud that his son had returned to the area as a trained geologist. Unfortunately, like most wildcats, the well was dry and my reputation took a beating. My Standard friends did not quite realize that I was not responsible for the lack of production at the location but only for the job of seeing the well drilled. After the well was abandoned, I returned to Calgary to resume logging wells.

At this point, however, an organizational development occurred that affect-ed the rest of my life.

In 1952 Socony decided to decentralize its operation and, although the main office remained in Calgary, district offices were established in Edmonton, Swift Current and Regina. The management in Calgary was sufficiently impressed with my organizational skills that I was asked to move to Edmonton and set up a Socony district office, which would be responsible for all exploration work in central Alberta.

I regarded this as a great opportunity, and I immediately accepted the assign-ment. I didn't realize at the time that it was the first of my many moves to cities across western Canada and North America. Many geologists in those booming years made discoveries and also had the administrative ability to become execu-tives. It was my chance to get out of the logging lab and prove myself.

One of the first things I did was rent office space in downtown Edmonton. The quarters were modest. The building was a nondescript two-floor walk-up

In Edmonton, taking a break from work (the photographer insisted on the big smile).

and the accommodations were unpretentious. We were a small group of only three geologists, two landmen—in Canada, landmen do what needs to be done to obtain government permits and participate in provincial land sales—and three non-professional staff. The other two geologists were Fred Trollope and Tony Mason, both excellent professionals, who became lifelong friends. Tony retired in Panama and subsequently died. Fred retired in Calgary and still lives in the city.

Funny, I revisited the street where the office was located a few years ago to find that the building that was the nerve centre for the discovery of the biggest oilfield in Canadian history, and the place where I made my reputation, had become a strip club!

In 1952 Edmonton was closer than Calgary was to the exploration action, closer to the drilling rigs and closer to the glamorous drilling targets. Edmonton was surrounded by the discoveries of large, light sweet-crude oilfields that had followed Leduc: Redwater, Golden Spike, Wizard Lake, Bonnie Glen, Duhamel (a Socony find), Joseph Lake, Stettler, Sundre, Fenn, Big Valley and more. Some of these names are remembered only locally or by oil-patch old timers like me, long since overshadowed by five decades of newer discoveries. Some are still part of the common memory of active oil and gas companies and their young professionals and leaders. A small few are still imprinted on the public mind. To us, back then in the early 1950s as we moved into our Edmonton digs, those names and discoveries were part of our daily conversations.

In those days, Edmonton was the province's oil town. Edmonton had at its threshold the wheat fields, the coal and oil and natural gas deposits, the university, the airfield and the access to the North. Also, with the development of the Cold War Distant Early Warning Radar Line (DEW Line), the radium and uranium mines for the emerging nuclear power industry, as well as the belief that the future resource wealth of Canada was north of the 60th parallel of latitude, it seemed at that time that Edmonton would be the economic powerhouse of the province.

Calgary's success as the oil capital of Canada has long since carried it past Edmonton as a business centre. However, in 1952, as our small band of Socony geologists started work in Edmonton, what mattered was the energy and enthusiasm that surrounded us. Soon, Tony Mason, Fred Trollope and I—all University of Alberta graduates—would make our own contribution to the excitement.

PART TWO

Exploration

8

Before Pembina

IN 1952, the year I opened Socony-Vacuum's new Edmonton district field office, petroleum geology had come of age in Alberta. My generation of petroleum geologists was better educated and better equipped than any generation had been. We had a powerful array of "modern" exploration tools at our disposal. Geophysical surveys, geological surface maps, well logs, well cores and accurate regional stratigraphic columns verified in every well drilled by samples of rock recovered in the drilling rig mud screens.

The first century of oil and gas exploration in Canada and Alberta was ending. In that pioneering era, discoveries were first made drilling surface seeps of crude oil and natural gas or surface deposits of oil shales and tar sands. Slowly, geologists began to understand the relationships between surface features and oil and gas traps below the surface.

The use of seismic surveys to map subsurface stratum and structures started in an experimental fashion before the Second World War and scored its first major success with the discovery of a large deposit of sour natural gas at Jumping Pound west of Calgary. The war was being won in Europe and the Pacific, so this breakthrough didn't make a huge impression on the public mind. The next big oil discovery, Imperial Oil's Leduc No. 1, on the other hand, became the most famous well in the Western Canadian Sedimentary Basin.

It is the nature of oil booms that when a discovery is made in a particular geological formation and under specific circumstances, everyone will try to imitate it. In the earliest years of oil drilling in North America, explorers in southwestern Ontario and shortly after that in Pennsylvania drilled the first commercial fields in and around surface oil seeps or where water well drillers found crude oil within a few feet of the surface. As geological understanding improved, explorers began to discover oil and natural gas in structures that could be identified by the distinctive rolling terrain and sharp outcrops that betrayed anticlines and synclines below. The introduction of geophysical survey technology gave North American explorers the tool they needed to find stratigraphic traps and structures that couldn't be seen at the surface.

After Leduc, which was a vast oil reserve trapped in a Devonian-era limestone structure that 400 million years ago had been a picturesque coral reef off a tropical beach in a warm shallow sea, every company wanted to find its own Devonian reef. Geophysical exploration, a seismic survey delineating the image of rock strata and structures thousands of feet underground, was the key to the Leduc discovery.

Because it allowed an explorationist to "look" beneath Earth's surface, deep into the geological layers of the basin, only a seismic survey could detect and map a Devonian reef. Even though they held sometimes hundreds of millions of barrels of oil, Devonian reefs were tiny compared to the thousands of square kilometres of oil- and gas-bearing sedimentary basin in which they hid. When Imperial discovered the Leduc oilfield, there were eleven geophysical crews exploring in Alberta.

We were singularly fortunate in Alberta to have the best exploration data available anywhere in the world. We had good regional surface maps. Dr. John Allen who, in 1912, established the geology faculty at the University of Alberta had also published the first geological map of the entire province of Alberta in 1920.

We also had the benefit of an extensive and growing publicly available bank of drilling cores and well logs. First the Geological Survey of Canada and then the Alberta Oil and Gas Conservation Board had encouraged the sharing of well data, and then the Alberta government eventually mandated it. (We aggressively "scouted"—spied on—confidential drilling operations to attempt to garner the exploration secrets of our competitors before they had to be disclosed by law.)

These tools and this knowledge produced a postwar wave of oil and gas discoveries. It was the perfect time to be a young exploration geologist with your career ahead of you, especially an Alberta-born and Alberta-educated one working in Alberta. Alberta was coming of age as a self-reliant, independently wealthy, self-confident province, and petroleum geologists were making the discoveries that were responsible for Alberta's dynamic new look.

The competing oil companies busily conducted geophysical surveys across central Alberta and studied the printouts looking for the big prize—the Devonian reef that might contain the light crude oil, that holy grail of oils that has low density, lots of hydrocarbon fractions and flows freely at room temperature; it also produces a higher percentage of gasoline and diesel fuel at the oil refinery, giving it a higher price than heavy crude—that would yield a highly productive well capable of producing hundreds of barrels, or preferably thousands of barrels, of oil a day. A young geologist couldn't hope to get the budget to drill a well unless he had a seismic survey in his hand that had a blip on it that might be considered a reef. Like all the others, Socony-Vacuum was conducting seismic surveys. We knew, however, that there wouldn't be enough Devonian reefs to go around. Those that were being discovered lay along a pretty big fairway that ran from northwest to southeast across the centre of the province near Edmonton. The Western Canadian Sedimentary Basin was much bigger than that, and other types of oil and gas traps had been discovered in it. We knew the basin had hardly been touched yet; it had much more to offer.

Meanwhile, the steam was going out of the boom that Leduc had triggered. Activity had been dramatic but oil exploration has its cycles. Alberta had already been through three boom-and-bust events at Turner Valley. By 1952, six years after Imperial spudded the Leduc No. 1 location, investment and new drilling activity was slacking off. It was almost imperceptible, but the slow-down was happening and was noticed with concern by the experts and authorities.

What was needed was a new idea. In that district office in Edmonton, poring over geological maps and data, my colleagues and I found what we hoped would be the next big thing: the Pembina oilfield. It was located in an isolated bush and pioneering community, just a few miles southwest of Edmonton, in a world that still operated in a manner that had become extinct elsewhere in the province, in a world still reliant on kerosene lamps and horses.

At Socony-Vacuum, we had our own well data that was still confidential because the deadline to give it to the regulator for public sharing hadn't been reached yet. The competitive advantage in the halcyon years of wildcat drilling and exploration that followed Leduc was the ability to see in data that everyone shared things that other people couldn't see. And working in that cavernous warehouse—too hot in summer and too cold in winter—had taught us, at Socony, to be pretty good at seeing things that others missed.

From March 3 to April 7, 1953, a group of Canadian corporate, government and academic leaders gave a series of Tuesday afternoon speeches in New York called *Canada on the March* to explain to the investment and business community the economic boom that had been unfolding in Canada since the end of the war. One of the speakers was Nathan E. Tanner who was Alberta's Minister of Lands and Mines from 1937 to 1952 and presided over the political management of the birth of Alberta's oil industry.

Tanner was a respected man in oil and gas circles, the rare kind of politician trusted by business. Before the war, he had earned the respect of the industry with his role in creating the Oil and Gas Conservation Board and because of his tireless and thankless campaign—which entailed arduous trips to London, New York and Montreal—to get Canadian, British and American investors to capitalize Alberta's oil development. In 1953 Tanner told his New York audience:

> It is true that the extent of the oil development and production in Canada is very small in comparison to that of the United States, and to some, at first glance, might even seem insignificant. On the other hand, it must be realized that practically all of the development has taken place in the last six years.
>
> At the beginning of 1947 when the [Imperial Oil Devonian reef, sweet, light, crude oil] Leduc strike was made, Canada had reached a low ebb in the search for and production of oil; in fact, serious consideration was being given to the possibilities of making synthetic oil from natural gas.
>
> Canada was producing less than 10 percent of her petroleum requirements, or just barely enough for the province of Alberta. Today [1953] her possible production would meet over 50 percent of all her requirements.
>
> In 1947, the total proven reserves of crude oil were sufficient only to meet Canadian requirements for less than a year. Today, just six years later, these reserves have increased by more than twenty times (from 72 million to 1.6 billion barrels) and are sufficient to meet Canada's requirements for more than ten years in spite of the fact that the nation's consumption has more than doubled.

Geologists had also discovered a great deal of natural gas in Alberta in the years between 1946 and 1952. In 1951 gas reserves increased 45 per cent, from

4.7 to 6.8 trillion cubic feet. In 1952 they grew another 50 per cent to 10.2 trillion cubic feet. *Daily Oil Bulletin* editor Carl Nickle, another man people listened to at the time, wrote in his year-end report: "the great questions of 1953" wouldn't be about oil at all but rather whether or not governments would clear the way for gas pipelines and exports that would, "put to use the gas resources which are among the West's biggest 'idle assets.'"

The Leduc discovery on February 1947, Tanner said to those gathered in New York, had changed the landscape. No one understood that better than geologists like me who had been hired to explore for oil as Alberta was flooded with American investment capital from companies who were scouring the Middle East and the world for crude oil to fuel postwar industrial expansion in North America, Europe and Japan.

Tanner described how that flood of capital—from $12 million a year in 1946 before Leduc to $50 million in 1948, $165 million in 1959 and $300 million in 1952—had changed the oil patch. Geologists like me were exploring 214 million acres of land at the end of 1952 compared to 20 million acres of exploration permits in 1946. The 840 exploration wells drilled in 1952 was seven times the 119 drilled in 1946.

Tanner showed his audience two maps of western Canada. One, dated 1946, indicated only four important oilfields in western Canada: Turner Valley, Jumping Pound, Lloydminster and Pincher Creek, all in Alberta. The second map, dated 1952, was black with forty dots stretching from Daly, Manitoba, to Fort St. John, British Columbia.

The future, said Tanner, depended on completing a network of interprovincial and international pipelines in Canada that would take the rapidly multiplying crude oil and natural gas reserves of Alberta and the Western Canadian Sedimentary Basin to consumers in its biggest cities and markets. And, he said, the future also depended on the commercial development of the oil sands, initially called tar sands, which had taken on a new life since the end of the war and, with Alberta engineers and geologists leading the research, was moving slowly toward its first postwar mining and extraction projects.

Behind Tanner's numbers lay two stark facts that defined the opportunities of my new career as a petroleum geologist. The first was that we geologists had our work cut out for us. There were thousands of wells to drill and hundreds of discoveries yet to be made. The second fact was that North Americans were buying cars and building homes and highways at an astonishing rate. My family heated our little farm house at Standard with coal, as did most Canadians before the war—coal or wood. Now families across the country were asking for oil or gas furnaces; factories were switching from coal, the fuel of the industrial revolution, to oil and natural gas.

In the early 1950s, Eric Hansen, an obscure young economics professor at the University of Alberta, was documenting the Canadian move from coal to oil. The age of coal was ending and the oil age beginning. In 1946 the world demand for oil was 8 million barrels a day, and 60 per cent of that was burned in North America. In ten years, Hansen predicted, that consumption would double. In Canada oil was replacing coal as the primary source of energy. In 1945 coal supplied 58 per cent of Canadian energy needs, and oil 22 per cent. In 1955, two years after I discovered the Pembina field, oil provided 50 per cent of Canadian energy and coal had fallen to 33 per cent.

I was just one among the 925,000 Albertans, both in and out of the oil and gas exploration and production industry, whose lives were being changed by the industry. Only one-third of Albertans lived in the largest cities of Calgary and Edmonton. Half lived as rural residents in remote, widely scattered locations in the counties and municipal, improvement, and special districts of the province. One in ten was the head of a farm family. As oil and gas exploration and production operations expanded, the human geography of the rural landscape—in which half of the population lived by farming, logging, fur-trapping or mining—was being transformed. Little hamlets and settlements that still relied on kerosene lamps for light and horsepower for work were turning overnight into boomtowns and future oil towns.

Two of those little places were the hamlet of Drayton Valley on the North Saskatchewan in Brazeau County southwest of Edmonton, and the neighbouring settlement of Violet Grove on the Pembina River. The forest surrounding these communities had been passed through by explorer David Thompson in 1810 but remained the domain of the Cree people until 1907, when the first lumber crews arrived to harvest the lush stands of timber and float the logs down the river to Edmonton. The area was so remote that it hardly noticed the Depression, and the only industrial development proposed for the area— a hydroelectric power dam—was never built. Likewise, railway lines were also planned for but never constructed.

Living conditions in these communities were as primitive as you could find in Alberta after it became a province in 1905. The first settlers—Dora and William Drake—spent their first winter in a tent. Their living conditions improved when they built a log shack whose walls were caulked with mud and pages from the Eaton's catalogue. The first homesteaders who wanted to farm had to work for cash on the logging crews or as trappers until they could clear the land, an arduous task that depended upon teams of oxen to pull the stumps. There wasn't much land to clear as this was a place of swamps, coulees and impassable streams. In the early years of settlement, the nearest supplies of coffee, sugar, flour and other staples could only be obtained by travelling to a larger town, a trip that most families only undertook once a year. There was at first no priest, no church; there was no school for the first ten years. People survived on garden staples—potatoes, rhubarb, carrots, turnips—supplemented by wild berries, which fortunately grew abundantly in the bush, and wild game and fish. Recreation consisted of box socials and card parties. Dances were held outdoors in the summer. Occasionally, a family was able to afford a radio.

As the logging industry subsided through the 1920s, Drayton Valley and Violet Grove became even quieter, surviving on the edge of subsistence only because of the courage and resourcefulness of the people. During the Depression, the area escaped the terrible drought experienced to the south. The people had so little cash in good times that they hardly noticed its absence in the bad times.

The only changes before the war came were the construction of a community hall, a school, churches and a local store. In 1952, the year before everything would change for these two communities, conditions in the settlements had been stable for forty years. Only 30 per cent of the land in the district was under cultivation. Second-growth forest was swallowing up much of the wilderness that had been previously logged. The houses were still basic wood-frame structures, the poorest little more than shacks. Most homes still lacked electricity and indoor plumbing; there were no telephones in the homes, just one at the general store. People heated with wood, read by the light of kerosene lamps and dug their own wells for water.

Drayton Valley had a population of seventy-five in 1952 and didn't even rank as a village in the government's eyes. Violet Grove was half that size. However, they were populous and important centres of a 1,864-square-mile rural improvement district with a widely scattered population of farmers, loggers and trappers numbering just seven hundred. Drayton Valley, with a narrow muddy main street and modest wood-frame buildings was the service centre for the farms and logging operations. Violet Grove was a place where more isolated people went for dances and social events. When oil companies first acquired permits to explore this desolate bush, we geologists called our new prospects "moose pasture" because that was the only use for the land before we arrived, or so we believed.

The moose pasture would change dramatically overnight, as exploration crews and their families poured in after the Pembina No. 1 discovery was announced in 1953. Within weeks, dozens of families living in vacation trailers were crowded into clearings around Drayton Valley. In Violet Grove, men were happy to have a bed in a garden shed, or in a thrown-together plywood and tar-paper shanty.

This was a pattern of change in the human geography of Alberta that would be repeated over and over again in the next twenty years, as seismic survey and drilling rig crews moved north and west in Alberta, pushing deeper into the wilderness in search of new drilling locations and new discoveries. They were preceded, as a rule, by fleets of bulldozers—Cats—that opened rough, muddy, access roads; running seismic lines; and cleared air strips, campsites and drilling pads, preparing the stage for the actual work of exploration. They moved like an invading army westward into the foothills and northward into the Peace Country and the borderlands where Alberta and British Columbia met the Yukon and Northwest Territories. Somewhere north of Edmonton, oil company aircraft flew out of civilian airspace and into the skies of bush pilots and Cold War military flight and radar defence.

The deeper the oil exploration crews penetrated into the boreal forest, the more seasonal operations became. Unable to move heavy equipment through swamp and muskeg, men waited until freeze-up to start work and evacuated the bush before spring thaw. And everywhere they went, small outposts populated by fur trappers, homesteaders, fishers, timber crews, including First Nations and Métis peoples, all of them scratching out a living in unforgiving circumstances. Frequently the crews noted that English was not spoken in these settlements, which were often immigrant or First Nations communities. Just as it had in years past, everywhere in Canada and the United States to the south, the frontier was disappearing. This time it wasn't pioneers in covered wagons or immigrant homesteaders crammed into Canadian Pacific Railway cars who were changing the landscape. Now, thin seismic exploration lines snaked out through the forests in an expanding web. Well-site pads and campsite clearings, where men lived in cramped trailers, sprang up beside traplines and remote cabins. And tiny hamlets that didn't even boast of a crossroad—just a post office, a priest or a Mounted Police detachment—were turning into boom towns of shanties and twenty-four-hour taverns and brothels, soon to be followed by modern houses, electric power lines, fresh groceries in the stores and paved roads as oil towns spread like wildfire across the province.

9

Discovering Pembina

LIKE MANY OTHER great western Canadian oil and gas discoveries, Pembina No. 1 defied conventional geological wisdom. In 1952 the conventional wisdom was that Alberta's best oil prospects were in the Devonian-era limestone reefs—ancient coral reefs of shallow seas now locked up in the province's geologic deposits. The Pembina discovery was made by going off in a completely different direction.

Before Pembina, Socony-Vacuum was still a small player in the Alberta oil boom. It had minor oil production from nineteen wells in a Devonian reef discovery made in 1950 at Duhamel, a small village near Camrose. That field gave Socony a taste of Leduc-style oilfields, and the company acquired more exploration prospects in central Alberta and southern Saskatchewan.

By the end of 1952, we had interests in 8.4 million acres across western Canada, including 3.8 million in southern Saskatchewan. In 1953 Socony increased its prairie exploration budget to $275,000, a sizeable sum at the time.

At the time, Socony-Vacuum's most active area in Canada was in the now-famous Williston Basin in Saskatchewan, where it had just made five oil discoveries. By comparison to the Devonian reefs of Alberta, however, the Williston Basin wells were small potatoes. In February 1953, Socony-Vacuum announced a major deal with the Seaboard Oil Company, an American outfit from Delaware. Seaboard held a Crown reservation—an exploration permit—for four townships totalling nearly 100,000 acres in west-central Alberta, the village of Drayton Valley centrally located in it. This area of forest and swamp was still unexplored for oil and gas, and we called the place a "rank wildcat" acreage because the first well drilled would be, we hoped, a wildcat well that would seem untamed. The company hoped that somewhere in those four townships we young geologists would find oil-rich Devonian reefs.

The terms of the deal with Seaboard required that Socony would pay all the costs of drilling two test wells—each about 9,500 feet deep—to earn a half interest in the entire block of land. The wells were to be drilled into the legendary D-2 strata or Nisku, in which the coveted oil-loaded Devonian reefs had been discovered at Leduc, Redwater, Golden Spike, Wizard Lake, Bonnie Glen and Pigeon Lake.

If we made a discovery, government regulations required that we turn half the subsurface rights on the 100,000 acres back to the province to be reissued in land sales so that other companies could compete for whatever we found. However, the remaining Socony 50,000-acre checkerboard would still be a very large development target.

As the district geologist in the Edmonton field office, it was my job to explore the Seaboard townships. I started by studying the logs of the handful of other wells that had been drilled in proximity to the Seaboard townships. Well logs are an electronic profile of the geology from the surface to the bottom of a well, made when it is drilled. I scrutinized those well logs for hour after hour. A well drilled at Buck Creek south of the Seaboard townships had found gas in the Mississippian strata, and I saw that the log showed the presence of the Cardium horizon just above the gas discovery. At the time, most oil and gas finds were in the Cardium, but then we started finding hydrocarbon in the Mississippian strata, which is lower and deeper than the Cardium.

North of what would be Pembina, in two wells drilled at Wabamun Lake, I could also see evidence of the Cardium, but in well logs for locations west of the Leduc discovery and east of the Seaboard townships there was no Cardium horizon. You had to be a pretty careful looker to see the Cardium signature, and to see when it wasn't there, but I was a pretty careful looker.

I recalled the summer working for the Geological Survey of Canada in the foothills of Alberta. I had literally walked on the Bighorn, a massive sandstone development that correlated with the Cardium in the deeper part of the Western Canadian Sedimentary Basin. The "keynote" of the correlation was in a fossil, the *Cardium pauperculum*, which is about the size of your fingertip. It is an index for the Cardium sandstone, and we'd found it in the Bighorn. It was

It might not look like much, but it was the harbinger of good fortune: the first Cardium sand core to be cut from the Pembina field, 1953.

the kind of geological evidence in which rockhound-style geologists like me, who had graduated from the Canadian Geological Survey, had confidence.

My geological premise for Pembina townships was that the Cardium was a major sandstone body in the basin, affirmed by the large number of wells in which I had found it. I remembered that as the Bighorn Cardium formation comes out of the foothills, it plunges deeply into the basin. Travelling eastward, it turns up and dips to shallower depths and disappears—pinches out—two to three hundred miles east of where I'd walked on its outcrops as a summer student with the GSC.

When I saw the Cardium horizon in the logs, I realized that I had found good conditions for a huge regional stratigraphic oil and gas trap.

Most geologists in 1952 disregarded the Cardium. It was good sandstone for hydrocarbon reservoirs, but it was always tight—lacking the porosity to produce oil or gas commercially. The wisdom at the time was that if it had previously produced oil in Alberta, as some old hands claimed it had, it was only in negligible amounts.

How did I know there was hydrocarbon in the Pembina-area Cardium? I went to see the great academic Charlie Stelck at the University of Alberta. He had been one of my professors. He had also done fieldwork on the Bighorn out-crops in the foothills and had detected oil staining in the rock. He reassured me that my theory of hydrocarbon deposits in the Cardium sandstone stratigraphic trap was a likely one.

How much hydrocarbon would there be? And would it be oil or natural gas? We had to drill to find those answers. But to drill for the stratigraphic trap, I needed the approval of bosses who wanted me to find structural targets in the form of Devonian reefs.

Somehow I had to placate them. An exploration geologist could not get a well drilled in those days without it being on a seismically defined location—Leduc had been drilled on a seismic location, and the reef discoveries that fol-lowed were drilled on seismic anomalies. There had been a bunch of dry holes drilled on seismic anomalies, too, but that didn't seem to matter. I needed a seismic anomaly that had a hint of at least one Devonian reef to get the money to drill the well.

An American geophysicist named Don Bigelow and I began looking at the seismic data that Seaboard had acquired. We were heavily staffed with Americans like Bigelow because Socony, with huge operations south of the bor-der, figured if it was going to drill some of these raw lands in Canada it would bring some of these smart Americans up to help these dumb young Canadians.

Seismic in those days was very poor compared to what was available in later years, and the seismic data I had to work with was the poorest of the poor. It was very much like an old, grainy, blurry, black and white photograph compared to today's high-resolution, colour, digital photos. Nevertheless, Seaboard had covered four townships with reconnaissance seismic in the previ-ous couple of years, so we had to work with it. Bigelow and I spent two days looking for something that was drillable and would get approval from the top men in Calgary.

Two of the senior managers were American geophysicists: Rex Mooreman, the president, and the chief geophysicist, Jim Kidder. The third was the chief geologist, Joe Spivak. Spivak was a veteran of the Geological Survey of Canada, not really tuned into geophysics. He was an old-time rockhound, and for him the key to exploration was in the field looking at rocks. He would understand my evidence for a hydrocarbon-bearing Cardium stratigraphic trap.

After two days, Bigelow and I chose the best-looking seismic high. We knew this was third-rate, just a geophysical hickey. It didn't look anything like those big, powerful anomalies that the Devonian reef discoveries were drilled on. Of course, we had another objective: a stratigraphic trap. But the only way to test

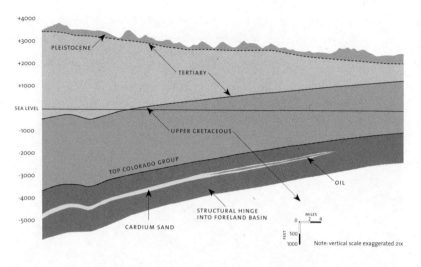

+4000
+3000 PLEISTOCENE
+2000 TERTIARY
+1000
SEA LEVEL
-1000 UPPER CRETACEOUS
-2000 TOP COLORADO GROUP
-3000 OIL
-4000
-5000 STRUCTURAL HINGE INTO FORELAND BASIN
CARDIUM SAND

MILES
0 2 4

FEET 500
1000 Note: vertical scale exaggerated 21x

Stratigraphic cross-section showing Cardium oil entrapment in the Pembina field.

it was to propose to drill a seismic "shadow" that looked like it might be a reef. In other words, we told our bosses what they wanted to hear. Our location was accepted and we immediately signed up drilling contractor Reading & Bates to get out to the location and prepare the well site.

Another geologist in the Edmonton office, Tony Mason, was critical to the decision to drill at Drayton Valley because his agreement with my theory was a clincher. The well-site geologist was to be Fred Trollope, who would oversee the operation as the well drilled into the Cardium.   ·

With the well approved, my next job was to put together the geological section and prepare a prognosis listing the names of the horizons and the approximate thicknesses the drilling crew and well-site geologist could expect to encounter. I knew that in the Cretaceous formation we would find sandstone and shale; the sandstone would likely be tight and the shale would also be non-porous. There would be sandstone beds in the lower part of the Belly River formation—a stratigraphical unit of Late Cretaceous, made up of carbonaceous sandstone and shaley coal seams; it underlies most of the Alberta plains—but I didn't expect them to be as potentially productive as the Cardium. We would also penetrate the Viking horizon. The Viking is higher up stratigraphically than the Cardium and therefore deposited after the Cardium was. It has produced a lot of oil in the Western Canadian Sedimentary Basin. It is fairly continuous but not as continuous the Cardium. The first Viking discovery that really caught the eye was Joseph Lake, some months later, and geologists began to say, "Boy,

Socony Seaboard Pembina No. 1, the discovery well of the Pembina oilfield on the day we brought it into production, June 17, 1953.

look out for the Viking." Ultimately, there were quite a number of other Viking discoveries and a lot of production from them.

Then, in my prognosis, came the Cardium, where I believed there would be a regional stratigraphic trap containing oil. Below the Cardium sand, a Mississippian strata formation would also be worth testing. For the benefit of management, I also said there was potentially a deeper Devonian reef.

For a long time afterward, other people in the industry said I'd just been lucky when the Cardium at Pembina proved to be a very large oil reservoir. Nonetheless, the original prognosis made before the well was drilled proved that we knew what we were doing.

The well location co-ordinates were 4–16–48–8W5 near Violet Grove, seven miles southwest of Drayton Valley and on the banks of the Pembina River. We began to drill the well on February 24, 1953.

Because this was a particularly important well for Socony, and because the competition for exploration acreage was particularly intense, major security precautions were necessary. Our routine communications with Drayton Valley were done via a telephone party line, to which the whole community had access. For the Pembina No. 1 exploration well, however, we had to protect the communication between myself and the well-site geologist in the field. This meant setting up a radio telephone. One end of the communications system was the radio telephone at the well site in the geologist's well shack. The other end was a radio phone in my bedroom. A drilling rig works around the clock, so I needed to get up at critical times throughout the night to communicate with Fred. Evelyn accepted this arrangement with equanimity in spite of the disruption.

We erected a pair of two-by-four poles in my backyard on which to hang the radio telephone aerial. This caused some difficulty with our neighbours, which I solved by asking one of Mobil's lawyers to come to Edmonton. He and I went to the homes of each of the neighbours to let them know that this was a temporary arrangement.

It was a great day for everyone concerned when we were able to establish one end of the communication system in our company office in downtown Edmonton and the two-by-fours came down and my wife could sleep though the night again.

Fred Trollope, the well-site geologist, had been on the lookout for the Cardium but didn't notice it immediately, so we missed noting the top of the formation. However, during the night of March 14, when the drilling depth reached 5,300 feet I received a radio call at my home from Fred telling me I'd better get out to the well site. Tony Mason and I jumped into my car and arrived at 3:00 a.m. on March 15.

After identifying oil-stained sand through our microscopes, we ran a drill stem test from an interval of 5,335 to 5,376 feet and recovered heavily oil-cut mud. I placed a jar of the oily mud on my credenza in Edmonton, and in a few days the top half of the jar was filled with light-gravity oil. For me, this was an exciting and significant development, as it verified my prognosis for the well in dramatic visual fashion.

We continued drilling for two more months until we reached a depth of 9,425 feet in the Ireton formation of dense green shale in the Nisku horizon. The Leduc-type reefs were always located in Ireton shales, but, as we expected this time, there was no reef. We logged the well on Friday, May 15, and clearly identified evidence of hydrocarbon in the Cardium. The log also indicated that we had missed at least 30 feet of porous permeable sand at the top of the Cardium formation.

There was considerable acrimony within Socony for the next couple of days over the decision to install production casing and test the flow of oil from the discovery.

I strongly recommended that we run casing—production pipe that protected people and maximized the production from the rig—and test the Cardium. The executives in Calgary objected because it would cost $30,000 to build a road into the well site to carry the heavy equipment needed to run the casing. The impasse was broken by Joe Spivak, who said the evidence was too strong to ignore and the company should back up the young geologist that they had put in charge of the Edmonton district. This was one of many occasions on which Spivak had a decisive impact on my life.

Final approval followed. On June 3, we proceeded to run casing, perforate it and test the Cardium. The result was a flowing oil well. We weren't positive how good a well it would be, so we tested it again on June 9. The oil was of a very high quality—sweet and light. It had a specific gravity of 37 degrees API, and was free of sulphur, all characteristics of superior quality, which made it all the more valuable.

We faced one more heated argument. The Cardium sandstone was tight and the flow rate of oil was minor compared to that at the Leduc wells: a mere five and a half barrels an hour and 132 barrels a day. This was no gusher. Operations were suspended because some of the executives didn't think it was worth pursuing our "little puddle" of oil.

Then Jim Warke, the well-site petroleum engineer, said that in the Middle East he had drilled wells like Pembina No. 1 and the solution was to frac them. "Fracking" or "fracturing" involves subjecting the oil reservoir to intense hydraulic pressure that opens tiny seams in the rock; the sand grains in the fluid keep the passageways open.

Warke's proposal represented a major Canadian development because at that time companies in western Canada did not frac wells, and they didn't know much about the technique. Jim, however, had learned all about fracking in the Middle East. With his impressive credentials and credibility, he prevailed. On June 17, we fracked with 3,000 pounds of sand in a fracking fluid, and the well "blew in" at 384 barrels per day: three times the initial production and as much as some of the D-2 discoveries were producing. Socony launched a major exploration effort across the four townships to determine the size of this newly discovered field.

We moved the drilling rig eleven miles to a location in the northeast corner of the townships and spudded a well called Pembina 33–7 on August 12. With better control of the geologic section, we were able to core and test the Cardium sand. The core samples showed that the Cardium at that location was "shaling out"—or, the sandstone bed had been replaced by shale; at the time,

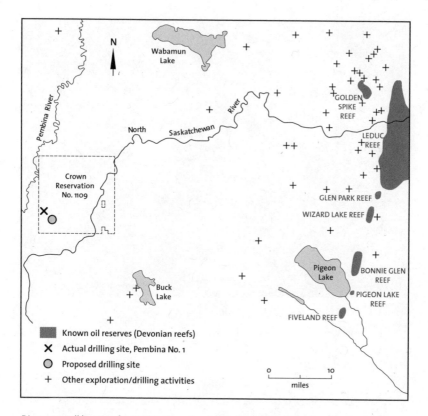

Discovery well location for Pembina No. 1, in relation to geological trends and exploration/ drilling activity in the area, 1953.

we couldn't produce oil from shale—although there was still some oil-stained sand with very low permeability. The subsequent drill stem test at the location only recovered oil-cut mud. We abandoned the well as a dry hole. I still felt confident that Pembina No. 1 had discovered a field and that Pembina 33–7 had penetrated the Cardium sand at the edge of the stratigraphic trap.

We now moved the drilling rig halfway back to Pembina No. 1 and spudded the North Pembina 33–6 on October 2. After two weeks of drilling, we cored and tested the Cardium sand. The cores showed that the Cardium was over thirty feet thick and that the sand was porous and permeable. In addition, there was a thick porous conglomerate lying on top of the sand. On October 18, we drill-stem-tested the Cardium and obtained a flowing oil well. I received the exciting news from the well-site geologist, Bob Cruikshank, in the middle of the night on the radio phone in our bedroom in Edmonton.

Carl Nickle, who founded the Daily Oil Bulletin, *and me at a conference in 1980.*

I immediately knew that we had discovered a large oilfield within the stratigraphic trap I had postulated.

I hardly ever get excited, but this time I really got excited.

We had discovered a multi-billion-barrel oilfield that for many years would hold the record for largest aerial extent in the world and remains the most productive in Canadian history. On the tenth anniversary of the discovery in 1963, Carl Nickle, the dean of oil journalists, would report that the oil industry had spend $700 million on exploration and production facilities in the field compared to the $450 million Canada invested in the St. Lawrence Seaway, built at the same time and opened on June 1959.

In October 1953, Socony's Calgary management began to plan the development of the field. Additional drilling rigs were contracted to begin drilling as quickly as possible on the 100,000-acre block to confirm the size of the field. At the same time, other rigs began drilling in the immediate vicinity of Pembina No. 1 to get the field on production as quickly as possible.

Our fifth well found oil in the Viking and Basal-Blairmore—primarily sandstone with one thin bed of limestone toward the middle—horizons and below the Cardium in the Mississippian carbonates, and we knew we had made a discovery that included multiple productive zones. We were also producing a good deal of natural gas associated with the oil. For the first few months, we simply flared this gas, but eventually Socony constructed gas processing and production facilities that were also the largest in the Western Canadian Sedimentary Basin.

Large blocks of Crown land in the immediate area were tendered for bids at the first sale following the Pembina No. 1 discovery. Amoco was already a large landholder in the area and was very competitive with Socony. Wells to obtain more information were drilled as close as possible to the land blocks tendered for the sale. Well-site security was high. We were able to core the Cardium in these wells, and I brought the core samples to my home in Edmonton and hid them under my bed for security.

The big sale was held in January 1954 and Premier E.C. Manning personally opened the bid letters in a little ceremony, which indicated the importance of the new field.

To our surprise, Socony and Amoco got nothing. I felt rotten because our management hadn't been willing to bid more money. The big winner was Texaco, who had done no drilling in the area and paid $13 million for a two-township block (13,040 acres). Imperial Oil paid $11 million for an adjacent block. Drilling resulted in Texaco's acreage being totally productive in the Cardium, whereas Imperial's acquisitions were dry.

Nevertheless, even after Socony turned back the 50 per cent of the townships that the regulations required us to relinquish, the company still retained about 49,000 acres. The huge Cardium stratigraphic trap meant that nearly all Socony's acreage was potentially productive. The company started on a major development drilling program with many rigs at work.

Since every exploration geologist dreams of discovering oil, not just chasing after other peoples' finds, Pembina No. 1 was a great moment for my associates and me. It was particularly a triumph for me. I had achieved the dream of every geologist; discovering a large oilfield through exploration based on sound geological principles.

10

Pembina's Impact

WHEN WE COMMENCED daily oil production from Pembina No. 1 on July 1, 1953, it was the most westerly oil well in the province and the first commercial Cardium sands production in the Western Canadian Sedimentary Basin. Those geographical and geological facts showed that the geological potential of the basin had been greatly expanded by the confirmation of an immense regional stratigraphic oil trap. Of course, it took several months for the significance to be verified and more time for it to sink into public and industry consciousnesses. After Pembina No. 1, however, the hunt for light, sweet, crude oil in Alberta and the West wasn't just about finding Devonian-era limestone reefs. Now there was another formation of equal importance—the younger, shallower, Upper Cretaceous Cardium sandstone.

In a relatively short time, follow-up drilling confirmed to Socony that we had found a large regional stratigraphic oil trap. Other companies were less certain, but joined the stampede to acquire drilling rights just in case we were right. Within a year, Pembina was the largest oilfield in the world in terms of aerial extent. Over the next three years, it overtook Leduc, Redwater and Golden Spike as the most productive field in Canada. Within ten years, it was acknowledged as one of the largest in North America; it still is, nearly sixty years later.

Also very important in the long term, Socony's follow-up drilling confirmed our hopes that, while the Cardium was the big target, we would find other productive oil horizons in the stratigraphic trap, such as the Belly River and the Viking, which became major targets in their own right over the next five decades. We didn't recognize the full potential right away, of course. In 1952 and 1953, petroleum geologists were steadily discovering new oilfields and there was a gold-rush type excitement in the air.

Socony kicked into high gear on a program of more drilling. Meanwhile, work began on the gathering lines, processing facilities to remove associated natural gas from the oil, and a pipeline to get the oil to Edmonton where it could be refined or shipped on the Trans Mountain Pipeline to Vancouver and the Interprovincial Pipeline (now Enbridge Pipelines) to Ontario.

By December, the company had drilled five wildcats in the new Pembina field. The Winter 1953 edition of *The Flying Red Horse*, a quarterly company publication named for the marketing logo of a galloping red Pegasus, featured an article titled "Pembina: New Discovery."

I gave my father my copy of the magazine, and we found it among his few possessions after he died twenty years later. He was a pretty laid-back guy, but he became quite animated when he saw this magazine, although my name and those of my geological partners wasn't mentioned in it. It did, however, note that five out of every six members of the exploration company were born in Canada. The remainder had been recruited from all over the world— Australia, Belgium, British West Indies, Denmark, England, Holland, Hungary, New Zealand, Pakistan, Scotland and South Africa—and had worked all across Socony's global operations—Europe, the Middle East, the Pacific and the United States. Western Canada had become a magnet of immense opportunity.

The article modestly stated that Pembina was possibly "another important oil discovery in Western Canada...It is good oil, too, 37 gravity, light, high quality, easy to transport and easy to refine (and) relatively shallow—only a little over 5,000 feet down." What meant the most to Socony, said the writer, was that the discovery vindicated ten years of exploration in Canada:

> The exploration effort that led to the Pembina finds...has been long and hard. It takes time to close in on a likely oil area and even more time to pinpoint the search enough to find oil in such an area. Looking for oil is almost like looking for a needle in a haystack. In this business, just finding the haystack is often tough...
>
> An area like the Pembina block, may atone for a lot of the headaches and heartaches our oil finders have endured elsewhere in Western Canada...

No matter how good the Pembina area may prove to be, many more hard years of searching lie ahead. It will be the same cycle, over and over again: first hunting for the haystack and then trying to find the needle—if it is there. But the needle—oil and its many products—is the lifeblood of a high standard of living.

Because of the years it takes to find and develop an oil area, our people in Western Canada are looking today for the oil the world will need tomorrow. In the oil business, tomorrow always comes.

In the first two years following Pembina No. 1, Drayton Valley changed completely. In the first year, the population grew from 75 to 2,000. In the second year, that number more than doubled and stood at 5,000 on the 1955 anniversary of the first oil showing in the discovery well. The *Toronto Star* sent a reporter to the town in February 1955, and he named Drayton Valley "the newest Klondike" and "Canada's most amazing boom town."

After the discovery, the reporter wrote, "Drayton Valley sprung from a barley field of a sleepy farm hamlet. There were no houses, so new arrivals bring their own, loaded on trucks or towed behind cars." A field of hundreds of travel and house trailers spread out from the town centre. Some families were living in skid shacks, an eight-by-sixteen-foot farm structure. There was a booming business for farmers who built the shacks for $100 and sold them for $400. Enterprising landlords bought them for $400 and rented them for $75 a month—a 225 per cent profit in a year. From spring to the following winter, men slept in steel highway culverts. Vacant schoolhouses in a fifty-mile radius were towed to the Drayton Valley town site so that all the migrant children could find classroom space, however crowded. Inevitably, two signature institutions of every gold rush, silver rush and oil rush in North American history were among the first to appear in Drayton Valley: the twenty-four-hour makeshift tavern in a shack outside the town called Shady Hollow, and in town the back-street house taken over for the "ladies of the night."

Two months later, another reporter working for Canadian Press went to Drayton Valley and came back with a story, printed in the *Calgary Herald* among other newspapers, that Pembina might contain more oil than all of East Texas! No one loves an oil rush more than a newspaper reporter.

The winter of 1954–55 was the busiest for oil and gas exploration in the province's history, with the level of activity lead by exploration around Drayton Valley. By 1955 Alberta was awash in oil—there was more production than pipeline capacity to ship it to markets outside the province, so every well had a production quota called an "allowable." In other words, we couldn't sell all the oil we were finding.

Meanwhile, as Socony's exploration and development program accelerated and other companies rushed in to compete, the drilling, well completion and construction activity required scores of men, who needed places to sleep and eat, and truckloads of equipment that needed a place to refuel. Along the road in Violet Grove, a series of rough shanties were hastily erected for accommodation. Fortunately winter hadn't arrived yet because these little hovels offered very little shelter. In Drayton Valley, vacation trailers used by seismic and drilling crewmen to keep their families with them as they migrated from field to field, were parked in open fields that grew more crowded every day. On some days, the lineup of traffic into Drayton Valley ran thirty miles back toward Edmonton, which was only sixty miles away to begin with.

Through the summer and fall of 1953, the new discovery gained momentum; our second productive well went on production at 612 barrels per day. Before the end of the year, we had drilled seven wells in the field, six of which were successful discoveries. The full size and significance of the Pembina Cardium oil discovery hadn't become apparent by year end because 1953 had been a record year for oil exploration in western Canada. Companies spent a million dollars a day that year on drilling and construction of production facilities, and the value of the oil they produced was half a million dollars a day. For the first time, the oil industry was the leading mineral industry in the nation, making more revenue and investing more new capital than economic stalwarts like the mining industries revolving around nickel, silver, gold, iron ore and coal.

Pembina was just one of three new Alberta discoveries of oil and "wet" gas rich in hydrocarbon liquids like propane and butane, fields that were in the race for geological eminence and capital investment. The other prominent oilfields were located at Sturgeon Lake in the northwest Peace River Country and Smiley in Saskatchewan, an exploration play in which Socony also had an interest. The wet gas field was located in the Homeglen-Rimbey area of central Alberta.

I should explain that back then, geologists considered gas discoveries a plague. Natural gas wasn't worth much, just four or five cents per thousand cubic feet. The only market was within Alberta because there were no pipelines leaving the province. However, wet gas was different because it contained condensate—high-gravity, very light petroleum from which liquids such as propane, butane and ethane could be extracted. Those products were very valuable and a significant petrochemical industry that used them as feedstock was starting up around Edmonton.

Even in west-central Alberta, the Pembina Cardium discovery wasn't the only thing going on. In the quarter-million-acre district that surrounded Drayton Valley, wildcat wells made discoveries in three Cretaceous and shallower Tertiary sandstone formations—the Belly River, Viking and Basal-Blairmore.

The Toronto Stock Exchange (TSE) was quick to pick up on the Pembina discovery; stock speculators always have a nose for opportunity. Smaller independent Canadian exploration companies, such as Nathan Tanner's Merrill Petroleums, which he started after his political career, zeroed in on the Pembina play and started to raise capital to acquire petroleum rights and drill wells. The Toronto newspapers were publishing immediate news of each new well, and every new report of production levels issued by the Oil and Gas Conservation Board. The stock speculators grabbed at the promise of fortune, as they always have in every Canadian oil boom. By the time we were drilling our fourth well, there was a "Pembina" group of stocks listed on the TSE, and investors followed the almost daily reports on their activity.

Oil and gas exploration produced a lot of good news in 1953, and it would take two years for Pembina to emerge as the best discovery of the year. By the end of the 1950s, however, University of Alberta economist Eric Hansen, in his landmark book about the impact of oil and gas development in Alberta following the Leduc discovery, declared that the Pembina No. 1 Cardium was: "the important discovery of the decade."

It wasn't until 1957, four years and 1,700 wells after the discovery of Pembina No. 1, that Mobil Oil of Canada (Socony's new name in 1955) allowed me to present the first geological paper on the structure, stratigraphy and lithology of the discovery, to tell our competitors and the geological world what we had found. The Alberta Geological Society had invited me to give a presentation on March 19, 1957, and the company consented. By then, my career had taken me on to Saskatchewan then back to Calgary, and I was about to be posted for the first time to Mobil headquarters in New York.

Many in the audience had participated in drilling wells for competing companies, and there were other Mobil geologists there, as well. Presenting the paper allowed me an opportunity to be reviewed by my peers on the work I had done. I felt sure that audience members would all be interested that we had determined from the lithology that the Cardium sands had been deposited in a shallow offshore marine environment. This type of formation would become a classic type of oil or gas reservoir found all across the Western Canadian Sedimentary Basin in the coming decades.

I devoted a great deal of my presentation to describing the Cardium formation and its five geological units: the upper shale, the conglomerate, the upper sand, the middle unit and the lower sand. I described as well-established fact, backed by hard evidence collected in hundreds of well bores, that my first prognosis of a stratigraphic trap rising from the west in a gentle regional up-dip and pinching out to the east was proven to be "dead right."

There was a good deal more technical data in the paper, which was later published by the society and cited again and again in later academic work. As I later learned, the paper attracted international interest and led to a friendship with Chinese geologists, who used it to develop fields that I toured when China opened up to Canadians. I loved doing that kind of analysis and might well have become an academic myself had I chosen to take a doctoral degree in May 1950, instead of a job with Socony-Vacuum. On that day, however, the pleasure was in standing before my peers and telling them that back in 1952, when I looked at the logs of wells that ringed the wildcat acreage that Socony wanted to drill on, I had seen something that everyone else had missed.

Leduc dominated exploration news in the 1940s; Pembina No. 1 dominated the 1950s. In the 1960s, the first pinnacle reef oil discoveries at Rainbow Lake, in which Mobil Oil had a 50 per cent working interest, was the primary find of the decade. In the 1970s, the last of these 100-million-barrel-plus discoveries in western Canada took place when Chevron drilled deep into the Devonian on the Pembina field's west flank.

After that, the Western Canadian Sedimentary Basin began to mature. The subsequent big discoveries were the trillion-plus-cubic-feet natural gas discoveries in northwest Alberta and northeast British Columbia. The new frontiers for oil exploration were in the North and the Atlantic offshore, including the discovery of the gigantic Hibernia oilfield on Newfoundland's Grand Banks, another Mobil Oil milestone. The excitement and competitive challenge of the oil boom years faded away in western Canada to be replaced by the awesome engineering challenges of unconventional oil and gas—oil sands and coalbed methane exploitation.

Petroleum geologists and their geophysical partners are the pioneers of resources; they open up continents, they remove the words "terra incognita" from maps and replace them with features and names that quickly become familiar.

As a new petroleum basin matures, the oil and gas development passes from the hands of the geologists to the petroleum engineers, the pipeliners, the accountants, the marketers and the lawyers. And as that transition takes place, the excitement and the public oil fever that came with it and our daily life in the early 1950s, is fading away.

The earth scientists—geologists and geophysicists—have had a second round of "frontier" exploration in western Canada in recent years because new technological tools, such as three-dimensional geophysical surveys and ultra-sophisticated computer imaging that could be paid for with high commodity prices, allowed explorers to wrinkle out and drill into small pools that we would have written off in 1953 as uneconomic.

Of course, in the 1970s, the 1990s, and in the first decade of the twenty-first century, the geopolitical conflict between the Organization of Petroleum Exporting Countries (OPEC) and the major Western oil producers, along with the supply crises created by embargos and wars, and the accompanying price spikes created a new kind of oil boom and a new kind of oil wealth. But the spirit, the excitement, the sense of creating a completely new economy and transforming a society are just a memory.

I was a young man—not yet twenty-eight years old—when we completed the well. I had made decisions that challenged the thinking of older, more experienced men, staking my career on the outcome. The thrill of that first discovery, what I learned from it geologically and in terms of exploration and corporate management, and the self-assurance that it gave me, indelibly marked the rest of my career. Many good, competent petroleum geologists spend their careers drilling wells to delineate and produce someone else's discovery. I had the satisfaction of being the guy who created more than a half-century—and still counting—of work for other geologists.

I have been fortunate to have subsequent opportunities, experiences and successes. I have lived a life of discovery that began but did not end at Pembina No. 1. Therefore, my life hasn't been spent looking back at, and constantly reliving a single golden moment in my youth. However, it is safe to say that discovery ignited my career. A petroleum geologist lives to find oil. Only a handful of them find an elephant. Such a discovery marks them: sets them apart. I would be falsely modest if I did not admit that nothing can ever quite match the emotions and the professional satisfaction of making a discovery that becomes a piece of history and the career rewards that follow such a discovery.

11

Oh, Saskatchewan!

I DIDN'T REALIZE it at the time, or for some years later, but following the Pembina discovery I was a marked man inside my company. In that era, oil companies planned the careers of its executives for years ahead. Underpinning their plans was the assumption that every employee would remain with the company until retirement, after which they would take pensions and remain connected as annuitants. I continued as district geologist for Edmonton until the autumn of 1954. There was a lot of exploration to be done on the Pembina Cardium trend, and I had some specific ideas of how to go about it.

In due course we geologists turned day-to-day operation of the field over to the production engineers. We then would go out and explore for more Pembinas. For a short time we had the best of both worlds: the delineation of the Pembina discovery along with exploration elsewhere in our district. We were young; we had a big discovery under our belt, and we were enthusiastic about making another.

One prospect that seemed particularly attractive was at Whitecourt, 112 miles northwest of Edmonton. Whitecourt was deep in the bush, an area of wild muskeg, rivers, a few rough roads and some isolated settlers. I had to fly in and out when I needed to be on the scene. I was preparing for one such flight when I received a telephone call asking me to come to Calgary to meet with

Joe Spivak. I was somewhat suspicious of the sudden decision, as I was ordered, in spite of my objections, to forego the trip to Whitecourt.

I drove to Calgary and met with Chief Geologist Spivak and Art Detmar, the exploration manager. They shocked me with the news that I was being transferred to Regina, to become the district geologist for Saskatchewan. The unexpected announcement came as quite a major blow, as I had just made the biggest discovery of my career. Being posted to socialist Saskatchewan where CCF Premier Tommy Douglas had been elected on a promise to "national-ize" the oil industry was not a reward, in my books; I felt like I was being exiled from capitalist, oil company–friendly Alberta.

To add to the misery, in the mid-1950s, Regina felt like a "hick" town com-pared to Calgary and Edmonton. After all, one only spent a certain amount of time on the job, so one had to consider what the prospects were for evenings and weekends. I knew there was really only one good restaurant in the city. Besides eating out, there was not much to do for entertainment in the evenings. Evelyn and I had a young family, and I worried that we would feel isolated.

It was a difficult year personally; my mother died in 1954 of a stroke at the young age of fifty years. The pioneers of my parents' generation in Standard didn't have much in the way of health care throughout their lives. They had a local doctor, a good man who coached our baseball team, but he just handled minor things like pulling teeth. When something was seriously wrong with you, he'd say, "You'd better see a doctor in Calgary." My mother would have lived a lot longer than she did if she had proper health care. When she had a stroke and we called the doctor, he said, "There is nothing I can do for you; you'll have to go to the city." Her death left my father and brother, Gerhardt, alone on the farm at Standard. I would have preferred to be nearer to them at that time, and this circumstance made the transfer to Regina even less attractive. However, I was under orders and certainly wasn't about to jeopardize my terrific job with Socony-Vacuum.

We bought a home in Regina, hoping at least to make some friends in our neighbourhood. Our neighbours were good people, but they had different political views than ours and our conversations were stunted because we couldn't get past the capitalist–socialist block. I must say that the landscape was also daunting. Saskatchewan has a great variety of geographical features—the entire province isn't flat and desolate—but the environment in which I did most of my work was south of Regina to the US border, a daunting, dry, flat prairie.

My younger sister, Miriam, moved with us to help look after our brood of children. By this time Evelyn and I had four children: Allan, Brian, Dianne, and

Robin. In the end, Miriam found a life in the province, got married and continues to live there. Her husband, Dean Richert, was a mechanic for the Regina police force, a good man with a good job.

My family and I lived in Regina for about two years. As things worked out, living there was not as bad as I'd feared, despite the socialist government and the lack of good places to eat. We established some excellent friendships during this assignment, one of which was with Bob Graves, another University of Alberta geology graduate. He was my best well-site geologist and supervisor, and we became lifetime friends. Bob spent his career with Socony and Mobil Oil, eventually moving into senior management positions in the New York head office.

My assignment to Regina came at the height of the Tommy Douglas era. The people of Saskatchewan thought the sun rose and set on Douglas, and on the new socialist policy of his party, the Co-operative Commonwealth Federation. It was tough for right-wing, dyed-in-the-wool capitalist oil guys like me. I came from a family that was so conservative my father thought William Aberhart was a socialist. Yet when Aberhart tried to export Social Credit to Saskatchewan, he was rejected as right-wing.

Tommy Douglas was elected as premier of Saskatchewan in 1944. He was like a prairie wildfire. His CCF party swept forty-seven of the fifty-two seats in the Legislature. The Liberal government of W.A. Patterson had held on too long, its life prolonged by the passing of a bill that extended its life to six years, a year more that the constitutional tradition in Canada, which calls for a maximum of five years between elections. The Liberals said that the election should be postponed because of the war. In fact, it was delayed because they feared the outcome, and rightly so.

The campaign, when it came, was nasty. The Liberals compared the socialists of Saskatchewan with Hitler's "National Socialists"—the Nazis. They said Douglas, like Lenin and Stalin had, would take over the farms of the province, "collectivize" them. Douglas was a Baptist preacher, and the Liberals warned he would also close the beer parlours and taverns of the province; oddly, they also said he'd close the churches. Nevertheless, on June 15, nine days after the Allies landed in Normandy on D-Day, Douglas was elected. He said that his party had established "a beachhead of socialism on a continent of capitalism."

To give Douglas credit, he said he was a socialist and he governed like one. In the years he was the premier, Saskatchewan's government developed a unique way of running the province, experimenting with things like Medicare, co-operatives and public insurance. By the time my family arrived on the scene in 1954, Canadian-style socialism was entering its second decade. The sun still rose in the morning, but we found ourselves—as did most of the people in the province's petroleum industry—living and working among people whose political and social ideas were different from ours. That said, one promise Douglas hadn't kept from his 1944 campaign was to take over the oil companies and nationalize the oil business. The province needed our investments, our jobs, the royalties from our production and the fuel from the oil and gas we discovered. However, it was still a difficult environment in which to work compared to Alberta because of a lingering hostility toward oil companies harboured not only by the government but also by the public.

Although we were concerned about the politics, there was no real economic risk to being in Saskatchewan. The government people may have been socialists, but they were not dumb. Even the Douglas government remained, on balance, fairly positive to oil and gas companies because it was in their best interest. Saskatchewan was strictly an agricultural province at the time, so there was no way they could say "no" to the economic importance that oil and gas exploration might bring. And there was a balance there, with Alberta right next door. Alberta had big reserves, so the feeling in Socony was that we can take a chance on those guys in Sask. They weren't likely to deviate in their policies too much relative to their neighbour to the west. And, in the end, they didn't deviate too much, at least as far as the oil industry was concerned. Saskatchewan actually had lower royalty rates than Alberta had at the time. Although its government was socialist, the province was competitive with Alberta in terms of oil and gas exploration and development.

Meanwhile, there was a positive outlook within the multinational oil companies toward federal politics in Canada. The federal government had a favourable attitude—in those days—to foreign investment. Company executives had figured out the relationship between the federal government and the provincial governments, and the federal government at the time really always remained positive. "Foreign investment" were magic words in the 1950s. Politicians like Prime Minister Louis St. Laurent and Trade Minister C.D. Howe knew they had to encourage investment. It was good for the country, good for the people: providing jobs, creating Canadian wealth and bringing all the good things that go with development.

The Douglas government may not have preferred capitalist oil companies on its soil, but if we had to be there, it wanted us to use as many people from Saskatchewan as possible. We hired geologists regardless of where they were born or lived, but the office people and other field people we hired locally.

I visited with Tommy Douglas when he was the premier to keep our relation-ship as smooth as possible. He was a nice guy who had a big personality, and lots to say!

Flash forward to 1973: after he retired as the party's national leader, Tommy Douglas was the energy critic for the New Democratic Party in Parliament. The issue of foreign ownership in the oil industry was at the top of the Liberal minority government's energy agenda. Douglas reached back thirty years to his first provincial campaign and again mused about the nationalization of Imperial Oil. Then he tempered his position and, instead, demanded the creation of a national oil company as a condition of the NDP's support for the Liberal minority. After that, it took Prime Minister Pierre Trudeau exactly one day to announce the creation of a Crown corporation that would be named Petro-Canada. Ironically, I was one of the first people who Maurice Strong, a wealthy businessman and trusted advisor to the Trudeau government, attempted to recruit as Petro-Canada's permanent president when he was its founding chairman. I declined the offer because I preferred to continue being the chief executive of a major multinational company rather than become involved with a government-controlled Crown corporation.

Years after I moved away from Saskatchewan, when I was president of Mobil, I went to see Saskatchewan Liberal Premier Ross Thatcher on behalf of the company and the Canadian Petroleum Association (CPA). The CPA recog-nized that things were different in Saskatchewan, even with the Liberals, who also leaned to the left. So we maintained a CPA branch office in Regina. I dealt with these two politicians the same way regardless of their party affiliation. I told them about our plans and progress. Tommy Douglas was reasonable to the extent that you always knew where you stood. Ross Thatcher was a busi-nessman and a good guy. He said we were welcome as long as we followed the regulations.

In 1954 Socony was the major oil and gas exploration company in Saskatchewan and remained so for many years. Prior to that year, the company had discovered six or seven fairly shallow, medium-gravity oilfields. Several men were prominent in this endeavour: Norm Elphinstone and Dick Slavin were geologists, and Jim Kelly an engineer. Elphinstone was a University of Winnipeg graduate, Slavin was from McGill and Kelly was a Calgarian who got his petroleum engineering degree from the University of Oklahoma, where many Canadian engineers received their education. Half a dozen of our geolo-gists and geophysicists lived in Swift Current, and it became a joke around the company that at one time or another you were going to have to do your time in Swift Current. "All careers lead to Swift Current," we said. We joked that we were being "sent to Siberia." I don't know why I escaped Swift Current, but I was never transferred there.

As district geologist in Regina, I was the senior Socony guy in Saskatchewan. Most of the people reporting to me were in Swift Current, but there were some other senior men in Regina. I had about half a dozen geologists working for me and three or four landmen. Each summer we hired two or three summer students, as well. We were busy, drilling between six and twelve wells at any given time in the peak winter drilling season. We had a certain number of field geological studies ongoing, as well, and were conducting regular seismic survey work. We also spent a fair bit of time assessing the provincial land sale postings because we wanted to maintain a competitive land position.

Although I had trouble with Saskatchewan's politics, I couldn't help but be impressed with that province's geology. Geologically, there was a complete stratigraphic section from Eocene to Cambrian if you wanted to drill that deep, although no one had. In southwest Saskatchewan, there was a lot of medium-gravity oil and relatively shallow production from the Cretaceous, as well as some Triassic reserves around Swift Current. While there was no production in central Saskatchewan and nothing at all in the Regina area, in southeast Saskatchewan, there was good Mississippian production around Weyburn and to the Manitoba border.

The exploration geology of Saskatchewan was interesting enough that it would keep a geologist busy for a good many years. We had three large fields at Fosterton, Cantuar and Success, as well as several smaller pools around Swift Current. They were all linked by a pipeline operated by Imperial Oil in which Socony was a working interest partner. Part of my job in Saskatchewan was to be a director of that pipeline company. Our production was taken by that system to Regina, where it connected with the Interprovincial Pipeline.

In southeast Saskatchewan Socony had a good group of Mississippian fields, Nottingham, Alida and Estevan, to name three. They continue to produce oil to this day. You can drill deep in Saskatchewan—the centre of the Williston Basin has the same kind of depths as those in western Alberta—but the production is from shallower horizons. The Williston Basin is an area that includes all of southern Saskatchewan and hooks up with the Williston Basin in North Dakota and Montana. It is a good illustration of the potential of Saskatchewan. We did well enough in the Williston Basin when I explored there, and it has continued to yield new discoveries over the intervening fifty years. Since my time there, geologists have found a lot of shallow gas, especially near the Alberta border, and Saskatchewan has built up good reserves of gas for future production.

One of Socony's core assets was a large farm-out of 13 million acres in eastern Saskatchewan, obtained from the Sohio Oil Company. It was equivalent in importance to the Seaboard farm-out in Alberta that included the Pembina field. The company drilled many wells on this Sohio acreage, but every one of them was a dry hole. The farm-out terms called for the acreage to be returned to Sohio by a fast-approaching date unless production was established. Finally, Bob Graves and I found some oil on the Sohio lands near a town called Roncott. The oil was in the Bakken sandstone formation. However, only a few oil wells resulted, and they depleted quickly, proving the field to be non-commercial. Since that time, large reserves of oil have been found in the Bakken shales, and it has become a major producing horizon in south Saskatchewan and North Dakota. It now leads the way in production in Saskatchewan.

The oil in the sandstones is of interest because it is generated in adjacent shale horizons. Not often do you find the source rocks and the reservoir rocks within the same horizon. This Bakken shale-generated oil is just the latest find in the Williston Basin. I would be extremely reluctant to say that the basin won't have a few more pleasant surprises for exploration geologists in the future.

A year before Socony transferred me back to Calgary, the company changed its name to Socony Mobil Oil Company. In Canada we were now called Mobil Oil of Canada. When I returned to Alberta, I took up a position as a staff geologist. I would report directly to my mentor Dr. Joe Spivak, the man who was originally responsible for hiring me. By this time, I considered him to be a role model and mentor. He never gave specific advice if I came to him with a problem. He would listen patiently and let me come to my own conclusion. "Arne," he would say, "you will always do the right thing." When I was a district geologist in Edmonton and Regina, he had been my point of contact with head office, the man I corresponded with and talked to by telephone on a regular basis. Not only was I being transferred out of my "Siberian exile," I was being taken under the wing of a mentor who had become as important in my life as my father was. At least, that's what I thought at the time.

In fact, when I set foot back in Calgary I was being lifted onto Mobil Oil's corporate fast track.

PART THREE

Executive and "Politician"

12

The Corporate Fast Track

WHEN I RETURNED to Calgary from Saskatchewan in 1956, to my new assignment as a staff geologist, I was overjoyed that I would be reporting to Dr. Joe Spivak, the general manager of exploration in Canada. Dr. Spivak had significant administrative responsibilities: personnel matters, exploration budgets, strategic geological evaluations and so forth. It meant an endless round of meetings, as he provided oversight to the geological work of the Canadian company. He needed a technical team to do the day-to-day detail work of reviewing reports from district geologists, supporting or denying their recommendations and directing the work done in the field. Those were the responsibilities of the staff geologists.

My new position at Mobil was not very stimulating, and I did not particularly relish a staff role. It was purely a technical job with none of the immediate excitement of day-to-day operations and no administrative or personnel responsibilities. Nonetheless, I was pleased to be released from Saskatchewan, to be back in an enterprising province friendly to corporations and capitalism, to live once again in a city with decent places to eat and a wider selection of recreational and entertainment options. I was closer to my father, and my brother Gerhardt, too. And Evelyn and the children were also glad to be back in Alberta.

The position worked somewhat as follows. The chief geologist received the geophysical exploration, field studies, drilling prognoses and land acquisition recommendations from the district offices and passed them down to the staff geologists. We analyzed these recommendations to decide what the company should do, then passed our recommendations up to chiefs of exploration, production and engineering. They gave a final recommendation to the exploration manager, who was a vice-president. He vetted all the work done by the exploration staff and brought the file to the president for a final decision. Similarly, engineering recommendations went back up to the engineering vice-president and manager.

It sounds complicated, but the process had three important elements. The first was that decisions passed through four levels of management: the staff; the chiefs; the vice-presidents and general managers; and then to the president and general manager. (In Socony we had many double titles.) This division of responsibility allowed people to focus intensely on their jobs. The result was discipline, accountability and a competitive advantage. During my years at Mobil, exploration didn't often get "bogged down" by internal red tape.

The second element of the system was that many points of view were brought to bear on exploration decisions. Mobil's process balanced its risks and its opportunities by thoroughly vetting investments in order to avoid mistakes. It is one thing to spend a few thousand dollars on a decision, but it is quite another to lose tens or hundreds of thousands, or even millions, by making a bad decision. Oil and gas exploration and production is a "knowledge business," and you can't spend your financial capital wisely unless you use your intellectual capital first.

The third element to Mobil's process was that we worked as a team. Great discoveries often come when one geologist sees something others have missed. However—and it is a big "however"—every one of those discoveries depended on collaboration with other professionals who had expertise in other technical areas in order to drill, complete and produce a well. The heroic image of a lone wildcatter striking it rich by discovering a gusher works only in novels and movies.

Mobil employees became a close-knit bunch and we were very competitive, especially against our chief rival, Imperial Oil and our peer companies such as Chevron, Shell, Gulf and Texaco. I made enduring friendships with men like Ed Barroll, who later became a production vice-president, and Ed Bredin, a future general counsel. Long after we retired from Mobil, we remained close as annuitants and continued to meet regularly for events such as annual Christmas parties. Most of these friends made at the outset of my career have passed on now, and it is the price of longevity that the circle of people with whom I shared in the memorable events of the 1950s and 1960s has shrunk significantly.

A few months after I returned to Calgary, a development occurred that surprised me considerably. My friend and mentor, Dr. Joe Spivak, accepted a position in the Mobil office in New York. Much speculation followed as to who would replace him as chief geologist of Mobil Oil Canada. It came down to a choice between me and another close friend of mine, fellow Canadian Don Axford. I was selected for the coveted position. I am pleased to recall that Don became chief research geologist, a new position developed especially for him that was equivalent in standing to mine.

Just a few months after Dr. Spivak was transferred to New York, I received the news that I, too, was on my way to Mobil's world headquarters in New York. I was to become the geological liaison between top executive management and the geologists in the company's operating divisions across North America. This was the third promotion and fourth transfer for me in seven years, and I was just thirty-two years old. No doubt the Pembina discovery had a great deal to do with my advancement—but obviously the company also liked what I had done as an executive.

Suddenly, I was on the corporate fast track.

My job as liaison was to maintain contact with all of Mobil's operating offices in North America. I was the communications link who reported to New York about what was going on in Houston, Midland, Denver, Calgary and Los Angeles in exploration as well as production. I talked to the top guys in each city, and they sent me reports, which I used to prepare myself for the meetings with the top corporate executives in New York.

The first year of my new position in New York was delightful for me and my family. We lived in New Canaan, Connecticut, a beautiful small town in a beautiful state. In the fall when the leaves changed colour, it was magnificent. It was the only place I could find a house big enough on my budget to handle my growing family. By August 30, 1956, Evelyn and I had six children, Allan, Brian, Dianne, Robin, and finally Garry, born in 1955, and Paul in 1956. From our home in Connecticut, I commuted to New York every day by rail, an hour and twenty minutes each way. Our house was a fifteen-minute walk to the train station, so I would often opt to walk to my commute. Sometimes, however, Evelyn would drive me to the station. My stop in New York was Grand Central Station: Mobil Corporation's office was right across the street from where I disembarked. That was just as well because it was already a long commute, and an additional subway ride would not have been appreciated! I used my commuting time in the mornings and evenings to work through the very large stack of reading that came with the job. I loved New York, and still do. There were compensations for being one of the tens of thousands of commuters moving in and out of the city each day. Living near to the Atlantic coast gave my family plenty of opportunity to explore the eastern United States from Florida to Maine.

The "fast track" would take me to New York, Denver and Houston in the next ten years, with one stopover back in Calgary. Each one of these transfers involved upheaval for my growing family, but they also brought us some great adventures and opportunities to see and do new things. Evelyn never complained about the inconvenience of packing up and moving on, she just got things organized and looked forward to the next destination. This can't be said for the wives of some of my colleagues, who hated the moves and said so. However, my children had the wrenching experience of making new friends and then leaving them behind. I was fortunate that there were no serious family rebellions. Meanwhile, they were exposed to life in New York and on the eastern seaboard, the Rocky Mountains, and the Texas Gulf Coast with its ready access to Mexico. We sought out new activities in each location, and we found many places to explore together as a family.

Professionally, I had an unparalleled opportunity to practice geology in the most prolific oil-producing American basins from the Gulf of Mexico to the Williston Basin and from the Rocky Mountain states to the Appalachians. I gained increasing levels of responsibility and the oversight of larger employee groups and bigger budgets. I also had the opportunity to understand how my company worked, why it was so successful and the ingredients of managerial and executive leadership.

When my tour of duty in New York was completed at the beginning of 1959, I came back to Calgary to resume my position as chief geologist, but within a year, I was on the move again. In 1959 there was another major reorganization of Mobil Oil Corporation. The large US companies associated with Mobil— Mobil Producing in Billings, Montana; Magnolia Petroleum Company in Dallas; and General Petroleum in Los Angeles—were dissolved and all become part of one very large corporation, Mobil Oil, headquartered in New York. Divisional offices were established in Houston, Denver, Midland, Texas and Los Angeles. Many offices across the United States were closed. A former president of Mobil Oil Canada, Fred Moore, became the head of all three divisions.

As part of this reorganization I was transferred from Calgary to Denver, Colorado, where I became exploration vice-president and manager of the newly constituted Denver Division. The Houston Division had its hands full big time with activity in the Gulf of Mexico, Louisiana and Mississippi. In West Texas, Midland was another centre of intense activity, primarily exploring for and producing deep gas. The Los Angeles Division had the California basin and Pacific offshore to deal with. For the rest of the United States, Denver was central, so Denver managed everything else. The responsibility ran from the Rocky Mountain states of Wyoming, Utah and Montana to the Williston Basin of North Dakota, all the way to the Atlantic coast. The basins that were the responsibility of the Denver Division were located in widely separated geographical areas that covered a large range of geological environments, each with unique challenges and a diverse range of activities to exploit them. At the time, our principal exploration and producing activities were in the Anadarko, Hugoton, Arkoma and Appalachian Basins. In striking contrast to my reservations about being a staff geologist in Calgary, I enjoyed this assignment very much. I made many changes when I began my new position, including setting up district offices in Casper, Wyoming; Wichita, Kansas; Oklahoma City, Oklahoma; and Denver, Colorado.

While in Denver, I started an exploration project in the Appalachians. The Appalachians had produced a lot of shallow gas. I asked myself, "What's wrong here in the Appalachians? They have all of these apparent structures a good geological section, and they haven't been properly explored." So I set up an·office in Pittsburgh and put a number of geologists there, closer to the scene of action. We drilled some wells and we got a bit of gas, but it didn't really work out the way I had hoped. In more recent years, however, in the same area, large volumes of gas have been found.

In central Oklahoma I participated in the discovery of a prolific four-well field called Craddock. Its wells were 16,000 feet deep and produced lavishly. It was an excellent discovery, one of the most memorable in my career, and I still have a piece of oil-stained core from the discovery well.

My position changed again in 1962, when I was transferred to Houston as exploration manager of the Houston Division. I had anticipated that such a transfer might occur. Our principal areas of activity were in East Texas, Louisiana, Florida and the offshore areas of the Gulf of Mexico. Houston was then and still is one of the world's premiere oil cities. It is the centre for exploration and production from several of the most prolific basins in the United States, as well as headquarters of great service companies, the focal point for technology research, and a refinery and transportation hub. I was responsible for all the exploration and producing activity in the Gulf of Mexico onshore

Texas, onshore Louisiana and onshore Mississippi. This included responsibility for budgets, drilling and land acquisitions. I was also responsible for recommendations and reports to New York on significant decisions and developments.

I enjoyed my life in Houston even though the city was very different from Denver and Calgary. The weather was semi-tropical—hot and muggy—but everything grew quickly with lush vegetation and many flowers. I had to get used to snakes, such as water moccasins and rattlesnakes, which could deliver fatal bites. In Houston, Evelyn and I established many new friendships, and I still enjoy visiting Houston on business trips. We made "fun trips" to New Orleans and Corpus Christi, Texas, where Mobil also had offices. Evelyn developed an interest in Aztec art, and we often travelled the short distance to Mexico so that she could pursue the acquisition of a small collection of ancient pottery. My good friend, Bob Graves, moved from Calgary to Jackson, Mississippi, so he and I were within shouting distance of one another again.

The offshore Gulf of Mexico was the big exploration play for the Houston Division. Mobil was the first company to drill a well in the offshore Gulf of Mexico, this event occurring in the early 1900s. Offshore Louisiana got a big chunk of Mobil's exploration budget every year. We spent some of it on "reconnaissance geology" conducted on Bourbon Street in New Orleans. As time went on, the drilling in the gulf moved out to deeper water and west off the Texas coast, and we discovered many more producing fields.

The Houston Division was also responsible for Louisiana onshore, and in Louisiana you can drill to hell and get big, thick, producing sands all the way down. The politics in Louisiana, however, were beyond imagination. Before I was there, the state employed a series of governors—Huey Long, for example—who were absolutely and totally dishonest, lining their own pockets. Their hold on power couldn't be broken. It was very difficult to cope with these guys. They wanted money under the table, and lots of it. In the past, they had received the money they wanted. But the companies eventually drew the line and said, "No more." By the time I was in Houston and responsible for the company's Louisiana interests, the governor was no longer receiving money under the table. Still, the big shots would get their "pay" in other ways. For me, a clean-cut young Canadian, it was difficult to swallow. Mobil was a big integrated company, and we were vulnerable to a lot of scrutiny, and we always kept our and the company's noses clean.

The independent producers were more accommodating, which made life difficult for us because the politicians couldn't see why we should behave any differently. Meanwhile, we wanted to get along with the independents. We had adjacent acreage to them on freehold land and produced from the same horizons as the independent operators next door. You didn't have to deal in a dishonest fashion. But if you were honest, you had to be patient. To develop a prospect in Louisiana and Texas might take three years, as you had to assemble the land piece by piece.

The land department in the southern states was much more important to the geologists than it was in western Canada, where 85 per cent of the mineral rights are owned by the Crown and acquiring them involves an orderly process of well-organized land sales and tenures secured by leases issued by the government. As a result, in Canada, landmen have a straightforward job description. In Louisiana, by comparison, landmen really worked for their money because they had to make deals and assemble exploration lands from freeholders, one piece at a time.

We had a landman in New Orleans, Basil Moss, who was unbelievable— he knew all the right guys, the politicians. I don't know how he got what he wanted; I guess he became one of them. He introduced me to people I would otherwise never have met, sometimes at private clubs that were taboo for African American people. In all the southern states, at the time, there were private clubs where African American people were not allowed. In Louisiana this racism was the worst. In New Orleans, there were "white" restaurants and there were restaurants in which only African Americans would dine. Of course there were successful African American businessmen and musicians and so forth. But no matter how smart or successful they were, they weren't able to join the private racist clubs. Experiencing this first-hand was something new and uncomfortable for me, and totally different from any club I'd been to in Calgary, or for that matter, in Denver, where my attention soon turned.

One thing that looked promising in western Colorado on the Utah border was the oil shales. You could take a sample of that shale and hold it up, light it with a match and burn it like a candle. At that time, however, there was no technology to extract oil from the shales. It has proven a lot tougher to get oil from oil shale than from oil sand. Today, we have technology that can help us access that oil, but environmentalists have fiercely resisted companies interested in pulling the oil from Colorado's shale because of the potential damage to the immediate area. Colorado is a beautiful mountain state, in some ways more lovely than the Canadian Rockies. Mobil has not pursued the oil shale vigorously. Unconventional oil, including that in the Canadian oil sands, was not a strong point for the company when I worked for it. As I write this book, however, the oil sands is a centrepiece of Canadian energy, and as part of Exxon Mobil, my former company participates in it.

I lived in Houston for five years, at which point I received a letter from the US government noting that I had been living in the United States for a number of years and soliciting me to consider taking out citizenship. It wasn't a legal requirement, but it was an opportunity to acquire dual citizenship. However, when I thought about it, my loyalty to Canada caused me to decline the offer.

My time in the United States was a golden age for a petroleum geologist. In Denver and Houston, I had opportunities to explore for oil and gas across the whole continental United States. In those years, the geologist was the "top dog" in a company like Mobil, which explored aggressively for new production and reserves. The really big discoveries in the United States were made before I moved to that country. Nevertheless, there was a lot of exploration work still to be completed. It seemed quite likely that if Mobil didn't leave me in Houston a while longer, my next transfer might well be to an executive management position in New York.

13

Leading Mobil Oil Canada

IN 1966 I transferred from Houston back to Calgary to become vice-president of exploration of Mobil Oil Canada. I held the position for a year to re-orient myself to Canadian affairs prior to becoming president of Mobil Oil Canada. On January 1, 1967, at the age of forty-two, I was appointed president and general manager of Mobil Oil Canada. I was both the first Canadian and the youngest person to have held the job. All of my predecessors, beginning with Dr. Cliff Corbett of Socony-Vacuum, had been Americans. It was Canada's centennial year, and I was very proud of being offered this position, not only because of its importance but also because I was the first Canadian to head up the Canadian subsidiary of a multinational oil company. It was not just any multinational but one of the "Seven Sisters," which at that time stood at the pinnacle of the world's oil industry.

The Seven Sisters were the world's largest international petroleum companies of the postwar era. Their membership included my company Mobil Oil Corporation, Exxon (formerly Jersey Standard), Texaco, Gulf Oil, Standard Oil of California, Royal Dutch Shell, and British Petroleum. They ranked in the fifteen largest Western corporations in the mid-1970s, controlling combined assets of $130 billion. The Seven Sisters were all integrated companies with exploration, production, refining and marketing operations that extended from the well-head to the gas pump.

Before the OPEC cartel—original members in 1960 were Iran, Iraq, Kuwait, Saudi Arabia and Venezuela; later joined by Qatar, Indonesia, Libya, the United Arab Emirates, Algeria, Nigeria, Ecuador, Gabon and Angola—emerged as a policy-making force in the early 1970s, the Seven Sisters dominated and virtually controlled world oil supply and price. They were as powerful and influential in energy matters as any government and wealthier than some smaller countries.

The international show-down over oil price and supply, which was about to take place when I became the president of Mobil Canada, was a battle between OPEC and the Seven Sisters for control of world oil markets. Before OPEC, the price of oil was relatively flat, year after year, because it was in the interest of the Seven Sisters to provide growing European and North American markets with inexpensive oil. When OPEC asserted national control over the largest reserves in the world outside North America, the resulting dramatic spikes in the price of crude oil, followed closely by increases in the price of natural gas, set the stage for big political battles in the United States and Canada.

The Mobil Oil Canada that I returned to in 1967 was different from the one I had left ten years earlier when I had my first US assignment in New York. We were no longer the pure exploration company focused on establishing a base of crude oil reserves and production. Now we marketed our production, and, in northeast British Columbia, we were also engaged in the search for natural gas. In 1966 the company changed its corporate name for a third and final time. In 1955 Socony-Vacuum became Mobil Oil of Canada; in 1966 we became Mobil Oil Canada.

In 1965, the year before my return to Canada, Mobil acted as a working interest partner in the last big conventional oil discovery in which we would participate in western Canada. The play was called Rainbow Lake in northwestern Alberta. The field was the first of the so-called pinnacle reef discoveries, named because of the seismic profile of these slender, oil-bearing, Devonian structures. The Rainbow Lake field was discovered on a Mobil farm-out to Banff Oil, a Canadian independent that had the Canadian subsidiary of the French company Aquitaine as a partner with a deep pocket. Mobil ended up with a 50 per cent working interest in the discovery. Rainbow Lake was what we called an "elephant"; for some time it was the last of the giant, billion-barrel-plus, light-sweet-crude oilfields. Like Pembina, it was the largest industry discovery in Canada for many years. It generated one of the last great oil booms in a remote muskeg and forested region of Alberta that resembled the Devon and Whitecourt areas of our big finds in my youth.

The Rainbow Lake discovery gave us the knowledge and confidence that the Western Canadian Sedimentary Basin still had plenty of light oil and even more natural gas for the exploration geologists to find. It was an exciting time in the company, a time of important new discoveries in western Canada that reminded me of the "oil rush" of the 1950s.

In 1967, the year I became president, Mobil Oil Canada also became the largest exporter of oil and liquids to the United States. Our parent company, Mobil Oil Corporation, had lots of refining capacity south of the border but none in Canada. They wanted as much liquid as they could possibly get from Canada. We shipped some of our production west on the Trans Mountain Pipeline to a big refinery at Ferndale, Washington, and east on the Interprovincial Pipeline to large refineries in Michigan. In those years, Alberta was capable of producing more oil than could be shipped on existing pipeline capacity. After Richard Nixon became president, independent producers in the US successfully lobbied him to constrict the flow of Canadian oil across the border, and the 1960 Canadian National Oil Policy barred Alberta production from Quebec and the Maritimes.

Nevertheless, we were making bundles of cash shipping Canadian oil to Mobil Oil's own refineries in the US. If we sent the money to Mobil Corporation in the US, the Canadian government charged a 15 per cent withholding tax. So, we delivered our oil to the Mobil refineries and sent them a bill. Then our parent took a long, long time to pay the bill. It infuriated the Canadian authorities and gave some ammunition for the politicians, who attacked foreign ownership, but it was a good arrangement for Mobil—a way of "borrowing" interest-free money from a subsidiary. Other multinationals in Canada copied the practice.

In the mid-1970s, we also had our first successes on a new frontier: the Mackenzie Delta and near-shore waters of the Beaufort Sea. We acquired a 25 per cent working interest in Gulf Oil Canada's exploration concession in the delta in a deal that gave us the exposure to the Canadian North that Mobil Corporation wanted after the 1968 Prudhoe Bay oil and gas discovery in Alaska. In return, Gulf received a 25 per cent interest in many of our East Coast properties.

One of our northern holdings with Gulf was in a play called Parsons Lake near the mouth of the Mackenzie River where, in 1976, Gulf discovered a good natural gas field. Selecting the Parsons Lake interest was one of the best frontier exploration decisions we made at Mobil. A quarter of a century of political impediments, mainly due to environmental and Aboriginal-rights issues, have forestalled the construction of a gas pipeline to southern Canada, but in the future, I believe these reserves will be produced to help fill a pressing need.

Meanwhile, Mobil looked at the West Coast offshore and rejected it as a possible exploration venue. Shell Canada had drilled a dozen wells in that area, all of which were dry. Mobil never seriously considered Shell's offer of a partnership. There were sediments and structures identified in the seismic surveys, but the sediments were very volcanic, except at the mouth of the Fraser River. Volcanic-influenced basins worldwide were bad bets for petroleum reservoirs at the time. The Fraser Delta has been drilled by a number of small companies as far back as the 1930s, but nothing has been found. We geologists never go so far as to say "there's nothing there," but the West Coast has been explored by some good companies who have found nothing.

Also in 1976, Mobil Oil Canada made its best-ever discovery in British Columbia when we found a giant natural gas area in the Sierra and adjacent Sahtaneh fields, just west of the Alberta border. Mobil had been one of the earliest companies to actively explore in northeastern BC, when it became an active wildcat exploration area after the Leduc discovery. Our first exposure came when Texaco, Mobil and Amoco formed the Northern Foothills Agreement (NFA), operated by Texaco. The NFA made an important oil discovery called Boundary Lake near the Alberta border, and a couple of smaller gas and oil discoveries.

After a time, the companies in the group separated their exploration interests but continued to operate amicably on the production. Mobil continued to explore and in due course discovered the Sierra and Sahtaneh gas fields. Mobil continued to explore in BC, eventually all the way to the Yukon border and then across that province to a Northwest Territories field called Pointed Mountain. We found large reserves of gas but never had the corporate profile in British Columbia that we had in Saskatchewan. In the 1960s, our work in Saskatchewan included some early waterflood-enhanced oil recovery; in other words, we pumped water into the formation below the oil to force it up. (This technique was also called "secondary recovery.") However by the mid-1970s, we were drilling no new conventional oil wells. We had moved on to heavy oil, and around Lloydminster were launching the Celtic heavy oil recovery project using a technology called wet combustion: wherein we used heat and water to force the hydrocarbon up. In short, Mobil was a company that had moved beyond the heady exploration era, the Golden Decade that followed the Pembina discovery, to become a well-rounded, mature, exploration and production company with an iron in every attractive fire from one end of Canada to another.

Most of my time as president was spent managing people, budgets, partners, and government and industry relations. We had several hundred employees, and we added people on a regular basis. I made a practice of meeting every new employee we hired. I thought that if you came to work for this company, you should know the man who ran it, and he should know you personally.

I had the human resources department contact me regularly after five or ten new people joined the company. I set aside a morning, and they came to my office, one at a time to visit and have a cup of coffee. The human resources managers provided me with a few personal details so that I could start the conversation. I told them about the company, our objectives and what we were doing at the time. We talked about their jobs, careers and family.

Afterward, when I toured around the offices, I knew them and could speak to them using their names. Occasionally, to this day, I run into former employees and they remember our first meeting in my office. They appreciated it, felt connected to the company soon after joining it and therefore more committed to doing what they did well. I have known too many senior executives—presidents, chief executive officers—who only knew the top few people who reported to them. I don't believe this is a good policy.

Our corporate budgets were set each year at big meetings nearly always held in Scottsdale, near Phoenix, Arizona. The heads of the various subsidiary companies came in from all over the world. There were always three of us from Canada in attendance: Don Axford, Ed Barroll and myself. The other participants were from Australia, the US Divisions, and all the other places in Mobil's world where we had operations. We spent a week, sometimes two, going through every single program. We sat through everyone else's presentation, too. Each subsidiary had a proposed program for next year and predictions of what the expenditures would achieve for the company. In Canada there was a year-round process leading up to the preparation of specific proposals for these meetings.

Alex Massad was the executive vice-president of exploration and production worldwide. He chaired these Scottsdale meetings, and we spent as many days as necessary to review all the various exploration and development programs. When we had his agreement on a program, he would phone New York. Then the president, Bill Tavoulareas, would arrive with his senior staff and we spent maybe two days going over our proposals in a more summarized version, making firm recommendations. The big boss would agree, or not. Ultimately, he would go to the board of directors and make a presentation to get their approval. Once it had been set by the top executives, the program worldwide was so high-graded that the board rarely, if ever, said, "No."

After we finished budget preparations, we spent a week evaluating people. In Mobil we filled out an evaluation form each year on every single professional, assessing the major pluses and minuses of performance. A second form evaluated the person's future: How high do you think he can reach? How many can be exploration managers? How soon will they be ready for this job? We developed highly disciplined plans based on, firstly, the quality of people and, secondly, the best utilization of their talents. That's the way Mobil planned its future. It followed the decisions made at those meetings—when a vacancy arose, when someone retired unexpectedly or someone got sick, there was a list of people who would be ready to take the vacant job.

At these meetings, the ability to get up on your feet and talk proved an important skill; communications is pretty important. When asked what I think the major attributes of an executive are, my response has always been the same: the ability to get up on your feet, make your point, and persuade people to agree with you—and do the same in writing. Of course, you also need to be able to get along with others.

I spent about 30 per cent of my time as president managing Mobil Oil Canada's relationship with New York. I had to go there about five times a year to meet with Bill Tavoulareas, Dick Tucker and Alex Massad to keep them completely up to date with what was going on in Canada. I presented them with ideas we proposed, to get their agreement. In Calgary, I was on the phone to them often to deliver reports, and gain approvals and instructions.

I spent another 20–30 per cent of my time managing our relationships with partners in projects, operations and exploration ventures, and with the other members of industry through the Canadian Petroleum Association. The balance of my time was spent running Mobil Canada. A large portion of that had to do with personnel matters and the discussion of operations and financial results with the people reporting to me.

Sometimes, I was even able to get out into the field and enjoy the exploration side of things, but not as often as I did before I was president.

14

Sable Island

DURING MY TWENTY-SEVEN YEARS with the company, Mobil had grown from a scrappy little wildcatter to a leading integrated oil and gas producer. However, if you think that our days of discovery were over in the years I was president, the discovery of natural gas offshore Nova Scotia at the fabled Sable Island will set the record straight. In 1966, while I was still the vice-president and general manager of exploration, we began to organize wildcat drilling on the East Coast, offshore Nova Scotia. The company's East Coast connection began much earlier and more speculatively when, in 1943, Socony-Vacuum's first exploration well in Canada was drilled in the shallow waters off Prince Edward Island. The wildcat took twenty-five months to drill to its ultimate depth of 14,696 feet, and was lauded as the "the deepest well ever drilled in the British Commonwealth." It earned only one other distinction: it was also the most expensive dry hole in the world to that time—a $1.5 million duster.

Since 1959, when Don Axford first persuaded Joe Spivak and our president Art Detmar to begin leasing oil and gas exploration rights around Sable Island, the arm-waving geologist had been consumed by a conviction that there was a large petroleum basin on Canada's Atlantic shelf. He proposed a multi-zone oil and gas trend offshore Nova Scotia, built around a Devonian reef structure. By 1966 we held 30 million acres of oil and gas exploration permits, and our interests had been completely surrounded by Shell, which had acquired about three times the amount of acreage we held. It was a typical Shell strategy to be second in on a wildcat play such as this: it let someone else make the first move and then came piling in to gain a strategic position. Shell originated its own big discoveries, such as the 1944 discovery of the huge sour gas field at Jumping Pound in west-central Alberta. However, Shell couldn't be everywhere, so it was also their policy to cover their bases on discoveries made by other companies, and they weren't the only company to do so. When we made the Pembina discovery, Texaco, Imperial and Amoco came in after us to acquire the acreage on the large exclusive block of Socony Mobil interest lands, which regulations required us to surrender after the first successful wildcat.

I give Don Axford the credit for Mobil's subsequent success. He led the way on the geological and geophysical study to pick some well locations. I may have been the vice-president and manager of exploration, and later the president, but Don was the inspiration for Sable Island. As chief geologist, he was considered the research head of the organization, and he had put together all the information for the site, gathered over several years. Mobil Oil proceeded on his advice, and in 1967 I appointed him exploration vice-president, one of the first major decisions I made as head of the company.

Don had joined the company a year ahead of me and our careers paralleled one another. We enjoyed working together and shared many discoveries, notably Sable Island. Axford was a top-notch explorationist. He found a lot of oil and gas for Mobil and later for Petro-Canada and subsequently as an independent oilman. He earned the media nickname of "billion barrel man" for his discoveries. In that regard, we were geological peers, having both found more than a billion barrels of oil. He got more newspaper ink than I did for his discoveries, however, because he enjoyed the spotlight whereas I didn't seek it out. He did not advance as far with Mobil as I did because he wasn't terribly interested in the red tape and bureaucracy of a big company. He wasn't a great organizer. The engineers, lawyers and accountants, and even the geophysicists of the industry, consider geologists "arm wavers" because we use our enthusiasm as a tool to persuade them to see oil and gas deposits that are hidden deep in the ground by thousands of feet of rock. Don's enthusiasm at times seemed to be a cover for his disregard for the corporate bureaucracy. He was like the stereotypical professor with bundles of reports and maps under his arm, always slightly disarrayed. Nevertheless, he was a great guy to work and travel with, and I admired his tenacity in chasing his deductions of oil and gas reserves in unexplored and underexplored basins.

Don said, later in his life, that he had planned to spend his career with Mobil. However, he was frustrated by Mobil's decision not to drill the Hibernia prospect but to farm it out to Chevron. Soon after that decision, he left the company rather than accept a transfer to Indonesia, which would have involved leaving his young children in Canada to continue their education. At that point I think he also knew that the proposed transfer was a signal that he would not reach the top at Mobil. So he left the company in 1976 to become vice-president of exploration and production at Petro-Canada when it was starting up. Don stayed at Petro-Canada for a year until his strong differences with Bill Hopper, who was taking over the presidency from Maurice Strong, prompted him to resign.

After that he devoted his career to the independent Canadian sector as a consulting geologist and entrepreneur who started up a couple of junior oil companies and made some very good oil discoveries. His career garnered lots of publicity. Don and I always got along well and his career after Mobil reminds me a great deal of my own. Don kept working to the end of his life, and I intend to emulate him in that, as well.

Back in 1966, as Don and I prepared to explore the Sable Island area, we had no geological information, absolutely none, to go on. No geophysical surveys had been conducted so what we knew was based on regional geology that we had put together based on what we knew in general about the East Coast. We decided to drill a stratigraphic test to find out what the geology was really like in the area. We couldn't justify the expense of contracting an offshore drilling rig for a proposal like this. But one of our leading drilling contractors, Peter Bawden, suggested we use Sable Island as the "drilling platform." Sable Island is a glorified sand bar forty-eight kilometres long and less than a kilometre wide, covered with sand dunes, tough grasses and shrubs, and at no point higher than a few dozen feet above sea level. Its wildlife consists chiefly of wild ponies, seals and a rare bird called the Ipswich sparrow.

Peter obtained a military landing craft designed for Second World War invasions, loaded his drilling rig onto it and piloted it up onto the sandy shores of the island. The first well we drilled was right in the middle of the island. When we had more data, we discovered that we had drilled our discovery well on the optimum location: a salt dome. Our drilling location was arbitrarily determined by the location of the island; it was by accident that we found the best spot.

Peter Bawden was a very remarkable man, an American who came to Canada early in his career and stayed. Peter was a superb oilman and executive; he was articulate and a great problem-solver. He became very successful and very wealthy and was an entertaining person to work with.

Drilling the first well at Sable Island, offshore Nova Scotia (rig owned by Peter Bawden), 1970.

When he became a Canadian citizen, he was elected as a Member of Parliament in 1972. It says a lot about him that he hated life as an MP! He wanted to get things done, and as an opposition backbencher, there was very little room for his talent. Had the Conservatives been elected as the government in 1972, he would have made a terrific Cabinet minister. But Pierre Trudeau, who had a terrible first five years as prime minister, won a minority government, with the New Democrats holding the balance of power. They say Conservative leader Robert Stanfield was the best prime minister Canada never had. Peter Bawden was the best energy minister we never had. He died at a premature age of cancer, a very sad ending to a great career.

One of Peter's highlights must have been Sable Island. We drilled the first Sable well down to 15,000 feet. We got gas shows in the upper part of the well, not what I'd consider to be commercial gas but promising gas shows in the sandstone. As we drilled deeper, the pressure began to build up. We weren't equipped with blowout-preventers to deal with high pressures. I, Don Axford and Ed Barroll, who was Mobil's production manager, faced the problem.

Ed said, "We're going to have to quit drilling." We were tempted to drill deeper when we recovered a little bit of oil, but Ed was against it. "The

*Premier Regan of Nova Scotia talks with the press about the Sable Island discovery in 1970.
I am the one holding the map, and Don Axford is on the premier's left.*

pressures will endanger the well, and if we have a blowout we'll have a public problem," he said.

Reluctantly, we decided we were going to have to stop drilling. We ran a drill stem test to the very bottom of the hole before we quit drilling and recovered some heavily oil-cut mud. But it was an indicator to us that this could be a major discovery and encouraged us to go ahead at that time.

We kept the Bawden rig on the island. We needed geophysical data before we picked the next location. The regulators allowed us to run one line of seismic down the island but only one because of the Ipswich sparrow, a small, Atlantic sand dune-dwelling bird that breeds exclusively on Sable Island and winters in the salt marshes of the Georgia coast. Our problem, of course, was that was our drilling platform on Sable Island was the Ipswich sparrow's breeding ground. Whether we were getting in the way of the sparrow or it was getting in our way is a matter of perspective. Nevertheless, a politically aware contingent of scientists and activists prevailed, and we had to capitulate. That said, it has always been my experience that oil companies, particularly geologists and geophysicists, tend to prevent damage to the environment as much as possible. We were willing to accommodate the sparrow; it just meant we had to be creative in our exploration.

The Halifax Chronicle-Herald *reports the major discovery at Sable Island, October 5, 1971.*
[Reprinted with permission from the Halifax Herald Limited]

Wild horses on Sable Island.

The seals and the wild horses carried on as usual during our various operations. For the seals, carrying on as usual involved lying around on the beach sunning. The wild horses had been on the island since they were abandoned in 1737 by an eccentric preacher named Le Mercier, who had planned to take up residence on the island but decided against it when a disagreement ensued with the British North American colonial government of Nova Scotia on the terms of his land grant. We weren't the first to be thrown off that particular island. Le Mercier beat us to it.

We ran the rest of our seismic survey offshore, including lines as close to the island as possible. We got an indication of structure at the end of the island, which gave us the opportunity to drill a second well from the island on the apparent structure. A well-known geophysical contractor named Wes Rabey ran the survey. Peter Bawden and Wes Rabey showed us that service contractors who'd cut their teeth on the prairies and in the foothills of western Canada would adapt well to the offshore environment.

The federal government was by now much involved, and we had to get numerous approvals working in that environmentally sensitive area, even though the world had not yet become as environmentally aware as it is now. It was easier to explore for oil and gas in those days; it would be impossible now to operate in any way on Sable Island. In the late 1960s and early 1970s, however, environmental protection was still a new issue. Public and political pressure for strong environmental programs was growing, and oil companies were gaining a better understanding of how to work responsibly to minimize the impact of their operations.

In 1971 we completed the second test of an oil well. We called it Mobil Tetco E-48, and it ranks as the first offshore crude oil discovery in Canadian history. A Mobil Corporation magazine that year included a cover photo of Sable Island and that discovery; Mobil rarely featured Canadian activity in its reports, so this was a special occasion. In 1972 we made a second gas discovery close to the island in a field called Thebaud. That discovery led, in later years, to a deeper find called Panuke, which has become quite well known in Nova Scotia. In 1973 we discovered oil at Cohasset, although nearly twenty years would pass before we produced it.

We drilled four wells using Bawden's rig on the island. None were commercial. Two were completely dry, and the other two had just a very little bit of pay. After four years of drilling, we really had one oil well and one gas well. These were expensive wells, so we accepted the fact that we had a non-commercial discovery. The Sable Island area had basically everything that was needed for a petroleum basin—sediments, reservoirs and hydrocarbons. It just turned out that the volume of hydrocarbons was insufficient to really make it into a major oil- and gas-producing geological province. Perhaps we shouldn't complain; a fair amount of gas has come out of the Nova Scotia offshore. Gas has turned out to be Sable Island's major producible commodity, next to the Ipswich sparrow. Peter Bawden's rig, which had been on the island for about six years, was finally taken off and the Sable Island play ended in 1973.

While it was there, Peter Bawden's rig on Sable Island was a curiosity: a modern drilling rig on a fabled island with its photogenic ponies, seals and Ipswich sparrows. A lot of people asked us to take them out to see it—journalists, a landscape painter and, of course, the politicians. I arranged for Nova Scotia's Liberal Premier Gerald Regan to tour it with a newspaper photographer. The next day, the premier's photo was in the paper. Well, a day or two later, on a weekend, I did something that almost never happens in life. I cleaned out my garage and took a lot of stuff from it to the city dump in Calgary. Back at home, the phone rang and my son, Robin, answered. A stranger asked for me and Robin said, "He's at the dump today," like it was something I did a lot. The man replied, "When he gets back from the dump, ask him to call John Buchanan in Halifax." The caller was the Conservative Leader of the Opposition John Buchanan.

When I returned his call, he said, "Arne, you have to get me out to Sable Island to get my picture taken. My caucus is on my back because Gerald Regan got there first." Mobil's operation on Sable Island had become a political commodity. I happily took John on the requested tour a few days later, and he got his picture in the paper. Meanwhile, I had learned a valuable lesson: the jobs we were creating and the economic activity we were generating were invaluable to the people of Nova Scotia. That meant they were also invaluable to vote-seeking politicians.

We also conducted tours for Mobil Corporation senior executives from time to time, as there was great curiosity about this drilling operation on a tiny strip of sand in the ocean. Mobil's chief executive was a man name Albert Nickerson, a real New Englander who loved to sail and fish in the Atlantic. He played tennis, of course, and golf and followed the horses. A real outdoorsman was he, and a sporting man. Well, Don Axford, Ed Barroll and I took him on a tour of the island one summer afternoon. We were walking along the beach, and Nickerson was gazing out over the ocean. Suddenly he stopped in his tracks and stripped naked. "Come on fellows," he said. "Let's have a swim."

Don, Ed and I were stunned. We looked at each other, not quite sure what to do. But he was our boss, and our naked boss, the CEO of a big global oil company, was now headed for the surf. We did what any good and loyal employees would do. We stripped too, hiding our reluctance, and waded into the water with him. Well, Don and Ed were pretty much able to keep up to him, but it was a different story for me. I wasn't much of a swimmer, and I was sure that I'd be swept out to sea where I would drown. I stuck as close to the beach as I respectably could and was glad when the boss had enough and came ashore.

In spite of the Cohasset, Tetco and Thebaud (Panuke) wells, the Mobil Corporation executives in New York were not happy with Sable Island because it was not commercial. We'd spent a lot of money, but we did not have a cut-and-dried discovery. So, Mobil style, they told us to "get some help," and Texaco became our main helper. Although Petro-Canada shared the cost of some of the wells, Texaco took the most important farm-out from under us. In 1979 Texaco discovered the Venture gas field when they drilled on the largest structure that we had developed. Venture became the foundation of the Sable Offshore Energy Project, which began producing offshore gas in 1999 for use in Nova Scotia and New Brunswick, and for export to the northeast United States. The Sedco rig Texaco used to make the Venture discovery was built in Halifax for Mobil Oil Canada. My wife, Evelyn, christened that rig! Also participating in the occasion was Premier Gerald Regan.

It would be decades before Mobil got a cent of revenue, much less turned a profit from this multi-million dollar investment. But it was already paying a

My first wife, Evelyn, christens the Sedco J, *the first offshore rig built in Halifax, 1970.*

dividend to the people of a province that had lost its coal mines and was losing the North Atlantic fishery. Nova Scotia had a political desire for activity to
help its economy, to have the employment and the business infrastructure
that would result. We had a lot of government support. Premier Regan was of
tremendous help in getting the industry moving. I can remember him introducing me at a bid dinner in Halifax when I was visiting our Mobil office, and he
rounded up all the businessmen he could in order to introduce me as "one of
the saviours of this province." He bent over backwards to foster the industry.

His successor as premier, John Buchannan, was a Conservative and was
equally helpful. In all provinces, the premiers were always looking at the next
election; they had to have the support of the people to get re-elected, and
what's better for that than jobs? The royalties would help them out, but those
come more slowly, in the future, after production. But in those long early

Merv Graham, Mobil's drilling superintendent (far left), me, and Premier Regan (second from right) on Sable Island, 1970.

decades of exploration and development that preceded production, what we had to offer was jobs. We hired provincial residents everywhere throughout our operations.

The drill ships and crew came from Houston; we couldn't just take a man off the street and put him in a drilling job because skilled people operate the equipment and there are dangers for which you have to be trained. Initially we needed those Texans, but as time went by we trained and employed a large number of Nova Scotians, and, later, on the Grand Banks a large number of Newfoundlanders. Oil and gas exploration and development was a big leg up for East Coast people, and their politicians.

The federal government wasn't as good at recognizing what we brought to the provinces. The political persuasion of the highest elected officials in the Liberal government included a bias against foreign investment. The federal government wanted the royalties when and if development happened, but it was hostile toward foreign investment, even though it was a big factor in Canadian economic development. The government wanted to make sure that the foreign-owned companies paid a high price for participating. The successive provincial governments said, "Welcome. Come on in." They wanted the activity and the federal government wanted to play ball with the provinces, but it also had to deal with the issue of US investment at the same time.

Over the years the issue of foreign investment slipped into the background, particularly when discoveries were made and the big projects were constructed and it was obviously a big political plus for the East Coast. However, the debate over foreign investment affected the oil and gas industry in Canada in a powerful way, and as president of Mobil Canada, I was involved.

15

My Political Initiation

POLITICS AND OIL are inseparable. When I became president and general manager of Mobil Oil Canada on January 1, 1967, of necessity I also became a politician and public figure. This was not of my choosing because I preferred to be low-key. However, the boss of an oil company is also its "chief executive politician."

Geology demands optimism. Who wants to drill a mile or more into the ground to hit a target that is a geologist's fantasy? Politics also requires optimism; but optimism in human nature is much riskier. In my career of sixty years, the only big mistakes that governments have made (in my opinion) happened when they changed oil and gas policies before talking to the industry thoroughly to recognize the impact—good or bad—that those changes might make. Mistakes are avoided and policies improved and perfected when governments take the time to ask companies: "If we do this, what will it do to you?"

There are many opponents to the oil and gas industry who say, "You can't trust these guys; they lie to you every chance they get. They are only interested in what's good for them." The record in Canada doesn't support those claims.

Time and time again, in war and in peace, in economic crisis or environmental challenge, companies have balanced their interests with other public interests. Meanwhile, oil and gas exploration in Canada has yielded immeasurable economic, social and political benefits to all Canadians. It has been and is part of our identity as a nation.

At the beginning of my career at Mobil Oil Canada in 1950, public policy was pretty stable and quite favourable for getting on with the job of finding oil and gas. In 1950, the federal government gave scarcely a thought to the oil boom in Alberta except to acknowledge that it was good for Canada. The Alberta government saw the opportunity through the oil and gas industry to transform the province from a rural agrarian backwater to a modern, resource-based, industrial economy.

However, by the time of my mid-career in the late 1970s and early 1980s, politics became a threat to oil and gas development in Canada, and the industry was very nearly destroyed by bad national public policy. At the end of my career in 2009, the political risks had subsided and exploration was again more about geology and less about politics, although the occasional crises—such as the federal decision to eliminate energy income trusts or the Alberta decision to increase oil and gas royalties—have come along to disrupt the orderly development of resources.

In the winter of 1967, the flashpoint for oil and gas politics during the rest of my career—wildly escalating crude oil and natural gas prices—had not yet materialized. A barrel of crude oil sold for about $2 and on an inflation-adjusted basis, it hadn't changed much for thirty years. The dramatic emergence of OPEC as the controlling body for world oil price was still just a rumour. However, there were seismic foreshocks that hinted at the turbulent times ahead. I had been president of Mobil's Canadian subsidiary for less than two months when the first shot of the coming Canadian energy war was fired in Ottawa with the release of the Carter Royal Commission on Taxation.

The Carter Commission recommended the abolition of federal tax oil depletion allowances. These tax deductions provided significant incentives for our investment in exploration and development work, enabling producers to invest in spite of the rising costs of oil and gas exploration and the high risk of failure. Fortunately, the Carter Commission suffered the fate that most royal commissions receive—it was largely ignored. But it sounded a note that was repeated in federal policy in the years to come: federal hostility toward the oil and gas industry that included hostility to the producing provinces.

For Mobil Oil Canada, the nation's centennial year was a politically sensitive one because it was also the year we became the largest corporate exporter of Canadian crude to the United States. This profile was dangerous north of the

border when, that year, US multinationals became the villains of foreign investment in the Canadian oil industry.

Not all the political threats faced by Mobil came from Canadian sources.
In April 1967, the United States, noting the sudden rise in Canadian oil imports
that year, considered curbing Canadian oil and gas shipments to protect its
independent producers. At the end of the year, the United States went ahead
with import controls in 1968 that effectively capped the growth of exports
to our neighbour. In 1968, we were nearly side-swiped by American curbs on
foreign investments by US companies. For a while it looked like we would be
limited in the amount of cash flow that we could reinvest in new leases, drilling and development. As those reinvestments were the crux of our competitive
ability to increase reserves and production, this would have been a crippling
blow. Fortunately, Congress and President Lyndon Johnson came to their senses
and exempted Canada from those provisions. In return, the Canadian government secretly agreed to limit crude oil exports to the United States until 1971.

Meanwhile, in the spring of 1967 the Six Day War between Israel and Egypt
was waged, and members of the Arab Oil Exporting Countries—the forerunner
of OPEC—tried to embargo oil shipments to the United States to retaliate for
its support of Israel in that war. It didn't work; there were just too many other
countries, including Canada, willing to sell oil to the Americans. But another
ominous theme sounded in the new politics of oil.

The first major crisis that landed on my plate as Mobil's "President and
General Manager of Politics" was the campaign in Canadian nationalist circles
against foreign ownership. The issue ignited in January 1968, on the first
anniversary of my promotion, with the release of a study done for the federal
government called *Foreign Ownership and the Structure of Canadian Industry*.
It became better known as the Watkins Report, for the University of Toronto
economics professor Melville Watkins, who headed the task force of academics
and government "aristocrats" who prepared it. I abhorred Mel Watkins, a radi-
cal socialist gadfly who fancied himself a powerhouse in the New Democratic
Party. It warmed my heart when my old nemesis from Saskatchewan, Tommy
Douglas, said of him: "Mel Watkins developed an overweening pride and
became completely unrealistic."

The real political power behind the Watkins Report, however, was wealthy
Toronto accountant, nationalist and Liberal Cabinet minister, Walter Gordon.
Gordon was an honourable—some would even say noble—man. He was also
of a type of independently wealthy politician who is on a crusade and doesn't

see the need to make the concessions, compromises and alliances that ordinary politicians make to achieve an objective. Gordon's single-minded goal was to save Canada from US domination through uncompromising nationalism. As president of the Privy Council in the government of Lester Pearson, Gordon oversaw the commissioning of the task force, its mandate, and he received the task force's report on behalf of the government. The political forces behind the foreign ownership report had been growing within the Liberal Party since Gordon's disastrous performance as finance minister in 1963, and his first and only budget in that portfolio. He almost destroyed Pearson's fragile minority government and left the Liberal Party deeply divided between nationalists and the conservative Bay Street businessmen who had been the stabilizing factor of the party since the long Liberal reign of William Lyon Mackenzie King.

Gordon gathered a following of journalists, politicians, businessmen and academics, who would form the Council of Canadians. Ironically, given the impact of the Watkins Report, Gordon recognized that the great threat of American influence to Canadian national identity was social and cultural rather than economic. Equally ironic, in the mid-1960s, Canada, at the behest of influential Liberals, had, at times, advocated a continental energy policy, which would have seen the kind of economic integration with the United States that Watkins, and perhaps Gordon, regarded as anathema.

The purpose of the Watkins Report on *Foreign Ownership and the Structure of Canadian Industry* was, "to analyze the causes and consequences for foreign investments, to assess the actual benefits and costs and to put forth proposals for legislative consideration." Watkins wrote:

> The extent of foreign control of Canadian industry is unique among the industrialized nations of the world. Canadians are aware of the economic benefits that have resulted from foreign investment. They are also concerned about the implications of the present level of foreign investment for Canada's long-run prospects for national independence and economic growth.
>
> Canada needs to attract and absorb capital and technology from abroad and to gain access to foreign markets. Canada has relied heavily on foreign direct investment to meet these necessities. This will continue. But there are other options. It is possible to some extent to acquire capital and technology without relinquishing control. It is important to devise national policies which will increase the benefits and decrease the costs of foreign investment.

In writing this, Watkins created a phantom of his own making by stating that foreign investment in oil and gas by Mobil and our competitors was part of a larger agenda to dictate Canadian foreign policy. Watkins wanted it both ways. He wanted to "maintain steady economic growth, equitable distribution of income, rising standard of living and job opportunities for an emerging work force" without the inconvenience to his ideology of foreign investment. So, he lauded the outcome of foreign investment while demonizing the investors.

It was all very well that he wanted to "maintain national independence [and] increase the capacity of the Canadian economy to grow and develop in ways determined by Canadians." But that's exactly what was taking place in the oil industry. Provincial ownership and control of oil and gas guaranteed that the multinationals recognized provincial control and recruited Canadians like me to put a Canadian executive fingerprint on everything they did.

Watkins's paranoia had a context. The Vietnam War was raging. A 1960 book, *Peacemaker or Powder Monkey*, by CBC's Washington correspondent James Minifie, had warned Canadians not to get drawn into such US military adventurism. Canada was working behind the scenes through Albertan diplomat Chester Ronning to broker a peace agreement. Meanwhile, it was Canada's centennial, national pride was at its height and the new national dream was an independent presence for Canada in the world.

The meat of the Watkins Report wasn't just in its sometimes fictional iterations of an ideological framework but also in the numbers. This is where the Watkins task force found the evidence to prove the verdict they'd already decided upon:

> In 1964, foreigners owned $33 billion worth of assets in Canada and Canadians owned $13 billion of assets abroad [so] Canada's balance of international indebtedness was $20 billion compared with a postwar low of $4 billion in 1949.

At this point, the report neglected to note that Canada was a much different country in 1964, and its economy much differently structured than it was in 1949's postwar economic boom. The report noted that "over the same period, GNP went from $16 billion to $46 billion" but didn't analyze why that happened. Canada had been transformed into a modern resource-producing and manufacturing industrial economy.

Watkins's condemning data concerned foreign investment, foreign ownership and economic concentration. "The major contributor to Canada's net foreign debt is the expansion of foreign long-term investment from $7 billion in 1945 to $27 billion in 1964." Foreign direct investment grew from $2.7 billion (or 40 per cent of long-term investment) in 1945 to $15.9 billion (or 60 per cent of long-term investment) in 1964 and $12.9 billion (or 80 per cent of long-term investment) came from the United States. Watkins had his villain: the United States. Not only did US companies own 80 per cent of direct foreign investment, they also held 84 per cent of foreign-owned funded debt (such as corporate, provincial and municipal bonds) and were being paid $1 billion a year in interest and dividends. The report said that the eighth-largest petroleum and coal firms had 93 per cent of the annual sales in the sector; the largest twenty had 99 per cent sales. Eighteen of the largest companies were foreign-owned, and sixteen were from the US.

"A substantial petroleum and natural gas industry has developed and absorbed large amounts of foreign capital," the report said, accusingly. In 1964 it was 64 per cent foreign-owned and 74 per cent foreign-controlled. Manufacturing foreign ownership rose from 38 per cent in 1926 to 54 per cent in 1963, and foreign control increased from 35 per cent to 60 per cent. In mining and smelting, foreign ownership had risen from 37 per cent to 62 per cent, and foreign control from 38 per cent to 59 per cent. Watkins accused Canadian firms of being inferior because of the small size of the economy, national tariff protection and control by an elite that protected the status quo. He said the structure of the economy had encouraged US companies to create Canadian subsidiaries to conduct their investments.

When Watkins tendered his report, his political mentor, Walter Gordon, was unable to persuade the rest of Cabinet to endorse it, so when he tabled it in Parliament, he had to say that it represented the views of the task force and "not the government." It was referred to the Standing Committee on Finance, Trade and Economic Affairs, and there it languished.

The Watkins Report was commissioned at a time when the multinationals—like Mobil—hadn't recovered the investment they had made in Alberta, Saskatchewan and British Columbia since the end of the war. We were reinvesting most of the cash flow that was coming from new oil and gas discoveries into more exploration and drilling ventures. Mobil had just become the largest exporter of Canadian crude oil to the United States, yet we had barely recovered the investments we made in the 1950s and 1960s. We were here for the long haul and our business would deliver enormous strategic economic benefits to Canada. We needed a stable economic and political environment to thrive. Yet we were being treated with suspicion and even contempt by federal politicians. This attitude would continue for some time in Canada, resulting in significant policies developed in the 1970s.

Before the Second World War, western Canadian oil executives and provincial leaders were unsuccessful in persuading the great financial houses of central Canada to invest in oil and gas. The banks were more interested in real estate and agriculture. The stock markets of Toronto and Montreal understood mining and forestry—not petroleum. One of the bitter legacies of the Great Depression in Alberta politics is the memory of Minister of Mines Nathan Tanner travelling to Toronto, Montreal, New York and London in an unsuccessful attempt to find backing for Alberta's fledging petroleum ventures.

After the war, with the exception of a few large insurance companies in Montreal and Winnipeg and a couple of the major banks, Canadian financiers left the western Canadian petroleum industry to Canadian independent wildcatters and the American and European multinationals that were searching the globe for oil reserves. Even after Imperial Oil's Leduc discovery, western Canada had less to offer than the Middle East or the continental United States. However, Alberta's potential was of interest to the big multinationals, which had seemingly limitless exploration money.

In spite of the benefits that foreign investment offered to Canadian oil and gas development, when Ashland Oil, a large American independent, made a bid to acquire Home Oil in February 1971, the Liberals orchestrated an "emergency" debate in Parliament about the proposed deal. Then Ottawa blocked the takeover. Prime Minister Trudeau revived the Watkins Report, tabled it as the government's policy and initiated legislation that established the Foreign Investment Review Agency (FIRA).

FIRA was to be "a screening body whose limited mandate was to ensure that it takes place in forms which carry some benefit for Canada." It was not intended "to block or discourage foreign investment," and it never turned one down. But it made things difficult—for instance it took a year (1984–85) to approve the Mobil Oil Canada takeover of Canadian Superior. And I can tell you, based on the experience of some bloody internal battles at Mobil over Mobil Oil Canada's annual capital budgets, FIRA created an environment in which it absolutely discouraged foreign investment in Canada.

The *Foreign Investment Review Act* was passed in Parliament on February 18, 1974, near the end of the Liberal minority government of October 20, 1972–July 8, 1974. Prime Minister Pierre Trudeau was skeptical about nationalism because of the negative influence of "Quebec nationalism" on the separatist movement. So, why did he go along with FIRA? He agreed to it because the NDP, which held the balance of power in Parliament, set it as a condition of propping up the Liberal government.

Although FIRA proved in the long run to be innocuous, Mobil Oil observed a significant change in the federal government's attitude toward foreign-controlled subsidiaries, especially American ones. As we developed our Atlantic discoveries around Sable Island and the Grand Banks, Ottawa bargained harder than seemed reasonable to ensure we paid a premium price for "foreign" investment in the offshore.

"Canadianization" of the oil industry became a primary objective of the National Energy Program (NEP) and was an excuse for the harsh fiscal terms of the NEP that proved, ironically, more damaging to smaller Canadian independents than to the multinationals. It didn't escape the notice of the oil industry that although Watkins identified high levels of foreign ownership in all Canadian resource and manufacturing sectors, the Liberals never attempted to Canadianize any other sector. For instance, it never challenged the big US automobile makers in southern Ontario.

It takes a high level of political maturity to not become bitter about hypocrisy and regional prejudice, maturity we in the oil industry have sometimes lacked. The bottom line is that Canadian governments of all political stripes have made bad energy policies, and as a result, oil executives are unlikely ever to trust federal political parties and governments. Of course, we still had to work with them, but we were always on our guard.

16

Political Tools

DURING THE TIME of the attack on the foreign ownership of the oil and gas industry, I became involved in a positive way with the federal government. Mobil Oil belonged to the Canadian Petroleum Association, and I was on the executive committee for ten years, and was twice chairman of the board of governors. In this capacity, I frequently represented the industry to the federal government on critical policy issues. The fact that I was a Canadian, whereas most of my counterparts were Americans, made me a more acceptable face of the industry than the others. I made numerous trips to Ottawa to talk with the energy ministers and other high-level politicians on matters relating to oil and gas policy.

In 1969 Minister of Energy Joe Greene set up an organization called the National Advisory Committee on Petroleum (NACOP). Joe was remarkably likeable. He looked like Abe Lincoln and was a terrific political speaker, one of the last campaign-stump orators in Canadian politics. He ran unsuccessfully for the leadership of the party in 1968 against Pierre Trudeau. Greene could have cared less about foreign ownership, but he worried about Canada's energy security. He was vilified on one occasion by the cynical press gallery for proclaiming that Canada had nine hundred years of oil reserves—that claim worried me, too. However, he welcomed any information we gave him, and he was thoughtful about substantial matters related to oil and gas. Oil industry opponents hated NACOP, criticized its secrecy (we were "sworn in" just like Cabinet ministers) and dismissed us as inconsequential.

In order to go on the NACOP board, I needed the approval of Bill Tavoulareas in New York, and I was dubious about getting it. I thought he would regard it as taking away from my Mobil work. There was a strong chance that he would say, "No," if I asked him, so Joe Greene made the call on my behalf. Tavoulareas said, "Yes," and I was on NACOP for the full time of its existence. The group met about every two to three months, usually in Ottawa. The secretary was a deputy minister named Roland Priddle, who subsequently became chairman of the National Energy Board.

The committee consisted of about a dozen individuals at any one time, who were chief executives of their companies. In order to gain a broad range of representation, the individuals invited were from major oil companies, smaller independents, and major pipeline and gas utility companies. A total of thirty-three men sat on it over the years, representing a couple of dozen companies. They were a Who's Who of the Canadian oil patch.

Their faces remain completely fresh in my memory: Bill Twaits and Jack Armstrong of Imperial; Bill Daniels and Harry Bridges of Shell Canada; Robert Campbell of Canadian Pacific Oil and Gas, later PanCanadian; R.W. Sparks and A.G. Farquarson from Texaco Canada; Jerry McAfee and C.D. Shepard from Gulf Canada; David Mitchell and Fred McKinnon of BP Canada; L.E. Richards of Hudson's Bay Oil and Gas; Gene Roark of Husky Oil; D.G. Weldon of Interprovincial Pipe Line; Ed Phillips of Westcoast Transmission; Kelly Gibson of Pacific Petroleum; Ed Bovey of Norcen Energy Resources; Alistair Ross of Western Decalta; Ken Heddon of Great Canadian Oil Sands; A.F. Campeau and Pierre Nadeau of Petrofina; R.F. Ruben of North Canadian Oils; R.B. Bailey of Canadian Reserve Oil and Gas; James Allan of Golden Eagle; Murray Paulson of Home Oil; James Kerr of TransCanada Pipelines; the Irving brothers of Irving Oil in the Maritimes; and O.L. Jones from Consumers Gas in Ontario. Jack Gallagher, the founder of Dome Petroleum, declined an invitation to join. I was disappointed because he was my neighbour and a great friend. Jack had his own back doors into government, although there were many times, I'm told, that he wasn't all that welcome.

NACOP operated for more than ten years under Liberal energy ministers Joe Greene, Donald Macdonald and Alistair Gillespie, and it dealt with every significant issue faced by the federal government, up to but not including the infamous National Energy Program of October 1980. The energy minister of the day, Marc Lalonde, foolishly told us we weren't needed and dismissed us. I don't think he ever regretted getting rid of NACOP and still supports the ideas behind the NEP. Such is the way of politics.

The NACOP agenda was a two-way street. The ministers asked our advice about most decisions that they planned to put into effect, and we offered them advance notice and an explanation of our position. The subjects included taxation, economic development opportunities arising from oil and gas activities, and the first two national energy policies developed in the Trudeau years. We discussed development of the Canadian frontiers, world oil prices, OPEC, United States oil import restrictions, the oil sands, as well as provincial policies. We often disagreed, but we always understood one another. Being a part of NACOP was a remarkable experience, and I wonder if it could be done today, so partisan is our political debate now, and so poisoned by incessant media scrutiny.

The most important tool of the political trade for me as Mobil Oil Canada's "Chief Political Officer," however, was the Canadian Petroleum Association. The CPA was formed after the Second World War and represented the mostly foreign-owned major oil companies who accounted for 80–90 per cent of the oil and gas produced in Canada. The smaller companies were represented by the Independent Petroleum Association of Canada (IPAC), whose roots went back to the Alberta Petroleum Producers, which had been formed after the 1914 Turner Valley discovery.

The CPA had about twenty-five large member companies, and twelve of those were directly represented on the board. They were nearly always the same twelve from year to year. Strangely enough, these companies were all extremely competitive in their oil and gas activities; however, when they came to the CPA, they were able to work together to find consensus on major issues to present to the government. The job of the CPA chair was to get all of these companies to work together to obtain a consensus that he could then take to Ottawa or the provincial governments.

As each major issue was encountered, the company was represented in CPA discussions by its top executive, the president or chief executive officer or chairman. Each company came with a view as to how the position of the organization should be relative to presenting the issue to the government. There was only one way to reach a common position—persuasion. The chairman had to persuade companies to take a position that was compatible with everyone else's, a position that he and two or three members of the executive committee could take to Ottawa. It worked marvelously, but that isn't surprising because, in most cases, the companies had the same stakes in major issues.

At an Oilmen's golf tournament in the late 1970s. From left: me, Don Lougheed (Peter Lougheed's elder brother and petroleum engineer at Imperial Oil); my wife, Valerie; and Don Harvie (a prominent oil and gas executive, philanthropist, son of Eric Harvie and president of Fina). Senior oil industry executives from across Canada and the United States attended this annual event.

The government also sought the viewpoint of IPAC. The position of the small companies on major issues usually differed from those of the large companies. IPAC put their views together effectively for presentation to the government. On all issues, the government sought the views of both associations.

The CPA was headquartered in Calgary. There was a division in Saskatchewan based in Regina because that province had a different set of issues to deal with because of its socialist government. When I was chairman of CPA for the first time in 1971, I set up an Ottawa office. We thought that the bureaucrats were the most important people to deal with in government, and we needed someone on the ground in Ottawa who would have daily contact with government and represent the executives in Calgary. As well, whenever I or any other CPA member went to Ottawa on behalf of his own company, the Ottawa office staff would help make the right contacts.

We also set up two CPA offices in Atlantic Canada when drilling began there, one in Halifax and one in St. John's, because we were dealing with a different kettle of fish in each of the two provinces. Newfoundland had a separatist attitude to Canada at the time. In Nova Scotia, Maritimers thought their interests were not represented properly without a CPA office because the Nova Scotia offshore exploration industry was smaller than Newfoundland's and would be overshadowed if there was just one CPA office in the region.

My wife Valerie and I share a drink at the Oilmen's golf tournament, 1980.

All of the CPA member executives got along well socially and personally. We had a network to cement our relations and that paid a dividend when it came to working on political matters. The premier networking event was the Oilmen's, an annual golf gathering alternating between the Banff Springs Hotel and Jasper Park Lodge. The Oilmen's went on for several days, and everyone always brought their wives. Even guys like me who didn't golf were involved. The dinners during the Oilmen's were the most important relationship-building nights in the industry, so most CPA board members participated.

I served an unusual two terms as chairman of the Canadian Petroleum Association. My first term was in 1970–71. Although he hadn't been elected yet, we were aware of the winds of political change in Alberta and were building a relationship with Peter Lougheed and the Progressive Conservative Party, which was the Official Opposition in the Legislature. Exploration was gaining momentum in the Arctic and East Coast offshore, so matters related to that were coming onto the agenda. In the larger world, the producing countries of the Middle East and Venezuela had led the initiative to form OPEC. My first term with CPA was a time of preparation; big changes and big crises lay ahead, and we were just starting to get a feel for what might unfold.

My election to a second term as chairman of the CPA board of governors came after my task force and I had completed the Alternative Energy Program, which we were selling to the Conservatives as the solution to the National Energy Program, and which I address later in this book. The members elected me because I was a Canadian, a necessity at the time of the National Energy Program. I'm not sure if the appointment was a "recognition and reward" for what I had done or an assignment to follow through and get the alternative policy adopted. I joked in a newspaper interview that all I had to do was drag out the speeches and presentations from my first term, because the issues hadn't changed much. However, things had become a lot more urgent.

I have some very warm memories of the people I worked with at the CPA, but none better than those of Ian Smythe, the president of the organization. I was very much involved in hiring Ian and became his friend. Smythe succeeded John Poyen, who had retired from Imperial Oil and had knowledge of the business and numerous connections. He was also the best golfer who ever held that job! Unfortunately, he was abrasive and raised hell big time in Ottawa. He absolutely hated the government and didn't hide it.

We needed a different kind of person, and Ian was it. John despised government but Ian had worked in it as a Deputy Minister of External Affairs and had a stint in the Foreign Service in Africa. He was diplomatic and persuasive and knew the right people. Shortly after he became president, we also began to click with the media, and that became an invaluable relationship in the troubled 1980s.

I had occasion to meet with a lot of top political people in Canada, particularly when I worked for Mobil. Among them I got to know former Prime Minister Jean Chrétien very well personally because he was energy minister for quite a long time. I took him to tour some of the exploration activities off the East Coast and met him at quite a few meetings. I first met him when he was Minister of Indian and Northern Affairs, on matters related to northern exploration. There was a lot of activity at the mouth of the Mackenzie River, the Beaufort Sea and Canadian lands off the East Coast that interested both of us, so our paths crossed. People either liked Jean Chrétien or disliked him. I like more people than I dislike. I liked him. He always made himself available for meetings and dinners. Chrétien had a lot of personality and in my opinion did a good job in his various government assignments.

I also met with Richard Hatfield, the premier of New Brunswick, when we drilled a well in the Bay of Fundy in New Brunswick waters and had a very pleasant evening with him. Shortly after, there was a national premiers' conference held in Nova Scotia. Premier Gerald Reagan, the host, asked me if I would help him out by taking the premiers to Sable Island. I did just that. Peter Lougheed was the only premier who did not attend. We had a catered barbeque dinner on the shore. When it came time to round up the premiers, there was one missing. This raised a huge concern in a hurry, particularly for me. Instantly, help was called to find the missing premier, Richard Hatfield. We found him lying on the beach about a mile from where we had the party! He had had too much to drink and was fast asleep.

I met many people in the public service through my government relations work; including the men who became Petro-Canada's founders: Jack Austin, Bill Hopper, and Maurice Strong. They were straightforward, honest, competent and well selected. Jack Austin was a deputy minister and is now a retired senator. He didn't always lean our way as he was very government-oriented, but I liked him as an individual. Bill Hopper and Jack worked closely on the development of Petro-Canada when they were both young deputy ministers. You couldn't help but like Bill, who I first met in 1973 in China, because he had such a great personality.

I became acquainted with Maurice Strong only slightly. He ran Power Corp and was well-known in Calgary before Petro-Canada. He had an unusual wife— she was Swedish and had unique religious ideas. They once invited about fifteen monks from China to stay at their ranch. Maurice had a big reception at the ranch and he invited a number of us from the oil industry to meet the monks.

I first dealt with Maurice when he asked me to accept an invitation to head up Petro-Canada. I declined. Maurice then became head of the company but had been at Petro-Canada for only about six months when I received a call from him asking me to visit with him in Ottawa. I wondered what he wanted to talk with me about. He asked, "Arne, why don't you take the Petro-Canada job?" He said he was leaving because he had too many other things to do. Again I declined, this time citing the administrative burden, which didn't interest me. Subsequently, Bill Hopper became the president of the company.

Another man in government I met along the way was Paul Tellier when he was clerk of the Privy Council under Prime Minister Trudeau. His position gave him a direct line to Trudeau. I liked him and he was very approachable. I thought he was on the industry side of issues generally speaking, or at least understood industry's positions. He eventually left the government and headed up Canadian National Railway and Bombardier. He is a good example of the value of having people in government who know business from first-hand experience, and people in business who know government first-hand.

During the years in which I handled Mobil Oil Canada's political affairs and represented the CPA on government matters, Mobil Oil Corporation's executives in New York never interfered and never issued directions. They knew that they should leave Canadian politics to their Canadian affiliate. I would go to New

York and review what was going on in Canada by way of government action that would affect Mobil. I received a considerable amount of advice, but the executives never said, "You must do this." The fact that I was Canadian and had a good relationship with provincial and federal governments gave them the confidence to leave the politics to me.

I recall an occasion when Bill Tavoulareas came up from New York and asked to see Ernest Manning. I couldn't think of two people with greater personal differences: Manning the Sunday preacher and Tavoulareas the hard-drinking profane oilman. Manning was gracious and they talked for half an hour, but it was just a courtesy call, they didn't say a thing of consequence to one another. On that occasion, Tavoulareas did not have any particular axe to grind—he just wanted to meet the famous Ernest Manning, who was a legend in American oil circles for his integrity and accomplishments on oil and gas policy. Manning welcomed us into his big office in Edmonton, and they had a good two-way conversation dealing with the industry.

I cannot recall any other occasion when the top executives visiting Canada met with the premier of a province. This was perhaps unfortunate as that one occasion, although it was just a "meet and greet," created a lot of goodwill.

In politics, goodwill is invaluable.

17

The Lougheed Years

WHEN I BECAME "chief executive politician" of Mobil Oil Canada, the iconic Social Credit premier of Alberta, Ernest Manning, was in his final year of power after twenty-five years in office. I didn't have many direct dealings with him on policy matters or socially, but I knew he was straightforward, extremely honest and great to deal with. When you met with him you got it straight from the shoulder. He set up the rules and regulations under which the industry operated for many years, and his system still provides the oil and gas framework in Alberta.

He did not think his job was to take care of the industry—it was to take care of the province and to see to it that the people of Alberta were treated fairly. He knew the importance of the industry because he had used royalty revenue from the pioneer fields, mainly Turner Valley oil and natural gas, to pay off Alberta's Depression-era debt before big discoveries like Leduc and Pembina launched the golden years of his premiership.

In December 1968, Ernest Manning resigned as premier of Alberta and was replaced by the affable Harry Strom, a good dryland farmer but out of his depth in politics. A year later, Manning gave up his seat in the Legislature and was appointed to the Senate of Canada. My first term as chairman of the Canadian Petroleum Association occurred during Strom's brief tenure in office. I can recall no outstanding moment in the industry's relationship with him; he left us alone, and we obliged him by leaving him alone.

In the general election of August 30, 1971, Peter Lougheed's Progressive Conservative Party defeated the Social Credit dynasty decisively, winning forty-nine seats to the Socred's twenty-five. Ernest Watkins (no relation to Mel), a previous leader of the Conservative Party, said, "This was not a campaign of political discussion. It was a contest between two schools of political behaviour." Lougheed patterned his campaign after John Kennedy's 1960 United States presidential campaign, using television, polling and sophisticated communications strategies. He hit the streets, went door to door and distributed his brochures at intersections during rush hour. His opponents spent the days on their combines and campaigned only in the evenings, at polite coffee parties.

At first the oil and gas industry was not sure about Lougheed. Ernest Manning was a tough act to follow. Lougheed expected big-time support from the oil companies in the election of 1971, and he didn't get it. However, he went to see the presidents of all the major oil companies to make sure they understood his program. He wanted us to feel we could safely elect him.

He came to see me because I was chairman of the CPA. He came on his own, and we visited for two hours. He was a straightforward person who didn't indulge in small talk. We were both young men, graduates of the University of Alberta and part of a generation of Canadians who wanted to control their own destiny. He had played football for the university's Golden Bears and subsequently for the Edmonton Eskimos, and I had seen him play a number of times, but not otherwise. It was a job for him to explain why his Conservative Party should replace another "conservative" party that had treated the industry well. The key advantage he had was that Manning was gone and his successor, Harry Strom, wasn't cutting the mustard.

Peter Lougheed was a well-educated urbane reflection of the new Alberta that had emerged from the prosperity generated by oil and gas. He was as tough as barbed wire and very competitive. He was the closest thing to a "blue-blood" aristocrat that was possible in a "down-to-earth" province like Alberta, and his fifteen-year term as the premier is remembered as Alberta's political "Camelot."

His grandfather, Senator Sir James Lougheed, had invested profitably in Alberta's first big oil discovery at Turner Valley in 1914 and campaigned for Alberta's control over natural resources after it became a province in 1905. Premier Lougheed inherited a sense of mission based on the premise that the province's resources belonged to Albertans and could be developed more aggressively for their benefit than Premier Ernest Manning had done in the sunset of his career. (Lougheed's brother, Don, was a noted and very effective oil and gas petroleum engineer who ended up running Imperial Oil's western Canadian activities. I knew Don well because he was Imperial Oil's representative on the CPA.)

Lougheed proved to be a providential successor to Manning, building on, rather than replacing, the legacy. Change was in the air in 1971; the oil and gas industry worldwide and in Canada was on the verge of a tumultuous revolution. When the boom of the 1970s opened, its possibilities matched the drive and determination of Alberta's new premier. When the political stakes escalated, and oil and gas politics became as violent as they can be without domestic or foreign bloodshed, Peter Lougheed was tough enough and smart enough to come out ahead of his opponents, most of the time.

The new premier saw oil and gas production as the first step in a diversified economy that processed more of its oil and gas rather than shipping it all raw to other markets. He was increasingly alarmed at the centralist tendencies of the Trudeau government and was quite prepared to intervene in the management of resources.

There were good people around Lougheed. One of the best was a lawyer from Edmonton named Merv Leitch. He had been a law student with Lougheed at the University of Alberta, and you could tell that they had a close personal relationship. After he became the energy minister, he was by Lougheed's side during the worst years of the National Energy Program and the battles with Trudeau. I went to see Merv a handful of times on behalf of the CPA. He was a very good person to relate to, but he had a tragic end to his life after a battle with illness. Put him into the "good guy" political category: he understood the industry and had an effective relationship with us.

Lougheed had a circle of Canadian oilmen with whom he conferred, Bob Brawn, Rod McDaniel, Bud McCaig and Doc Seaman were some of the men in that circle. His rapport with most of the industry, however, was somewhat tenuous, and his demeanour ranged from diffident to frosty. He seemed driven to prove he wasn't in anyone's pocket.

During the 1971 election, both the Conservative and Social Credit parties promised to increase oil and gas royalties, provide more fiscal incentives for exploration and find ways to market the growing surplus of oil and gas that we were discovering. Albertans chose Lougheed to deliver on the promises. Soon after he was elected, Lougheed announced that he would review oil sands policy to speed up its development. Five months later, his Cabinet approved the first expansion of production from the Syncrude mine and upgrader. In March 1972, Lougheed announced a comprehensive royalty review.

Clearly, the passive days of Ernest Manning were over. The new premier was going to get in up to his elbows in governing the province and the industry. He coined the phrase "think like an owner" because oil and gas reserves—with the minor exception of old freehold lands—belonged to the province constitution- ally. The exploration companies, as welcome as they were, were just tenants on the leases and didn't take possession of their production until they paid the rent—i.e., the royalties. We were taken aback by Lougheed's aggressive new approach. However, he was generally fair. He did what he thought he had to do in the interest of Alberta and in the interest of his party. I visited with him a number of times on CPA issues and I found him to be a very straightforward honest person. He was—and still is—sunny and optimistic, friendly and confi- dent. The oil industry respected him, and that says a lot.

He was on top of every issue and had an informed intelligent answer to every question, whether or not you agreed with him. However, access to Lougheed wasn't as open as it was to Manning. You could get to see Manning almost any time you wanted and had a reason. With Lougheed, you needed the support of the energy minister before you got in to see him.

In his first term, Lougheed showed that he was no patsy for the industry. He wanted it to thrive, but public policy would be made on his terms. He formed the Alberta Petroleum Marketing Commission (APMC) as a vehicle to sell the province's royalty oil. Instead of paying royalties in cash, he collected it in pro- duction, and the APMC sold it. It began to sell the industry's share of production, as well, and did a very fine job of it, using its market power to garner top dollar.

The industry had looked with favour upon having Lougheed as premier, but then he made the controversial move to increase royalties. It was hard for us to accept the idea of higher rates with pleasure when they had been low since the discovery of Leduc. On the other hand, it was hard to argue against Lougheed's principle that the people of Alberta should get more because the world price of oil had increased by 20 per cent in less than two years (going from $1.80 to $2.20 per barrel). That doesn't seem like much now, but at the time after thirty years of flat prices, it was dramatic. He reminded both the public and industry that OPEC producers had increased their take from American producers and the Seven Sisters. Lougheed took the position that if the OPEC countries were tak- ing more, why shouldn't Alberta?

Industry moved in quickly to make sure there was a thorough discussion about the royalty hike, and royalty changes were forestalled until the impacts were discussed and understood.

Valerie and I meet with Alberta Premier Peter Lougheed and Sheik Yamani of Saudi Arabia, 1978.
Yamani was oil minister for Saudi Arabia and a very influential person in the world industry.
This was the first time he visited Alberta, and he gave a speech to the CPA. I introduced him.

A curious duality developed in the producers' attitude to the young premier. They applauded his toughness with the federal government. But his interventionist mindset and his eagerness to tinker with royalties made them apprehensive. As their relationship with Lougheed cooled, producers became openly critical, and at times hostile, especially when he raised royalties from a longstanding level of 10 per cent to over 20 per cent.

In August 1972, a year into government, the premier announced a royalty compromise. By now, world oil prices had jumped to $3 per barrel. Changes to natural gas royalties were postponed indefinitely and oil producers were offered a choice. They could pay a reserves tax or a modest increase in royalties from 16.67 per cent to 22 per cent. Meanwhile, drilling tax credits and a five-year royalty holiday for new discoveries would be provided. Producers were to make their choice within a year. On the deadline in 1973, eight major companies, including Mobil, representing 60 per cent of Alberta oil production, opted to pay the reserves tax. After the royalty rates were increased, there was more for the Alberta government and the people of the province, but the industry was not seriously damaged.

Less than two months later, however, after the world price of oil had reached $5 per barrel and the federal government froze domestic oil prices and introduced an oil export tax, firing the first shot in the federal–provincial oil wars that culminated in the National Energy Program, Lougheed was forced to change the plan. He repealed the reserves tax, tied oil royalties to the price and substantially raised them. The net effect was that subsequent to Lougheed's election, oil royalties had increased from 16 per cent to 23 per cent and it lost him some face as premier. Nevertheless, he stuck to his argument that if OPEC was raising oil prices in the interest of their citizens, we should do it in the interest of the people of Alberta. He was one tough customer, standing up to the intense pressure of the industry, and we admired him for it, even if we were unhappy with the new royalty bill.

There was more to come. In January 1974, with world oil prices now at $11.25 per barrel, Lougheed hiked royalties yet again, this time for both oil and gas. Again, the new system was complicated, as the government tried to maintain incentives for investment while capturing the Crown's share of the new wealth being generated. In simple terms, oil royalties escalated from 23 to 40 per cent for old producing wells but to just 28 per cent for new discoveries, and royalties were tied to world price.

The producers were now in a double bind: the federal government had frozen domestic prices so that they were getting only $6.50 per barrel, $4.75 less than the price in the United States. Meanwhile, the way the calculations worked, although the nominal royalty rate for old wells was 40 per cent, for some production the royalty would be as high as 60 per cent.

It was irritating, but it was unavoidable and therefore being irritated was as far as our reaction went. The Canadian independents, however, were angry and accused Lougheed of "tearing up" the 1973 royalty agreement. For the CPA, there was a certain amount of face-to-face complaining with the politicians but no public action. At Mobil, I was somewhat fortunate because Canada was minuscule within Mobil Oil Corporation's world. Mobil had problems around the world as OPEC took control of the market. It was one of the Seven Sisters, which formerly had set the price quietly by telling Middle East producers, which made up the majority of OPEC members, what they would pay. Now OPEC was telling the multinationals what they must pay. The Canadian issues were small potatoes by comparison.

Meanwhile, the people of Alberta were buying the program Lougheed was selling. In 1975 he was re-elected with a massive majority of 63 per cent of the popular vote and sixty-nine seats. All his opposition was shattered: there were just six opposition members elected, divided between three parties. That meant oil and gas was voting Lougheed.

In July 1976, Lougheed amended the terms of oil leases. Previously we had held them for ten and twenty-one years, depending on when we had acquired them. Because of the long lead times in these leases, large companies accumulated vast holdings and held them until they had the budget to explore them. Lougheed believed that practice locked the door to the growth of smaller independent companies, so he implemented a "drill it or lose it" policy, and companies had to give up undrilled permits after five years. The Lougheed policy would make certain that permits were drilled, not banked. I believe it was reasonable, although it affected Mobil because we had a fair-sized "land bank."

Still, Mobil had bigger fish to fry.

The oil wars with Ottawa were underway. Even the foreign ownership issue seemed minor by comparison to the multinational CPA members. We were engaged in a full-fledged battle to keep the federal government's hands off our wallet.

Only on one other occasion did Lougheed incur the anger of the industry to the same degree as the royalty reviews. In 1981, during the bitterest days of the National Energy Program, after arduous and acrimonious negotiations, he signed an oil price agreement with Prime Minister Trudeau. It was an attempt to resolve the problems created by a federal government two-tiered oil and gas price policy, which held the domestic price in Canada well below the world price.

The industry had stood behind Lougheed in the forceful campaign to get some fairness back. Eventually, they made an agreement. Lougheed was photographed toasting Trudeau with a flute of champagne—a moment orchestrated by Trudeau's clever handlers, which caught the premier off guard and took advantage of his good manners and good nature. When that happened, there were mutterings that Lougheed had settled for too little. The CPA and the companies went to Ottawa and protested privately, but we didn't embarrass Lougheed publicly.

Lougheed's successor, Don Getty, was a likeable person who grew up in Montreal and attended university in Ontario where he established his reputation as a football player. When he graduated, he came to Alberta to play for the Edmonton Eskimos; he was the team's first Canadian quarterback. Imperial Oil gave him an off-season job—companies did that in those days to support the football team. Imperial spoke very well of him for the work he did as a planner in their crude-oil marketing division.

Getty became energy minister after Merv Leitch. He was not considered to be really knowledgeable in the oil and gas industry, in spite of his previous job with Imperial Oil. However, he played an outstanding role in keeping the

Syncrude oil sands consortium together when one of the partners, Atlantic Richfield Company (ARCO), bailed out. He and Lougheed hammered out a deal in which the Ontario government participated with Alberta and Ottawa in replacing ARCO's investment. In the end, when Getty became premier, he was always compared negatively to Peter Lougheed. He didn't last long in office by Alberta standards.

Being part of a large company like Mobil allowed me to have a more global perspective on events at home in Canada. What was happening in Canada was important, even earthshaking when you were on the ground and involved in discussions, as my memories of the NEP and the Alternative Energy Plan will prove, but when I was given the opportunity to compare Canadian events to those of the world around me, I was able to take some things in stride and assert myself in a calm manner. One particular experience in the wider world of petroleum exploration and development allowed me to keep my perspective: a trade trip to China in 1972.

18

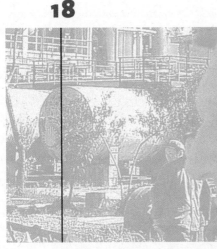

Behind the Bamboo Curtain

IN THE AUTUMN of 1972, my political experience as the president and general manager of Mobil Oil Canada was beginning to add up to something. I had been a member of the National Petroleum Advisory Committee for three years and had developed a friendly and fruitful relationship with the federal energy and mines minister of the day, Donald Macdonald. I had completed my first term as chairman of the Canadian Petroleum Association and learned how to navigate the treacherous waters of petroleum politics and to build consensus with friends and foes alike. Peter Lougheed's Progressive Conservative government in Alberta had completed its first year in office, and we had faced our first challenges in the post–Ernest Manning years. Lougheed had also given us an early taste of the looming rivalry between the federal and provincial governments over energy, and we had seen a preview of the role that made his reputation as defender of Alberta's constitutional control over its natural resources.

Then, in November of that year I had my first brush with international energy relations and a preview of the economic and political globalism of the future when members of a fact-finding petroleum mission from the People's Republic of China came to see me. They wanted to talk to me mainly about the Pembina oilfield: how it was discovered and the techniques Mobil was using to produce it, particularly the water floods for tertiary recovery. They had discovered an oil and natural gas field with striking geological similarities to Pembina called the

Taching field some fourteen years previously. It was located in Manchuria in northern China, three hundred miles from the border with the Soviet Union. Taching was the largest discovery in Chinese history, and they had a great deal riding on making the most of it.

They also wanted to talk about Mobil's Sable Island offshore discovery, and I arranged a brief visit to the operation. At the time, they were getting their first offshore experience at an oilfield called Takong, which straddled the low-lying coast and shallow waters of the Gulf of Chihli in the Yellow Sea, and they wanted to learn more about the way we did things here in Canada. That petroleum mission, a visit by a mining and metallurgical group in January, and reciprocal trade exhibits in Peking and Toronto in August, launched a new era in economic relations between our two countries.

After the Maoist revolution in 1949 overthrew the Imperial government and replaced it with a Communist one, a Bamboo Curtain had fallen over China, much like the Iron Curtain between Western Europe and the Soviet Union. European nations and the United States had earned a terrible reputation in China in the two hundred years before the Second World War. They had been the purveyors of the worst kind of colonialism in the nineteenth century. They had, among other ills, fostered and expanded the opium trade. Without a similar negative colonial record in China, and with a large Chinese population in our major cities, Canada was better positioned than any other industrial nation to break down the barriers of mutual ignorance, hostility, suspicion, fear and prejudice.

The Korean War had pitted Chinese and North Korean troops against United Nations forces lead by the United States and Britain, including Canada. In the aftermath of that conflict, which ended in a stalemate on the 38th-parallel border between North and South Korea, Canadian federal ministers, principally Liberal Trade Minister C.D. Howe, simply refused to consider any thawing of postwar hostility toward China. In the 1950s, Canadian officials in Hong Kong tried to persuade Howe to open trade talks, but with the memory of the war still fresh, Howe turned them down.

It is a fact largely forgotten now, except by historians and diplomats, that Canada was a world leader in establishing normal economic and trade relationships with China. Canadians went behind the Bamboo Curtain to begin selling wheat to China during the Diefenbaker regime, thanks to Minister of Agriculture Alvin Hamilton and Minister of Trade Gordon Churchill—both western Canadians. In June 1957, immediately after John Diefenbaker came to power, Churchill gave the green light for our diplomats to put out feelers to

China. China needed food, needed it badly and needed it fast after severe floods crippled its agricultural production and distribution.

In 1960 Canada and China signed a groundbreaking trade agreement: a three-year, 200-million-bushel deal worth $400 million. It was one of the largest nation-to-nation commercial transactions of its day—a real megadeal. Over the next five years, Canada signed two more agreements, worth hundreds of millions of dollars. These deals, overshadowed by subsequent events, gave Canada credibility with the Chinese and a competitive edge that can still be seen in dealings between us a half-century later.

The Bamboo Curtain was lifting, at least as far as Canada was concerned.

In the same year as the first wheat contract, future Prime Minister Pierre Trudeau travelled as a private citizen in China for six weeks and co-wrote, with academician Jacques Hebert, a slim volume about the experience. It was his second visit; he had been to China in 1948 on the eve of the revolution that brought Mao to power.

In 1968 now-Prime Minister Trudeau initiated steps that in October 1970 resulted in Canada formally recognizing China and establishing normal diplomatic relations with Beijing. We beat both the United Nations and the United States in this extension of political goodwill, and only France among the G8 nations got there ahead of us. Unlike us, France had an established presence in the region through its colonization of Indochina.

Canada, through its star diplomat, Alberta-born Chester Ronning, was a strong player in the Vietnamese peace process, which placed us in good stead with the Chinese. US President Richard Nixon made a much-publicized visit to Chairman Mao Tse-Tung in February of 1972, and Trudeau wouldn't get there as prime minister for another year—but the bottom line was that we had an inside track with the Chinese based on respect and confidence in one another.

I enjoyed meeting the Chinese Petroleum Mission to Canada in November of 1972, and felt good about helping them understand Mobil's geological and engineering operations in Alberta and offshore Nova Scotia. Nonetheless, I was surprised as well as delighted when early in 1973, just a few weeks after their visit to my office, I received an invitation from Minister of Energy, Mines and Resources Donald Macdonald to travel to China in late April and early May 1973 on an exchange visit.

The thirty-three members of the Canadian mission included Minister of Energy, Mines and Resources Donald Macdonald, two of Macdonald's assistants and his wife, Ruth, the only woman travelling with us. The bureaucrats included Bill Hopper, director of energy policy co-ordination and review, and later

The Canadian delegation to China in 1973. (Ruth Macdonald, wife of Canada's Minister of Energy, was the only woman on the trip.)

president of Petro-Canada; Dr. Y.O. Fortier, director of the Geological Survey of Canada and R.D. Howland, chairman of the National Energy Board. There were ten other civil servants from Energy, Mines and Resources; Industry, Trade and Commerce; Transportation; and External Affairs.

There were five oil people associated with producing companies invited by the Department of Energy, Mines and Resources, and thirteen who represented oil equipment companies and were guests of the Department of Trade and Commerce. The corporate oil executives, in addition to me, were Bernard Cloutier, the president of SOQUIP; "Doc" Seaman, the vice-president of Bow Valley Industries; and senior vice-presidents from Gulf Canada and Imperial Oil. The oilfield services and manufacturing concerns included geophysical and seismic services, drilling rig, petrochemical, transportation, civil air and other equipment and supply companies. We also took along two interpreters.

We were the fifth Canadian trade mission to China following diplomatic recognition. Previously, there had been an omnibus trade mission, and missions for textiles, grain, and minerals and metals. Many Canadians, especially those in government, believed, somewhat naively, that a strong commercial relationship with China was right around the corner. These bilateral missions allowed both countries to develop a better understanding of specific opportunities and to initiate relationships between senior officials in government and business on

As a child, I dreamed about walking along the Great Wall of China. In 1973, I did it.

both sides of the Bamboo Curtain. The hope was that the visits would lay the groundwork for future deals.

The specific purpose of our mission was threefold. The Canadian delegates would acquaint the Chinese with the type of oilfield equipment and supplies manufactured in Canada, with the long-range objective of trade deals between the two countries. We would evaluate the Chinese petroleum industry and its capability, concerning which very little was known in the Western world. And we would exchange technical information on all aspects of the petroleum industry. Mobil Oil Corporation had given me an extensive briefing book, and I had several opportunities to pitch the company's capabilities, and to keep my eye out for information that Mobil could use in future dealings with the Chinese.

We travelled more than three thousand miles in China by air, rail and bus. We visited major oilfields, refineries and petrochemical plants. We were the first Westerners to see the Taching oilfield and refinery complex since its discovery in the late 1950s. Indeed, we were the first Western oilmen to be allowed behind the Bamboo Curtain to get an accurate picture of the progress of China's oil and gas industry since Chairman Mao's revolution.

Our hosts made sure we saw the most famous sights: the Forbidden City, an exhibit of archaeological relics, the Great Wall and Ming Tombs and the Peking Man fossils. In Kwangchow we visited a trade fair, and in Shanghai we were taken out for an evening of Chinese theatrical performances. As we were in

We visit the Ming Tombs (I took the picture). Note that Chairman Mao's portrait was everywhere.

China on May 1, the most important anniversary on the Communist world's calendar, we spent that morning witnessing the May Day celebrations and parade.

The trip proved to be arduous. We got up at 5:30 a.m., regardless of the previous night's festivities. We ate prodigiously of foods somewhat difficult to identify; we drank orange soda pop to avoid the water, and wrestled with plumbing that often was nothing fancier than a hole in the floor. Travel on trains and buses, and even planes, did not match our North American expectations for comfort. Throughout the tour, we attended five formal dinners hosted by local revolutionary committees in Taching, Tientsin, Shanghai, and twice in Kwangtung. The Canadian Embassy in Peking (now called Beijing) had us over for a buffet dinner and Donald Macdonald hosted a dinner for us and our Chinese hosts at the famous Capital Restaurant in Beijing. The 5:30 a.m. wake-up call always loomed in our minds; enjoying these festivities came at a price.

We arrived in the Chinese capital of Peking on the evening of Sunday, April 22. On Monday afternoon, my presence was required at an orientation meeting, as one of six Canadians, including Donald Macdonald and Chinese Vice-minister of Fuel and Chemical Industries Tang-ke, along with a half-dozen of his officials. That evening, we had the first of the tour's official dinners, this one in the Great Hall of the Forbidden City hosted by Minister of Foreign Trade Pai Hsiang-kuo.

The Honourable Donald Macdonald, Canada's Minister of Energy, and Chou En-lai, the number-two man in China, 1973.

Before the formalities, we were invited for a brief guided tour of the Forbidden City, and the reason for this tour soon became obvious. There were a few others in the area besides our group, and shortly we were approached by one group of officials and security people accompanying an attractive but rather severe woman, dressed in the military-style collarless jacket and matching slacks that were the uniform of politicians in China. It was Chairman Mao's wife, Jiang Qing. She had been an actress in her youth, and she presented herself well. We were all introduced to her individually by Premier Chou En-lai, who was with our tour, and she spoke to us briefly through an interpreter. She showed interest in our tour and was pleasant in a formal diplomatic way.

We knew that this "coincidental" meeting was a carefully orchestrated event. We concluded, correctly I believe, that the Chinese took our tour and their new relationship with Canada very seriously and at the highest levels of government. We did not meet her husband, Chairman Mao, as he was already in the steady decline of health that marked his final years. What little we knew of Chinese politics, however, was enough to know of her fearsome power as an instigator and overseer of the turbulent Cultural Revolution and as a member of the infamous Gang of Four, which effectively ruled the country for a time. When we met Jiang Qing, she was just four years away from her downfall and arrest in 1976. At her political trial in 1980 and 1981, one of the statements that

These top Chinese officials accompanied our small Canadian party everywhere we went during our trip to China in 1973.

she made in her defence was that she was "Mao's dog and if he told her to bite, she bit." I suppose we would call her Mao's "pit bull," and it is a strong memory for me that I shook hands with the most powerful woman, and one of the most powerful politicians, of my time.

The next day, we got down to business.

China's chief geologist and director of the Ministry of Fuel and Chemicals, Yen Tun Shik, gave us an overview of Chinese exploration history and its progress up to the modern era. He said oil was discovered in west-central China 2,200 years ago and was used for lubricants and medicines. Long before the European settlement of North America, oil and gas wells drilled by means of animal power reached 3,609 feet in depth. Pipelines were constructed of bamboo. Natural gas was a cottage industry; with agrarian peasants and artisans utilizing it for domestic and processing heat.

Yen Tun Shik told us the petroleum industry in China entered the modern era with Mao's revolution in 1949—a political milestone that would spur on the development of oilfields equivalent to Canada's Leduc geological discovery. Previous to Mao's seizure of power, there were only seven petroleum geologists and eight mechanical rigs, and production amounted to less than 500,000 barrels of oil a year. After 1949 the new government made petroleum exploration a priority and began surface geological surveys in northwest China. Oil was discovered at Tsiadam, spurring the effort on.

From 1949 to 1958, the Soviet Union provided extensive technical and scientific help, but after a violent ideological disagreement in 1958, the Soviets withdrew. Mao had a policy of self-reliance in all things, so the Chinese oil industry pulled itself up by the bootstraps, expanding exploration by training its own personnel, building its own equipment and expanding the number of crews. The way Chief Geologist Yen told it, it was a real Horatio Alger story of enterprise—but with a Communist twist.

In 1959 self-reliance paid its first dividend with the discovery of the Taching field, which, by the time of our visit, had ended the need to import foreign crude. By the mid-1960s, China was exploring in all its sedimentary basins and had begun offshore work on its continental shelf.

We learned that China had already discovered seven very large and numerous smaller sedimentary basins with attractive Jurassic, Triassic and Tertiary sediments. At the time, there was a single state-run petroleum company. Within the Communist dictatorship, there were no regulatory impediments to exploration and the matters of mineral rights and access to surface locations were straightforward. Exploration and drilling crews were pretty much free to go where they needed to go and drill where they wanted. They conducted regional geophysical and geological analysis of a new basin, treating it as a single geological unit.

The exploration process was familiar to geologists worldwide: geophysical reconnaissance, gravity and magnetic surveys were followed by a geological survey of the entire basin, including geochemical and hydrological surveys. Stratigraphic tests based on the seismic profiles were then drilled to establish the sedimentary section, as well as detect structural tends and major fault zones. Discoveries were not developed at this stage. This first phase of exploration took four to five years for each basin, depending on physical accessibility, logistical issues and infrastructure.

Yen Tun Shik told us that during the second phase of exploration, the geologists zeroed in on structural targets, conducting seismic surveys and drilling wildcats to determine which structures in the basin bore oil. They concentrated their resources, exploring one basin thoroughly before moving on. The time from discovery to production was about three years. We got the impression that environmental conditions were never permitted to interfere with economic progress. However, agriculture had priority over oil and gas with respect to seismic surveys, which always took place after the crop year had ended.

Development of discoveries started with the drilling of a network of delineation wells three or four times farther apart than the ultimate spacing of wells in the field. Geologists and geophysicists seemed to call all the shots; drilling and completion engineers weren't part of the professional teams that managed these projects. Some of their methods—for instance, not coring rank wildcats but relying instead on logs for completion decisions—seemed to be geared to ensure rapid development. The Chinese didn't bother with blowout-preventers or shale shakers, which were basic equipment in North America at the time. Blowout-preventers were mechanical features attached to rigs, designed to prevent ignition of hydrocarbons. Shale shakers were devices used to sift the mud from the rock that is thrust up when a well is dug, allowing for the rock to be disposed of.

They placed an emphasis on discovering the position and distribution of the source rocks, believing that if they found a source more than 650 feet thick there would be an oil reservoir not too far distant. We learned that most of their continental basin reservoirs were sand bodies—channel sands or more massive continuous beach sands—in direct contact with source rocks, and most of their discoveries were related to sand pinchouts across structural features. Taching, at the time China's biggest oilfield, is an excellent example of a pinchout of a large sand body with well-developed source rock bodies on both sides of the reservoir sand. Carbonates were not a major factor in their exploration.

They were committed to Mao's policy of self-reliance: the People's Republic of China would carry out its own oil exploration and development. Never again would they rely on outsiders because the Soviets had let them down. However, their geologists were hungry for any information we could give them. They wanted to know more about detailed reservoir practices at Pembina and about the development of complexly faulted reservoirs. Now we knew why they had shown us the fields at Taching, which is similar to Pembina, and Takong, a complexly faulted oilfield. They had organized this mission and shown us fields and facilities related to their knowledge and technology gaps. The tour was more about what they wanted to learn than what we might want to know.

They wanted to pick our brains in exchange for some great dinners, tourist experiences and celebrity encounters with the likes of Premier Chou En-lai, of whom we saw a great deal, and Mao's wife Jiang Qing.

19

Chinese Petroleum Frontiers

THE HIGHLIGHT of the 2,983-mile trek taken by the Canada petroleum trade mission to China in the spring of 1973 was the visit to the Taching field on a "secret" trip. The Chinese were unbelievable in the way they kept everything "secret." They weren't telling anything to the Western world, which is how the term the "Bamboo Curtain" developed. When we went to Taching, we didn't know precisely where it was at, and they didn't tell us or show us a map. There was nothing published that indicated the location of the field. We had a rough idea of where it might be, but no one knew exactly.

On our way to Taching, we went first to Harbin—a significant city of 2 million people at the time, 5 million now. Our hosts took us on a parade down through the main street. They showed us off to the population—a bunch of white visitors who looked different than they did. Then we had a meeting with them. We didn't really know where Harbin was, as China had published and distributed no maps to Westerners. From Harbin, we took a train and they kept the route secret. We went along with the program and got on the train.

They had a field office in Taching, and some technical people were working there. We had two interpreters: one provided by the Chinese, who was pretty good, and our interpreter from Imperial Oil, who was excellent. He was a geologist and spoke excellent Chinese (whether Cantonese or Mandarin, I can't say), so he couldn't have been better equipped for our mission.

Our party travelled through China by rail. Sometimes, it was a tight fit!

We saw the field from end to end. Their major facilities were all underground because of the military threat from the Soviet Union. At this time, the USSR and China were at odds with one another, although they were both Communist countries. They couldn't get along and wouldn't even talk to one another. The Chinese were afraid of the Soviets. The border between China and the USSR was spitting distance from Taching, and our hosts feared that the Soviets would come over the border and bomb their field. We, of course, were from a country where everything is clearly visible on the surface; none of us would think of having our operations underground on account of danger from another country. Taching made a sobering impression on us.

The Soviets had built some big beautiful homes at Taching, and they had stayed in them up until the falling out between the USSR and China. In fact, we were billeted in those mansions, which had initially been built for use as guesthouses for VIPs.

When we were in China, the Chinese and Soviet political leaders were Mao Tse-Tung and Premier Chou En-lai, and President Leonid Ilyich Brezhnev and Anastas Ivanovich Mikoyan, who was a proven survivor because he managed to be the number-two man in the USSR under both Nikita Khrushchev and Brezhnev. At the time of our visit, Brezhnev was still very hostile to the Chinese, accusing Nixon and Trudeau of fomenting the differences between the two Communist "brother-nations."

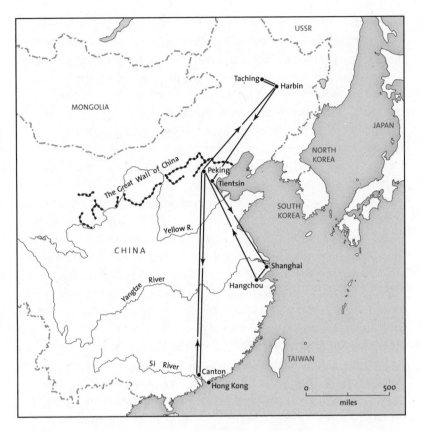

Itinerary map for the trade mission to the People's Republic of China, 1973.

Upon our arrival at Taching, the basic facts of this frontier discovery were clarified. The Taching oil and natural gas field was discovered in Manchuria in 1959, fifty miles north of the city of Harbin and less than three hundred miles from the border with the USSR. Development drilling began the following year, and within a remarkably short period of three years, the Chinese completed enough wells to supply newly built processing and refining facilities and to ship petroleum and petroleum products by rail to markets. Using Taching as their showpiece, the Chinese were determined to debunk the conventional wisdom that China was poor in oil; they claimed that production in the country was doubling every five years.

As we toured the field, we became familiar with the details. Taching is distinctive because its sediments—some 15,000 feet in thickness—were continental depositions, not the usual marine deposits. That oil could be found in non-marine environments was a controversial idea at the time. Otherwise, Taching strongly resembled Pembina. It was a Cretaceous reservoir at a depth of 3,500–5,000 feet. The oil lay in sandstone beds separated by shale. We were shown the data on one well with twenty-two productive zones. The field had been on production for more than ten years, and it appeared the entire field was already undergoing tertiary waterflood recovery.

Our hosts told us that 40,000 workers were employed in exploration, production, processing, refining and transportation. They lived in small villages; food was grown in well-tilled fields nearby; and small factories produced various types of oilfield equipment and supplies.

The work in the early years must have been gruelling. The vast grasslands of Manchuria in China's far north are a place of hostile winters, of ice and snow. Success depended upon hard physical labour with very little in the way of mechanical aids. Everything from rig moves to earth-moving to hauling the parts and supplies for heavy facilities construction was done by hand. Workers lived in tents for months, no matter the season, until they were able to build their own housing. Grain and vegetables were raised on farms carved by hand from the Manchurian steppes; the land was broken, crops planted and harvested and outbuildings constructed all by the manual labour of the workers' families.

This story of physical labour and community-building reminded me of how my father and his Danish friends had broken the ground at Standard, Alberta.

We were given a little pamphlet, published a year earlier, on the history of the Taching oilfield, called "Taching: Red Banner on China's Industrial Front." It is written in an intense, earnest and florid style, full of Communist Party slogans, quotations from Chairman Mao, and sentimental anecdotes about the hardships, diligence and commitment of the oilfield workers. The booklet was written to inspire a nation.

As the Bamboo Curtain opened to outsiders, China was becoming famous for its national five-year plans for economic growth. Our mission arrived in the oilfield during the second year of the fourth of those planning cycles. During this five-year plan, Taching was held up as an example of what China's Communist cadres could accomplish. Mao envisioned decades of patient economic growth that would make the country rich, and oil development was a shining example of what was possible in the future. According to this booklet, "the exploitation and construction of the Taching Oilfield is a great revolutionary practice in China's industrial history," and, "an example in studying Marxism–Leninism–Mao Tse-tung Thought."

Oil refinery worker, China, 1973.

The text was accompanied by black and white photos, some of oilfield facilities and others of workers going about their jobs, which seemed to include a considerable amount of manual labour. In one snowy winter scene, a swarm of workers in a half-completed processing plant are hauling lengths of pipe by hand while a second group is hauling a heavy piece of machinery across the ground with tow cables. In a second, a group of smiling kerchiefed "workers wives" are holding thick-handled shovels. Other images in the pamphlet included ones of women and children picking a field of squash, and a score of men in Mongolian-style winter hats with fur earpieces sitting outside a tent around a blazing campfire reading selections from the writings of Chairman Mao. Needless to say, the Soviets had been written out of the story; their role in the discovery and development of the field was missing from the text.

The hero of the pamphlet was the "Iron Man," Wang Chin-his. He was an oil well driller who had volunteered to work in the field when he heard of the discovery in 1959. He was, by this account, a remarkable man: incredibly strong with determination and fortitude, having a capacity for hard work and the charisma of a born leader. He was able to motivate men and women working with primitive tools in the harshest of conditions. Every Communist revolution needs a hero, and the Iron Man was that man for Chinese Communists working in the oilfields of Manchuria.

The Iron Man died of gastric cancer on November 15, 1970, two and a half years before our mission, but he lived on in gigantic billboards along the highway, in which he was depicted as a brawny champion. In the minds of Chinese workers, he was still out there somewhere in Manchuria, hard at work for the Communist cause. He occupied the same mythical place as hero of the revolution that Canadian physician Dr. Norman Bethune attained after he died on the battlefields of the 1949 revolution. Bethune was the son of a Presbyterian minister and grandson of a co-founder of the University of Toronto medical school. Born in Muskoka, Ontario, and educated at the University of Toronto, he was wounded while serving as a stretcher bearer in the Great War. He contracted tuberculosis while running a clinic for the poor in Detroit. During the Spanish Civil War, he joined the anti-fascist soldiers as a battle surgeon. Afterward, he went to China during the Sino-Japanese Wars, where he treated wounded Chinese soldiers. He died from a blood infection contracted during one of his surgeries while serving with the Chinese Communist army in 1939. After Mao's revolution in 1949, Bethune was remembered as a great hero, and although his Communist politics were anathema to us, he nonetheless paved our way, as Canadians, in building a relationship with our Chinese hosts.

There was one thing that endeared to me the Iron Man of Chinese oil myth and legend. He exemplified the idea that working in the petroleum industry isn't just a job or a career. It is a way of life. Politically we could not have been more different. He was a self-taught engineer; I was a university-educated geologist. We had nothing in common in our way of life, our beliefs or our values. But we did love the petroleum exploration business, and we worked our hearts out to succeed in it and make it a success for our respective nations.

The Chinese proved to be hospitable hosts and proud countrymen eager to show off their many thousands of years of recorded history. However, they rebuffed our interest in joint exploration and development ventures, equipment sales and other transactions. They had us more or less captive for two weeks and relentlessly picked our brains. We toured places where they had specific informational needs and we had specific knowledge. I admired that practical turn of mind and their determination to benefit from our time with them, even if we didn't get anything from it.

Only one of the Chinese senior industry and government officials—Chaio Li-Jen—a geologist and the director of the Petroleum Department of the Ministry of Fuel and Chemical Industries—spoke English, so essentially all communication was through the interpreters; this gave the Chinese some control over the flow of information. It was my good fortune to spend a great deal of

A Chinese refinery, antiquated by modern standards.

time with Chaio, especially on the buses, trains and planes, and I did my best to
get as much knowledge from him as possible.

I reached several important conclusions during the tour. The most important was that, with seven major basins and a handful of smaller ones, the
Chinese had great potential for oil and natural gas reserves. They had barely
scratched the surface of exploration and discovery. Their methodical exploration and development process and their practice of proceeding one basin at a
time meant that it would be many years—perhaps decades—before they knew
their full petroleum potential.

The entire exploration and development process they used completely
ignored economics and they didn't take as many safety precautions as we in

A Chinese service rig in the early 1970s.

Canada did. There wasn't much concern about the immediate impact of exploration and development. Ownership of mineral rights was irrelevant as it belonged to the state to dispose of as the Communist Party saw fit. Surface land access was automatic, regardless of the consequences for the local people. Environmental protection was scarcely considered.

The Chinese were determined to be self-reliant and prepared to take advantage of our goodwill to improve on their knowledge without reciprocating. They needed technical help. They wanted to buy oilfield equipment from Canadian companies. They had almost no pipeline experience. They were shipping most of their crude oil by train and truck. They needed more geophysical instrumentation. They wanted technology for making synthetic rubber. They had surprisingly well-advanced onshore geophysical capability but needed help offshore. Their onshore drilling technology was adequate, but no more. Their offshore drilling capability was purely experimental and ineffective.

In many areas—reservoir engineering, gathering systems, refining—what they were doing was conventional, but the equipment was usually technologically dated. At the Shanghai Industrial Exposition and Canton Trade Fair we observed that their electrical, computer and mechanical capability was far more advanced, scientifically, than their ability to manufacture equipment using it. There was a huge gap between what they were capable of and what they were actually doing.

For me, the mission turned into a rare and unique experience both from the standpoint of gaining knowledge of China's oil and gas industry as well as from a personal point of view of seeing intimately existing conditions in that great land which had been isolated from the rest of the world for so long. It was clear to me by the end of the tour that China had tremendous potential for the discovery of large, economically viable oil reservoirs, but that it would require many years for them to fully evaluate what they had in terms of national oil and natural gas reserves.

At the level of practical business, seemingly little was accomplished, and certainly nothing immediate. At a final meeting with a small group of the most senior Chinese and Canadian representatives on the tour, we were told in no uncertain terms that the Chinese were not interested in exploration and development joint ventures. In fact, we were told that they had rejected such proposals from Imperial Oil and British and Italian firms. They cited the great difference in "social systems"; by which I believe they meant the "enmity" between Communism and capitalism. The Cold War was still being waged, and while the Chinese were at odds with the Soviet Union, with rumours of war on their joint border, this did not mean that China was ready to line up with the West. They were fully committed to Mao's philosophy of self-reliance and bitter about the failure of their working relationship with the Soviets in 1958.

They would pick our brains for as long as we were forthcoming. In our geological discussions, they seemed reasonably transparent about their knowledge, and the discussions were informative and stimulating. However, their people were obviously tightly controlled. Whether the restrictions, in terms of the translation arrangements and the large number of Party officials at each meeting, constrained them to some degree is difficult to say, but given their philosophy and long adversarial relationship with the West, it's a good assumption.

The one essential that Chinese people had in abundance was confidence in themselves and their future. They were convinced that, with patience, intensive effort, total dedication and unlimited manpower, they would accomplish great things for themselves in spite of the lack of current technology.

I believe that their attitude to the West and to working with foreign, capitalist countries was changing, albeit slowly, so that today's "no" would be next year's "maybe" and the next decade's "yes." The way ahead, it seemed to me, was to keep the lines of communication open and to continue to liaise with China, but to remain low-key about future relationships: apply no pressure; make no proposals that they'd be forced to reject.

In the long run, my prognosis proved to be correct. They needed our technical ideas. Eventually, years later, they recognized that they had made a mistake, and they invited big companies over there ad infinitum. There are quite a few big companies in China now including Texaco, Shell and Exxon Mobil.

Canadians have probably forgotten how important we were in founding the Western world's trading relationship with Communist China and introducing modern Western economic, business and political ideas to them. Canada became a significant window for the Chinese on the Western world. Those years of the early 1970s, with Canada's wheat trade and the Canadian Petroleum Mission to China, were a prelude to the globalism of the twenty-first century and the emergence of China as one of the world's most sophisticated, powerful and dominating economies. There is a straight line-of-sight between the China we encountered in 1973, with its tentative openness to the world, and China's presence in world oil and gas—including the Canadian oil sands— thirty-five years later.

20

The Famous Lawsuit

I RETURNED FROM CHINA and took up my day-to-day duties, once more, as president of Mobil Canada. I didn't realize that my work would change considerably in only a couple of years' time. In 1974 Mobil Corporation proposed to transfer me to New York where I would become a vice-president and the general manager of worldwide exploration. I had made it to the big time; a Canadian-born and trained geologist and executive with the opportunity to move into the highest executive level of one of the largest and most influential multinational oil companies. Financially and professionally, this was an incredible opportunity. I was forty-nine years old. Such a move meant a very challenging and fulfilling job and the possibility of further advancement if I was successful in my new posting. When I had been in New York twenty years previously as Canadian liaison, my family and I had loved it. In Houston in the mid-1960s, we had been on the verge of taking out American citizenship on the assumption that my career would keep me in the United States. Had I not returned to Calgary to run the Canadian subsidiary, I would have gone to New York without hesitation. Nevertheless, for family reasons, I wanted to stay in Canada.

One of my sons was wheelchair bound and required special assistance in pursuing his education and adult life. My other children were at various stages in their education and launching new careers. I turned down the transfer.

This may not have been unheard of, but it was somewhat unusual, and I knew that the bosses in New York would not look kindly on it. Declining the transfer was a career-limiting decision. Meanwhile some tension had been developing between New York executives and me over the amount of authority and flexibility I had in making decisions about the Canadian operation.

I began to quietly look around for alternative employment. By this time, I had been courted by Petro-Canada. The facts that I was a Canadian and the head of a multinational company's Canadian subsidiary were assets for an unpopular Crown corporation looking for legitimacy. I might have been engaged as its president except that I wasn't very keen on it, and some influential people in Ottawa decided that I wasn't "political" enough.

I think that verdict was a compliment.

At about the same time, the partners in PanArctic Oils looked me over. PanArctic was a consortium of some thirteen companies with exploration permits in the Arctic Islands where there were attractive petroliferous structures to explore. The companies had combined their interests and were entering a joint venture with the federal government, which had promised to provide 100 per cent of the exploration budget for several years to earn a 45 per cent working interest in whatever was discovered. PanArctic was an interesting company, but nothing came of our courtship.

As 1975 commenced, things were coming to a head. After a quarter century of service, it was time for me to leave Mobil Oil because of my deteriorating relationships with New York executives and family considerations. I felt confident that I would have no difficulty locating another worthwhile position. It was largely a matter of where and with whom I could work out a relationship that would result in my having a top position with a satisfactory compensation level, in addition to being satisfactory to my family.

As my career prospects changed, another major event occurred, this time in my personal life. In the spring of 1975, I suffered a severe blow with the premature and unexpected death of my wife, Evelyn. We were enjoying a quiet dinner at the Owl's Nest in the Calgary Inn, when she suffered a massive heart attack. Paramedics rushed her to hospital, but she succumbed before morning. She was just forty-three years old. Evelyn had been a great oilman's wife. She never complained about our many transfers, and wherever we lived, she looked for opportunities for the children to enjoy the unique experiences offered by new cities and new states. I was crushed by her death and left a widower with my six sons and one daughter. In the aftermath of her passing, my children and I slowly adjusted to life without her. The change in my circumstances certainly influenced the decisions that came next.

By this time I had already been approached by Canadian Superior Oil, a well-known and successful Canadian subsidiary of a large US company. The first person who contacted me was the chief executive of this company, Art Feldmeyer: he had requested retirement after many years of service. I had great respect for Art, whom I had known personally for a long time. The American parent of Canadian Superior was Superior Oil, a successful independent head-quartered in Houston, Texas.

Like many American independent oil companies, Superior Oil had been created and built by an enterprising American family: the Kecks. They held the controlling interest, the equity of which was distributed among several members of the family.

The company's major activities were in California and it also participated in a number of oil ventures in foreign countries, particularly Venezuela where it was founded by William S. "Bill" Keck, an American expatriate drilling contractor. He had learned to drill wells in Pennsylvania before the Great War of 1914–18, then he moved to California to establish his first drilling company. He got into oil and gas production by the simple strategy of accepting leases or working interests in leases for payment when an operator was unable to pay his bill, a frequent occurrence in speculative wildcatting fields of California, especially during the Great Depression. He pursued the contracting business in Venezuela, but he moved back to the United States because his company became so successful there. Operations were based in Bakersfield, California, the centre of a great deal of oil exploration for over a hundred years. When Superior transferred its head office from Bakersfield to Houston, the family continued to reside in Bakersfield. Keck purchased a jet for his commute to Houston.

The principal shareholder of Superior Oil in 1977 when I got to know the company was Howard Keck, the billionaire son of the founder. Howard and his brother, Bill Keck Jr., worked for their father and, in due course, inherited the company and built up its US oil and gas production and reserves, although it continued to operate as a drilling contractor for many years.

The company entered Canada in 1943 and established itself here under the name Rio Bravo Oil. One of the four job offers I rejected when I graduated from the University of Alberta in 1950 came from Rio Bravo. The Canadian company's first president was a genial geologist named Art Feldmeyer, a Californian who had explored for Superior Oil in New Zealand, of all places, before coming to

Canada to open exploration and production operations here. Howard Keck, who had run the company since his father's death in 1964, gained notoriety around Alberta in the company's early years in Canada by flying in and out in his A-26 attack bomber, a demobilized Second World War aircraft that he had spartanly converted. He chose it because it had a cruising speed of seven hundred kilometres per hour, faster than any available alternative, which included most small private jets.

On a trip to Calgary in 1976, Howard Keck invited me to have dinner with him at Hy's Steakhouse. At the dinner, he offered me the position of president of Canadian Superior Oil to replace the retiring Art Feldmeyer. Howard had selected me to take Feldmeyer's place because of my reputation as an oil finder (a result of the Pembina discovery), my reputation as a good administrator, and because I was a Canadian. This dinner was the first meeting of several between Howard Keck and me, all of them at Hy's Steakhouse. Howard said that Hy's had the best steaks in North America. I preferred Caesars, just down the street in Calgary, but I wasn't going to argue with him on a minor matter like that.

I gave Howard Keck's offer very serious thought over a length of time. I had been with Mobil for more than twenty-five years and had worked for them not only in Canada but most of the United States. Most of my best friends I had gained through my association with Mobil. It was therefore very difficult to make the decision to leave this company and join a new one. Although the work would be the same, the philosophy of the company would be entirely different.

Of course, there were some strong positives to joining the Superior world. Particularly, I was promised almost total autonomy in running the Canadian affiliate of Superior. I would be reporting directly to Howard Keck with no other intermediaries involved. Furthermore, Canadian Superior was a very successful company in its own right with well-established exploration and producing departments. Financially, the company had no debt, and it was Howard Keck's policy that all Canadian earnings were deposited in Canadian banks.

Of course, then there was the money. Howard offered me a salary far in excess of what I was earning at Mobil, and compensation included stock options which, at that time, Mobil did not grant to executives in affiliated companies.

Therefore, in November 1977 I made the big decision to leave Mobil and join Canadian Superior. I strongly wanted to do this with as little acrimony as possible. I wrote a letter of resignation, then flew to New York and personally gave it to Alex Massad on November 22. He was very surprised. I think most people thought I had the word "Mobil" emblazoned on my chest.

He expressed his disappointment and then we talked about timing and a potential replacement for me in Canada. I strongly recommended that my replacement be Ed Barroll, the production vice-president in Calgary. Alex did not make a decision at the time—that came some days later when he advised me and the company that my replacement would be Dorey Little. Dorey was then the president of Mobil Oil Indonesia. I knew Dorey, as we had met frequently at budget and management meetings, and I knew that he was a capable executive, but I was disappointed that Ed lost his one and only opportunity to be the top executive at Mobil Oil Canada, the company for which he had worked his entire career.

During my twenty-seven-and-a-half year career, Mobil had grown from a minor player to one of the most accomplished multinationals in the Canadian exploration and production sector. When I resigned, we ranked among the top five companies in Canada and were number one in gas production. We had major activities in very large fields in the Western Canadian Sedimentary Basin and the East Coast offshore. Our staff, which had been about twenty when I joined the company, was now approaching some 1,000 employees. More than 90 per cent of them were Canadians, including most of those in senior management.

I announced my decision to the Mobil employees at the annual Christmas party. The room of five hundred fell completely silent: my colleagues couldn't believe that Arne Nielsen was leaving the company.

When I began to work for Canadian Superior, I recognized the danger of a possible conflict with my previous employer Mobil Oil Canada. I was therefore extremely careful. I took with me only the most personal items I had in my office. I took no maps or documents of any kind. Furthermore, in order to protect myself, I obtained the assistance of my secretary, Muriel Jones, in making the move. Over a ten-year period I had collected a substantial number of personal items that I kept in my office. In order to avoid conflict, Muriel checked and listed each item that I took with me to ensure that everything I took was personal and not related to Mobil.

This procedure protected me in the days ahead because Muriel had worked for Mobil for many years and her integrity was beyond question. She began in the accounting section of the company and subsequently became the executive assistant to seven presidents of Mobil Oil Canada, including me for the full ten years that I was president of the company. She was the most senior secretary at Mobil Oil Canada. During this time, I was also the Honorary Consul of Denmark for Southern Alberta, because of my Danish background and the fact that I could speak the language. It added a substantial workload to my daily activities. However, Muriel actually did most of the consul's paperwork.

In the past, Howard Keck of Superior Oil had recruited a number of senior executives from Mobil Oil Corporation in the United States, including top-level exploration and production personnel, to improve the quality of his upper-echelon executives. He only hired people who were highly regarded professionally and who had a considerable level of experience. I knew many of the professional associates who worked for Mobil south of the border who Keck hired, having worked closely for a number of years with half a dozen of them in Denver and Houston. This migration of its people created serious concern in Mobil Corporation's corporate offices, particularly at the top level in New York.

I soon became very engrossed in my new job, but I maintained contact with Mobil on a personal basis, particularly with the new Mobil Oil Canada chief executive, Dorey Little. About six months after I began my new job, an unexpected major development occurred. It was unwarranted and unwanted. One day, as I was working studiously, a sheriff arrived with a large brown package. He asked me to sign a document indicating that I had received the package and then he left. I didn't think it was important until I opened it. The contents of this package indicated that Mobil Oil was launching a lawsuit against me. Among other remedies, it asked the court to order me not to talk to Canadian Superior for a year from the day I left Mobil Oil Canada. Obviously, they wanted to cripple my ability to do my job.

This is how *Time* magazine described the lawsuit in its February 20, 1978, issue:

> In the bruising, competitive oil industry, raiding a competitor's talent is a common tactic—but there are limits. Mobil Oil Corp. has charged that pesky Superior Oil has gone too far. In suits filed in Houston and in Calgary, Alberta, Mobil accuses Superior of luring away no fewer than 32 exploration and production experts to acquire top technical secrets. Mobil wants the courts to enjoin the defectors from spilling the beans and to force Superior to pay damages for any information already obtained.

> *Time* said the case was like Goliath accusing David of dirty tricks because in 1976, Mobil's revenues were $25 billion, more than five times Superior's $441 million. However, said the magazine, "Superior has long had a brass

knuckle reputation." It described the founder Bill Keck Sr. as "a flamboyant wild-catter, ever on the alert for new oil, fresh profits and the main chance." Howard Keck was described as "relentless" and "reportedly offered" some of the men 100 per cent pay increases to desert Mobil.

As for me, *Time* said I "was well versed in highly classified and arcane Mobil technology, including its airborne radar propane seep detector and computer graphics modelling system. Mobil is particularly concerned about protecting information obtained from its highly expensive seismographic survey of land and offshore sites [as its] spending for exploration tops $200 million a year." *Time* claimed that there was a "thriving black market" among firms smaller than Mobil for "oil maps and aerial surveys" and that Mobil was "hoping that, if nothing else, the feisty wildcatters will have second thoughts about seducing people who hold secrets."

The reaction of the Canadian business and oil trade media ranged between astonishment and puzzlement that Mobil would advance such an allegation. I benefitted because Canadian journalists knew me and didn't know the faceless men of Mobil in New York, who were accusing me of dirty deeds. The word "far-fetched" was more than once used to describe the allegations. Not only that, my supporters in the industry and media said that I had become the embodi-ment of Mobil's reputation for integrity, and if anyone was to get the benefit of the doubt, it was me. "What was Nielsen supposed to do," asked *Oilweek* editor Vic Humphreys, "leave his head on his desk as he walked out the door at Mobil for the last time?"

Mobil was not alleging that I had removed any confidential data or maps at the time I left the company. Their basic charge was that I could not work for my new company in the exact same job that I had with Mobil without utiliz-ing confidential Mobil information. They particularly emphasized that I had attended Mobil budget meetings shortly before leaving Mobil, and I would therefore have in my head knowledge of the location of all of Mobil's prospects.

These were obviously charges that were going to be difficult to defend, and there was no precedent of any such lawsuit, either. Mobil suggested that my punishment be that I should not be permitted to work for Canadian Superior, or any other company, for a full year, during which my knowledge of Mobil's secrets would fade.

The Canadian oil patch had existed in a boom-like atmosphere for most of the time since Leduc and was heating up again as world oil prices rose under the new influence of OPEC. This meant there was job fluidity after years in which professionals were devoted to one employer for their entire career. A few senior people had even left the big companies to start up their own small exploration firms.

The statement of claim started a chain of events that occupied a large part of my time for the next year. The first thing I did was call Dan Love, the lawyer in charge of Canadian Superior's in-house legal department. He studied the statement of claim for a few hours and returned to say Mobil Oil was suing me for changing jobs. It was the first such lawsuit in the energy industry. To me, it seemed ridiculous. Many people had changed jobs in the past and why that should become a legal matter in my case didn't make any sense.

Dan Love, however, told me that it could become a major problem and suggested that we should obtain outside counsel. Superior Oil faced a barrage of suits from Mobil and was very worried. The cloud of uncertainty over my lawsuit was that it was breaking new ground. There were no precedents; seldom, if ever, had the head of one Canadian oil company been persuaded to quit his job and become the head of a competing company. Love said this could go either way, and I ought to mount a vigorous defence led by an independent lawyer.

I agreed, and a few days later I met Don Sabey, a senior lawyer with the Bennett Jones law firm and a very experienced litigator. Bennett Jones is one of the largest law firms in Canada and was actively engaged by Superior to assist Dan Love in the burden of legal matters. I quickly determined that Don Sabey would be totally suitable for me. He went to work immediately to learn all the details about the charges against me. Meanwhile, Mobil contracted Macleod Dixon, another law firm in Calgary, to proceed with the action against me.

For the next two years, I spent approximately half my time with Don Sabey. Don was older than I, an outgoing and articulate individual of the Mormon faith. He was extremely personable and very sensitive to any problems that surfaced within my personal life during this arduous process, as such issues would distract me. He learned about my family in every detail in order that he could advise me on dealing with them so that I could remain focused. I gained a tremendous respect for Don throughout this process and came to know him extremely well due to the amount of time we spent together. We remain friends to this day.

Don immediately went to work to develop a defence on my behalf. In so doing, he became immensely knowledgeable about how the exploration aspects of an oil industry functioned. By the end of the year, he was almost as good a geologist and geophysicist as our own professionals.

In preparation for the lawsuit, we made a trip to Bakersfield, California, where we met with Howard Keck and Superior Oil's lawyers to co-ordinate our activities. It was of interest that, although a number of Mobil Oil Corporation people—Bob Hirsch, Charlie Barney, Pete Dickinson—had left Mobil to work for Superior, no lawsuit was launched against them personally. I was being sued as an "example" in order to dissuade other senior executives in Mobil Corporation (US) and Mobil Oil Canada from leaving the Mobil organization.

On returning from California in the company plane, we stopped in Reno, which was one of Howard Keck's favourite cities. In fact, every year Superior Oil held its annual meeting in Reno. I was exposed to the slot machines big time and managed to lose some money. However, in compensation, I had one of the best dinners I had had in many months at one of Reno's premier restaurants. This brief break provided some respite from the pressures of the legal battle.

We went through the examination for discovery process after which Don thought that perhaps Mobil would withdraw its case because at best, it was shaky. An attempt was made to settle the lawsuit. Alex Massad, Howard Keck and their respective lawyers met in Denver to discuss a settlement. Being a principal in this matter, I was invited to attend and found it most interesting. For a while, I believed that a settlement was possible and that I would be able to avoid a lawsuit, but Mobil demanded that Howard Keck apologize for his actions. Keck, being a proud man, positively refused. From that time on, a lawsuit was inevitable. We went through several more months of intense preparation before the trial finally commenced in the Alberta Supreme Court in Calgary.

On the other side were Robert Montgomery and Gordon Dixon of Macleod Dixon. Both Montgomery and Dixon were the finest of gentlemen but, of course, they were on the other side of the argument. Montgomery eventually became a judge. Dixon remained a highly successful lawyer who was well known in Calgary for his excellent investments. The trial judge obviously was not acquainted with the oil and gas business. However, he was very astute, and he asked excellent questions throughout the proceedings. I was somewhat up-set to see, on the other side, the presence of Ed Bredin who had worked for me for many years as general counsel at Mobil Oil Canada. After the trial, he told me that he had not wanted to participate but was told to do so by Alex Massad.

Throughout the trial, which lasted close to two weeks, Howard Keck and his wife sat in the back of the courtroom and attended every session. My eldest son, Allan, who is a lawyer, attended a number of the sessions as did some of my other children. My daughter, Dianne, was in tears on occasion and was advised by the judge that no emotions were allowed.

I don't want to dwell on the details of the trial. Legal conflicts are the roughest brand of hardball. Moreover, Mobil later admitted the lawsuit was a mistake on its part, and we were happily reconciled. And since I won, I can be magnanimous, the more so because of the passage of time. However, since the essence of Mobil's case against me was essentially an attack on my integrity, I should, for the record, briefly outline my side of the story as Don Sabey presented it to the trial judge.

In the courthouse, Don was very articulate and showed all the characteristics of a top-notch litigator. He was visibly empathetic toward his client, ruthless and merciless toward Mobil and respectfully businesslike with the judge.

Don obtained the help of two well-known senior oil executives—Walter Dingle of Imperial Oil and Lindy Richards, the retired president and CEO of Hudson's Bay Oil and Gas. They testified at my trial as to my high level of integrity. They said I would never, never, never do anything to damage Mobil's interests. Their evidence carried particular weight because they were my competitors. Don also called George Govier, the chairman of the Oil and Gas Conservation Board, as a character witness. As he was the regulator of my operations in Alberta, his testimony also carried weight.

Don also established in evidence the measures I had taken to ensure a firewall between my work for Mobil and for Canadian Superior; that I had not removed anything from my office except for personal items. He emphasized the distance between me as Mobil Oil Canada's president and me as president of Canadian Superior and the detail of operating matters. He addressed the efforts I made in my new job to steer clear of situations in which I might inadvertently compromise sensitive matters I had learned about at Mobil.

Then we put Mobil on trial for its treatment of me, to show that my reasons for leaving the company were fair and reasonable, and that Mobil was fortunate I hadn't sued for constructive dismissal—a legal term that protected people from being forced to quit instead of being fired and receiving large settlements.

Mobil wasn't using my expertise by the time Superior came along with its offer of employment. In spite of my incessant pleading, Mobil's New York office had declined to approve participation in the two hottest exploration plays in western Canada—the discovery of prolific oil-bearing pinnacle reefs at West Pembina and deep, natural gas–saturated sands at Elmworth. As the name implies, the West Pembina reefs flanked the Pembina field I had discovered southwest of Edmonton. They were located much deeper than the Cardium and were discovered by using the latest, most advanced geophysical survey techniques. These reefs were comparable to the Rainbow Lake discovery and revived the prospect of finding more elephant-sized fields in western Canada.

The Elmworth prospect, made famous by Canadian Hunter founders John Masters and Jim Grey, straddled the Alberta–BC border in north-central Alberta and was the tip of an iceberg. Over the subsequent years it lead to a dozen gas discoveries and changed the way geologists thought about the deposition, discovery and production of gas along the eastern slopes of the Rocky Mountains.

In addition, just before I left Mobil, New York had ruled out Mobil Oil Canada's participation in exploration of the Arctic Islands even though aggressive exploration by PanArctic Oils was finding between 20 and 70 trillion cubic feet of natural gas reserves, along with one good oilfield. So, if my expertise was so valuable to Mobil, why weren't they using it?

We presented more evidence of conflicts between me and the senior executives of Mobil Corporation, which author Peter Foster summed up by saying, "as the full and somewhat sordid story of Mobil's treatment of its Canadian subsidiary and of Arne Nielsen unfolded, Nielsen, if anything, emerged as more of a hero than he had been before."

It became increasingly clear that Mobil had no case. On the last day of the trial, Mobil's lawyers said that at least I should have to pay the cost of the ticket I had used to go to New York to advise them of my departure from the company. They said that I could have done it by telephone and did not need to make the trip. At the end of the trial, the judge said that he would need some weeks to consider all of the evidence and that he would announce his decision as soon as he had completed his review.

A few weeks later, he dismissed the lawsuit. His decision was announced when I was on a business trip in the Andes in Chile. The decision was as we had expected it would be. Don Sabey, proving again his good character and his concern for me, called with the good news that we had won the case. As it happens, many people in the industry had come to feel that this lawsuit was frivolous and Mobil couldn't win it under any circumstances.

Nonetheless, it was a huge relief to me that we had won so convincingly. An important legal principle was established that senior oil executives with highly confidential knowledge at their disposal could change employers, and in the coming years several did. Later, some people said it was an easy case to win, but it didn't seem all that easy at the time. Don's call was obviously a moment of great satisfaction and relief. That night I had an extra martini to celebrate our victory!

21

Canadian Superior

WITH THE LAWSUIT now in my past, I was able to embrace my new job with Canadian Superior. I started work as the chairman and chief executive officer of Canadian Superior on January 1, 1978. My years with the company were some of the best of my professional career. Howard Keck was as good as his word. I had virtually complete autonomy to run the company. Of course, there was a board of directors that provided guidance and took care of the necessary legal matters required of a board. Both Howard and Bill Keck were directors and obviously had a very strong influence on its actions. However, the board never interfered with control of the company.

Not long after I joined the company, Howard Keck reorganized his own affairs and I began to report to a man named Fred Ackman, which turned out to be a good move for me. Fred was a geologist who'd joined Superior Oil from Exxon, and Keck wanted two things from him: to run Superior on a day-to-day basis and to make the company larger. Keck remained chairman of Superior. Fred had a reputation as a tough guy. He once made a *Fortune* magazine annual issue as one of the ten toughest bosses in American business, but I think he must have earned that reputation at Exxon because I didn't see that side of him.

Still, working for Fred gave me the distinction of having worked for two of the reputedly toughest guys in the industry: Alex Massad made that *Fortune* list, too. My esteem for the magazine went up when they listed Massad, but I completely discounted it when they said Fred belonged there. Fred was a totally great guy on a personal level and supported my business decisions. We had the perfect business relationship. He had only one characteristic that bothered me. He was the worst smoker I've known, and when visiting my office from Houston, he filled the big glass ashtray on my desk with cigarette butts in the course of a meeting. Sadly he contracted lung cancer and died prematurely.

The Keck family had a notoriously difficult time agreeing with one another. Howard, Bill and their sister, Wilhelmina, all had very different ideas as to how to deal with the Keck fortune, which was very large. Each one of them had a corporate jet. At one time, Bill placed an article in *Fortune* to the effect that his brother, Howard, had used his jet to try to run him down on an airport runway. Wilhelmina once placed a full-page ad in the *Wall Street Journal*, describing how she was being mistreated by her two brothers and how none of them could agree on financial matters.

Howard was the most responsible of the three. He had, at one time, been an alcoholic and ran horses in the major American horse races, actually once winning the Kentucky Derby. Eventually, after he was sober, he obtained control of the Keck fortune. Although he had only a Grade-12 education, he was very interested in scientific matters. One of his legacies is a giant telescope in Southern California. It is one of the most powerful telescopes in the world and has been used by astronomers from most countries. The telescope was given the name "Keck" and is being used even today by scientists from many countries. Howard was also responsible for donating money to many scientific endeavours, particularly in California. Bill drank to excess and, as a result, he would fall asleep at board meetings and even snore. Howard would always give him a strong nudge in order to keep him awake.

One of the things I did early on in my career at Canadian Superior was to hire a new number-two guy, Andy Janisch. He was my equal in terms of ability. Austrian-born, but educated at the University of Manitoba as the son of Canadian immigrants, Andy was one of those quiet Canadian stalwarts who made the oil and gas exploration and production sector tick. He had already established a reputation for himself during twenty-four years with Gulf, rising to the position of president of Gulf Oil Canada. Then he went to Petro-Canada as a vice-president for five years. Then, he moved over to Canadian Superior as president. I was a geologist and Andy was a petroleum engineer, a good one. We had a great partnership as we pooled our technical knowledge to maintain oversight of the company. He was also excellent in administration, so I could leave those details up to him and, to a large degree. I did. I sincerely regret that Andy died not many years ago from cancer.

I hired Andy about the time the National Energy Program was imposed upon the industry. As a governor of the Canadian Petroleum Association, I immediately took on the responsibility of chairing a task force to write an Alternative Energy Program as the basis to lobby the federal government for change. The task force took the best part of my time for a year. It was Andy's Trojan strength that enabled us to make that commitment of my time; he was fully capable of running the shop in my absence.

Howard Keck fully supported the political activities that I engaged in because he knew they were undertaken on behalf of the company, as well as the industry. He also understood that when he hired me, he got my political skills as well as my geological and executive skills. My engagement in industry matters was part of the package he had hired.

South of the border, Superior didn't have many government dealings. They went to Washington, DC, occasionally with other industry representatives to meet with people in that city, but no more than they thought was absolutely necessary. Art Feldmeyer, my predecessor, thought government relations was a waste of time. When he attended CPA meetings, he would leave shortly after the meetings started and he never really participated.

Nevertheless, I knew it was important, and Howard Keck agreed that in Canada things were different for Superior than they were in the United States. He recognized that my political involvement could be an asset for the company, especially because Canadian Superior was a bigger fish in a smaller pond here in Canada compared with Superior in the United States.

There was one condition to my political involvement. When Howard came to visit in Calgary, I had to focus on explaining to him what we were doing. When he was gone, he didn't really know what I did on a daily basis, so I could take as much time as I wanted to be involved in CPA activity.

By this time I had eight corporate directorships in addition to being on the boards of Superior Oil and Canadian Superior. These boards were Toronto Dominion Bank, Rockwell International of Canada, McIntyre Mines, Excelsior Life Insurance, Ingersoll-Rand Canada, Phillips Cables, Costain, Sultran, and Pacific Coast Terminals. Howard supported my memberships in all of them, not in the least because we could rely on Andy Janisch to take care of the home fires while I was away meeting my board obligations.

For the most part, Howard Keck thought that oil and gas made his dad, Bill, rich, and that's how he'd become rich and that's what Canadian Superior was

The Alberta members of the Toronto Dominion board: John Poole, Edmonton; Reg Jennings, Calgary; and me, circa 1970.

going to do. However, he happened to have an interest in minerals. He had strong likes and dislikes and one of his "likes" was minerals, as well as the international adventures that mineral exploration brought. Canadian Superior had a lot of money in the bank, so Howard figured we could find and develop new mineral properties. As a result, we conducted some mineral exploration in the Northwest Territories.

Before I had arrived at Canadian Superior, Howard had decided that Superior Oil would concentrate on domestic activities in the United States, and Canadian Superior would not only oversee Canada but also would be responsible for foreign oil and gas and mineral activity through a company located in Vancouver that nominally reported to me, although it also reported to Howard Keck. The Canadian oil and gas revenues bankrolled the international operation, which was a hit-and-miss operation that produced nothing of value. It included mining properties and a few small oil and gas interests in many countries of the world. Among these were the North Sea, Spain, France and South Africa.

After I'd been with the company awhile, the international guys wanted me to see these far-flung properties. They lined up a trip for me that would have taken me around the world and I would have visited all the locations where we had land. Well, I looked at this planned trip that was going to take between a quarter and half a year and I said to myself, "Where can I do the most good? Here in Canada where we have something to work with that is worthwhile,

Howard Keck, major shareholder of Superior Oil Houston, and I visit a copper prospect in Chile, 1980.

or making this trip, which looks like a boondoggle?" So I said, "No, thanks." Furthermore, I felt that the so-called international effort needed to be downgraded in a big way. Howard Keck agreed that we should spend more of our time and money in western Canada, and that's what we did.

Copper was the exception. We had six or seven copper properties scattered around the world, and we organized them into a separate little department. We pursued one opportunity in Chile, on permits that looked like they might be worth something. I made three trips to Chile, once with Howard Keck, which allowed me to see an eccentric side of him. He was terrified of getting sick travelling in South America, so he would refuse to shake hands when introduced to someone in business or politics. He brought his own doctor and nurse with him so that he wouldn't have to seek treatment locally if he became ill. He also brought along his own food and drink, and people to prepare them. It was interesting watching Howard's reactions to the conditions around him as we travelled through Chile. Today, that copper prospect in Chile we visited is now in full production and has, for some years, been a major revenue producer.

When I joined Canadian Superior, we had an annual cash flow of $250 million a year. Our exploration and production activities were self-financing and what we didn't reinvest, we put in the bank. The size of the staff was quite small. I increased the size of the current staff by one-third in order to get more exploration and production power into the organization.

The chief objective of Canadian Superior during my tenure with the company was to increase its production. One of Howard Keck's comments to me when he hired me was: "Arne, find another Pembina." We conducted a large exploration program in a number of places in western Canada. However, we weren't really geared up for a big operation like Pembina. So we grew the company by an accumulation of smaller wells and fields.

While I was there, Canadian Superior grew to rank fifth in Canada in natural gas reserves, twelfth in oil and liquids reserves and eleventh in net income. We took the company from being an intermediate player to a major producer. Our work produced no new Pembinas but a whole new scale of company. We made a lot of money for Superior Oil. Howard Keck continued to keep that money in the bank in Canada.

We had so much money that we became a "bank" ourselves, making loans to smaller companies. Howard Keck didn't want the money leaving Canada. Superior was doing so well in the US that it didn't need our revenues. There was also a 15 per cent withholding tax to move that money across the border. He didn't want to pay that tax unless he had to. We had money in big accounts in all the major Canadian banks. We financed everything we did out of cash flow. We didn't have any debt, so when the National Energy Program came along, we were able to wait it out. When interest rates hit 18 per cent for oil company bank loans, we didn't have a problem because we had no loans to service.

22

The National Energy Program

WE SAW VERY LITTLE of Prime Minister Pierre Trudeau in Calgary. He seemed uninterested in our well-being. When he did appear, during election campaigns, he was a dynamic vivacious man, and the "Trudeaumania" that developed had a lot to do with his distinctive personality. However, for the most part, he was perceived of as a man whose only contact with Alberta was to cross its airspace while flying somewhere else.

Although Trudeau knew of me because I was approached at different times to become president of PanArctic Oils and Petro-Canada, I did not have a personal conversation with him until many years later when I was invited to the prime minister's residence in Ottawa at 24 Sussex Drive to meet Trudeau's temporary successor, Joe Clark. I was asked to wait my turn in the garden. Also sitting in the garden, was a scruffy-looking fellow with an untidy beard, dressed in casual clothes. I didn't recognize him. Then he stood up and came over to introduce himself. It was Pierre Trudeau. He was very friendly, and when I gave him my name, he sat down for a chat. It turned out that he was sporting a beard and casual clothes because he had just returned from a canoe trip across the Barren Lands in the Canadian North. I told him we had something in common and described to him my days as a summer student with the Geological Survey of Canada at Lac de Gras. He was delighted with this story and had lots of questions for me, and he told me a bit about his recent canoe trip.

We had a very pleasant half hour until I was called in to meet the "interim" prime minister, Joe Clark, and the moment passed. For a few minutes, I actually liked Pierre Trudeau—however that conversation about the Barren Lands, mineral exploration and canoe trips was prior to the National Energy Program.

The story of the Canadian energy wars of 1973–84 between the federal government on one side and the oil and gas industry and the Alberta government on the other has been told often in the intervening years, particularly the chapter on the National Energy Program. I lived it; I was at the storm centre. I watched helplessly as the Liberal government squandered the relationship of mutual consultation built by three energy ministers and the oil and gas producers between 1969 and 1979. I watched as they put the future of Canadian energy security and the fate of the petroleum sector at terrible risk. In due course, when we—Canadian Superior, the Canadian Petroleum Association, the oil and gas industry and the producing provinces—had exhausted other means of redress, I led the development of the Alternative Energy Program that in the 1980s and 1990s enabled the Canadian petroleum industry to rebuild itself into a healthier and stronger economic sector.

But before the remarkable recovery came the debacle.

The National Energy Program was woven from three strands of Canadian economic history: the first was skyrocketing world and Canadian crude oil prices throughout the 1970s, the second was Canada's quixotic campaign against foreign ownership and the third was the repeated attempts of the federal government to steal, unconstitutionally, several billion dollars from the producing provinces, mainly Alberta, and the oil companies, particularly those that were foreign-owned and controlled. The disguise for this political theft was to "punish" us for "windfall profits" that we didn't deserve. The goals were to keep the West from becoming the economic powerhouse of Confederation and to Canadianize the ownership of oil and gas exploration and production.

The oil price strand of NEP history can be told by recounting the numbers. As the decade of the 1970s opened, a barrel of oil sold for $1.80 or its equivalent anywhere in the world including Canada. That price had been more or less constant for the postwar years. By mid-1973, however, after OPEC took control of the market pricing, it had risen to $3.40 per barrel. A year later, Pierre Trudeau's Liberal government, using a sequence of what were called "federal–provincial agreements" for cover, set the price of a barrel at $6.50 in Canada when in the rest of the world it went for more than $11. In the summer of 1980, as the

National Energy Program was being crafted, oil in Canada was selling for $14 per barrel, but on the global market, it fetched $28.

An enormous reservoir of anger and resentment is captured in that chronology of price changes. So-called "protection" for Canadian consumers penalized oil companies and producing provinces without a commensurate benefit to the Canadian economy, which staggered under the impact of world oil price inflation. The federal government essentially frittered away the opportunity to incentivize sensible conservation actions that would have paid both economic and environmental benefits in the long term.

Several attempts to capture the federal government's so-called "fair share of oil revenues" can be summed up in the two Liberal budgets of 1974 drawn up by Minister of Finance John Turner. In May the Liberals were in a minority in Parliament and trying to placate the NDP, which held the balance of power. Turner presented a budget to the House of Commons with a measure to end the practice of allowing companies to deduct provincial royalty payments when calculating federal corporate income taxes. He also proposed to reduce the allowable deduction for capital expenditures on exploration and development from 100 per cent to 30 per cent to increase our industry's corporate tax rate and to cap earned depletion deductions. The net result was to grab millions of dollars for the federal treasury at the expense of jeopardizing the future financial viability of scores of smaller, independent, Canadian-owned companies, to give the multinationals like Canadian Superior and Mobil a big incentive to spend their capital in some other country, and to devastate the service and supply companies like drilling contractors in the wake of massive reductions in oil company's capital spending.

Thousands of jobs were put at risk, and the drilling rigs started to head south to find work in the United States. I will never forget the image of Prime Minister Trudeau arriving at the Palliser Hotel in downtown Calgary to give a speech and being greeted by several hundred neatly dressed oil industry employees carrying placards and banners with messages decrying the budget. They got the idea from trade union strikes and student protests, and they knew that they needed to speak out, but they looked ill at ease in the stance of protesters. Trudeau was startled, and the city's mayor, Rod Sykes, who escorted him that day, was mortified.

John Turner came to Alberta, too, to defend the budget in speeches in Edmonton, Calgary and Lethbridge. He got pretty beat up, verbally, but to give him credit, he had the courage to face the music. As chairman of the Canadian

Petroleum Association, I led the way in publicly "beating him up," and I enjoyed doing it.

Fortunately, these budget proposals died when Prime Minister Trudeau called an election for July 8. When the Liberals were re-elected with a majority, and the pesky NDP were off their backs, we hoped for a change—a return, perhaps, to the more business-friendly government of Lester B. Pearson's days. We had no such luck. In November Turner was back with a budget that again ended the practice of allowing provincial royalties to be deducted as a business expense when calculating corporate income tax. We were angrier than we were in May, and exploration and production activity started to wind down. Now, not just the drilling rigs were crossing the border, but dozens of talented geologists and technicians were going with them. At a CPA meeting with Turner, I expressed our collective disappointment. We had thought that, with his background as a corporate lawyer, he would understand the oil and gas industry better than others might, that perhaps he would be on our side. But he wasn't, and we were surprised and very angry.

Five months later, in April 1975, the Liberal majority in Parliament passed the *Petroleum Administration Act* that gave Cabinet—a body that met privately and kept its minutes secret—authority over gas and oil prices. In July Petro-Canada was incorporated. The establishment of this federally owned company, with its numerous and considerable competitive advantages imposed by law, was unfair and accomplished nothing of permanent worth for the country.

The public backlash against it included a campaign to boycott Petro-Canada service stations. A popular bumper sticker read "I'd rather push this car a mile than fill my tank at Petro-Canada." Later, when the National Energy Program was created, many western Canadians who once were willing to do business with the government-owned service stations tore up their Petro-Canada credit cards.

Blow after blow was directed at oil and gas producers and producing provinces by a Liberal government motivated by federal greed for oil revenues. Their actions were overriding economic common sense and the constitutional rights of the provinces. By law the federal government didn't own the reserves and couldn't charge royalties. But they were claiming that oil and gas belonged to Canadians and that the federal government had a right to a big share of the wealth. For a guy who claimed to be a constitutional whiz, Pierre Eliot Trudeau was either missing in action, not following events, deliberately playing dumb or playing fast and loose with the facts. In the outcome, he, his advisors and ministers made a series of mistakes, and then they wouldn't admit they were wrong.

In April 1976 the government released *An Energy Strategy for Canada*, which purported to focus on creating energy self-reliance. No one in the government seemed willing to take the time to come to grips with the fact that the trend of their policies would make Canada less, rather than more, self-reliant by reducing oil and gas exploration activity. For the next four years, the federal government waded deeper and deeper into the swamp; regulating and taxing exports and managing prices to the detriment of the producing provinces, the industry and ultimately the economic good of all Canadians. The revenue grabs continued with one hand while with the other, the Liberals were destroying the goose that laid the golden egg. I persisted through the National Advisory Committee, CPA and on behalf of Canadian Superior to attempt to reason with the government.

It was to no avail.

These were some of the toughest days of my career. It seemed to me that the Trudeau government wanted to drive foreign-owned companies out of the Canadian oil industry. But I wasn't about to cut and run.

Most oilmen and many Albertans can still remember where they were and what they were doing on that perfect autumn day of October 28, 1980, when Minister of Finance Allan MacEachen brought down the Liberal budget that contained the National Energy Program. MacEachen was not the chief decision-maker; the real architect—the number one bad guy—was Minister of Energy Marc Lalonde. It was a crystal-clear blue-sky afternoon in Calgary. The autumn sun was almost hot; poplar and aspen trees throughout the city of Calgary shone gold. We sat in front of television sets in our offices, mouths agape. Prior to that afternoon, we couldn't have imagined anything the federal government could have done to us that would have been worse than what they'd already done.

We were naive.

I don't think Lalonde and his colleagues ever understood the colossal mess they made, in spite of the obvious damage the oil and gas industry sustained at the time, and the fact that not one of the government's objectives was achieved. Years later, reminiscing in his 1990 book *Towards a Just Society: The Trudeau Years*, Lalonde defended the NEP and tried to discredit its critics. In the book he said the NEP "was based on three precepts." They were: self-sufficiency through increasing domestic production, energy substitution and conservation (1979 international oil crisis); Canadianization of petroleum industry ownership with a target of 50 per cent by 1990; and a petroleum price and revenue sharing agreement that would be fair to all Canadians as well as to the federal and provincial governments. Of the three precepts, price and revenue sharing "were the most critical issues for a policy that sought to manage energy as a strategic commodity for nation building."

Wrote Lalonde: "The national energy program introduced new federal revenue and expenditure instruments which would increase the federal share of the revenue split." Exploration and development tax deductions were replaced by the Petroleum Incentive Program (PIP) Grants, which were to be a tool of Canadianization. And there would be an 8.5 per cent wellhead Petroleum and Gas Revenue Tax (PGRT), a Natural Gas and Gas Liquids Tax, a petroleum compensation charge (for Syncrude), the Canadian Ownership Special Charge to finance public ownership and the Special Compensation Charge. Another major tool of Canadianization would be the reservation of a 25 per cent Crown share in frontier lands preserved in exploration permits.

In his book, Lalonde said the NEP was used by its opponents as a scapegoat for all the problems faced by the petroleum industry in the 1980s, "even though the industry in Texas and elsewhere in the United States suffered as much as in Canada." But he admitted that the NEP and the energy price agreement with Alberta were seriously flawed.

The first error, he agreed, was to base the program on the premise of ever-increasing oil prices; prices collapsed during an economic recession. The second flaw was its administrative complexity, particularly the replacement of tax incentives (deductions) by grants in order to encourage Canadianization. It had been, Lalonde said, the only way to achieve Canadianization without contravening international tax treaties but proved to be burdensome, especially to smaller producers.

Regrettably, writing ten years after the fact, the former energy minister still did not see that the gravest error in the package was the Petroleum and Gas Revenue Tax. The PGRT was murderous to corporate finance. It skimmed 8.5 per cent of revenue off the top, at the wellhead, before we'd paid a nickel toward the expenses of producing whatever had been found, and couldn't be used as a corporate tax deduction. That was money that companies had been reinvesting, so it reduced capital budgets dollar-for-dollar. Most damaging for the long term, the PGRT reduced the value of oil and gas reserves on the company's balance sheets by 30 per cent and shattered investor confidence in the petroleum sector. The tax was enough to seriously damage—even cripple—the financial viability of most companies and destroy many. As well, industry correctly saw the 25 per cent Crown reservation, a so-called "back-in," as expropriation without compensation. The reservation entitled Petro-Canada to take a 25 per cent interest in any offshore discovery without paying a proportionate share of the finding costs.

My opinion hasn't changed in the thirty-odd years since the NEP. Combine all the fiscal measures with the domestic price schedule and the Liberal energy policy was the most damaging economic instrument in the history of petroleum policy of the democratic industrial nations, certainly the worst anywhere in Canadian economic history. It was beyond belief.

I wish Lalonde had understood that Canadianization had been implemented in a negative way. It drove foreign capital away by destroying the value of the investment that thousands of Canadians had made in the industry, wiping out a great deal of the wealth created by Canadian companies.

Prior to the budget of October 28, 1980, the CPA had an inkling, a suspicion that the federal government was going to do something that would dramatically affect the industry. We asked for a meeting. The CPA board of directors went to see Marc Lalonde with an agenda of matters of concern and some recommendations. He was very evasive. He was not yet ready to break the bad news. But he made it very clear to us that anything we had to say was not going to be of great importance because the government was planning some policy announcements in a very short period of time. It was obvious he had already made up his mind about what he was going to do. Although we were offering some advice on various energy matters, and we were prepared to provide support in helping him develop policy, he said to us very clearly: "There is no sense talking. The decisions are made. And you will hear of them in a very short period of time. I don't need your help."

I saw Lalonde in Calgary a few days before the National Energy Program was announced. I was invited by Alastair Ross, a prominent Liberal and independent oilman, to a dinner where he and I and Louis Lebel, Chevron's corporate lawyer and another Liberal, represented the industry. There were several Liberals there in one of the Westin Hotel's private suites. The purpose of the dinner, it seemed, was for Lalonde to give us a "heads up" that something big for the oil industry was in the coming budget. I kept pretty quiet, but Alastair Ross hammered him pretty hard, especially on foreign ownership. "Don't do anything to hurt foreign investment," he said. Lalonde was unresponsive. He had already made his decision. The National Energy Program was announced a few days later.

Lalonde didn't understand what he was doing, nor did the prime minister. Lalonde represented the policy as good for Canadian companies and in the best interests of Canada. He said foreign-owned companies—and he was including Canadian Superior and Mobil in that group—would find the program less palatable. But the Canadian companies would like it, and that was who it was intended for. Therefore, it should be acceptable to all; it was good for the industry and good for the country.

Lalonde expected, I'm sure, that Canadian Superior, Mobil, Chevron, Esso and Shell would complain, and it was obvious that we had to challenge them. The NEP was against our best interests. But he did not expect that the Canadian companies would find the new policy as unpalatable as the foreign multinationals did. He thought there was enough sugar in it—particularly in the PIP grants, tax incentives, and a requirement of 50 per cent Canadian ownership to acquire a production licence on federal lands—to make Canadian companies happy.

The way the numbers worked in practice was that Canadian companies had at least 30 per cent less internally generated cash for exploration and drilling and couldn't raise new equity from the markets because their value to shareholders was reduced by up to 40 per cent. They were eligible for PIP grants to drill on the frontiers—the Canadian lands under federal jurisdiction—but most companies couldn't afford the big budgets for frontier drilling, and the ones that could lost the gamble because either they didn't find anything in drilling in areas that were much riskier than producing provinces, or they found reserves that were years away from the development of transportation to markets and the cash that would come from production sales. Ironically, the large foreign-owned companies had the cash to hunker down and wait for the inevitable collapse of the NEP or to spend their money drilling in other friendlier countries.

It was argued that nationally owned Petro-Canada's acquisition of Atlantic Richfield and PetroFina represented Canadianization, one of the goals of the NEP. However, I believe that the loss of Dome Petroleum and its affiliate, Dome Canada—jewels of Canadian enterprise and ownership—more than offset the alleged benefits of Canadianization. Dome was the largest and highest profile Canadian company to fail in the wake of the NEP.

In retrospect, the exploration and production companies, IPAC and CPA were, under the circumstances, incredibly patient and probably naive in persisting with Lalonde, attempting to show him the error of his ways and asking him to amend the NEP. He and Prime Minister Trudeau were adamant, however. Either they didn't believe us, or trust us or didn't care.

Perhaps it was the service and supply companies, lead by the Canadian Association of Oilwell Drilling Contractors (CAODC), which suffered the most. These companies made the biggest layoffs and went bankrupt long before the exploration and producing companies started to tumble. The CAODC hired a

737 jet, filled it with more than one hundred executives and went to Ottawa. There they conducted the biggest one-day lobby in Canadian history. Not a protest, but a lobby—going door to door to see any politician who'd give them the time. Their voices weren't heard.

The petroleum industry languished, and trouble piled up like Biblical plagues. Interest rates soared and oil and natural gas prices plunged. Jobs disappeared. Drilling rigs were hauled into farmers' fields and laid out for the weeds to grow around. People couldn't pay their mortgages so they walked away from their houses and mailed the keys to the bank. The cranes of the construction boom disappeared from the skies. The mayor of Calgary, Ralph Klein, looked at the impressive office towers on the downtown skyline that the industry had built in the good years and joked, with coffin humour: "At least they can't repossess them and drive them away." Those years are indelibly inked in Alberta's political memory. However, many of us were not prepared simply to wait for things to improve. We prepared to act.

23

The Alternative Energy Program

IN THE BLEAK DAYS of the early 1980s, as the National Energy Program dev-astated the oil industry, there was a Cabinet shuffle. Jean Chrétien became the energy minister. This gave us high hopes that there would be some help from him. Chrétien was a more experienced Cabinet minister than Marc Lalonde. He had been in government since the Pearson years and was close to the prime minister. For much of the time that he was in government, I was in a senior position in the industry. He was the Liberal Cabinet minister I got to know best, and I regarded him as a friend. We were somewhat the same in that we liked people and enjoyed our working relationships, as well as our social networks.

When Chrétien moved into the energy portfolio, he said that he didn't like the National Energy Program. He met with the CPA and said, "The NEP needs to be changed." But these were just words. He let the policy ride even though he knew it was wrong. He was too much the loyal Liberal. It seemed as if the Liberals had two stories about the NEP: one was for Alberta, told by Chrétien in his "aw, shucks" charming way, and another for the rest of Canada, told by other ministers. In the end, Chrétien was distrusted and despised because he did not correct the damage the NEP had done when he had the power to change it. In spite of our good personal relationship, I was deeply disappointed.

Years later, when Chrétien became the prime minister, we continued to have a pretty warm relationship. On one occasion in St. John's, Newfoundland, his wife christened a drilling vessel bound for the Hibernia field and I was also at this celebration. I remember it as a very happy occasion. Nonetheless, there would always be a shadow over our friendship because of the manner in which he dealt with the NEP.

Chrétien's hypocrisy made me realize that the industry would have to act, so we set about creating the Alternative Energy Program. It's due time to put on the record what a little task force of CPA members was able to accomplish once we realized that we were wasting our breath trying to persuade Liberal energy ministers that the NEP was a mistake.

I regard the Alternative Energy Program as the major accomplishment of my political career. My role in its creation was overshadowed by Pat Carney, the Conservative minister who implemented it. However, she deserves the credit for saving the Canadian oil and gas exploration and production sector and paving the way for it to become the top national resource sector and main pillar of economic growth in Canada at the beginning of the twenty-first century.

Where the role of Canadian oil producers in influencing Carney has been noted, they have been dismissed somewhat contemptuously as simply part of one of the minister's "study groups." A few who have looked a little deeper have labelled the CPA's involvement in writing the alternative policy as just another one of those "secret" influence-peddling exercises engaged in by faceless oil tycoons. I've never thought of myself as a "faceless oil tycoon," but I guess that's what I am to some people.

Before her political career, Pat was a great oil and gas and politics journalist for the *Vancouver Sun*. One story that illustrates her determination, intelligence and street smarts concerns PanArctic Oils, about which she wrote frequently. The company's operational headquarters in the High Arctic was at Rae Point on Melville Island, in the eastern Arctic Archipelago. Although there was a "no females allowed" policy at Rae Point, she was determined to see it. She managed to hitchhike her way there on one of the cargo charter aircraft that serviced the operation. When she arrived, the head guy took her to his office and told her she was going back south in the morning and could spend the night in a sleeping bag in the boiler room. Then he called the company's president, Charlie Hetherington, to tell him she was there. What Hetherington said has been embellished in the retelling, no doubt, but it amounted to this: "Miss Carney will not spend the night in confinement. You will give her your best dinner and install her in my executive suite. If there happens to be an executive in the suite tonight, kick him out. Take her around to wherever she wants to go tomorrow. We are not going to make an enemy of a person this clever and determined."

Another insight into her character is the way in which she dealt with her battle with arthritis. Although it was at times crippling, she never complained and always met her responsibilities. When she went to the Senate, she raised the average IQ by about twenty points. She is very personable, outgoing and forthright. She had all the qualities of a good politician, a good minister, and she was very well respected.

Pat Carney also raised hell at the Calgary Petroleum Club when women were not allowed to become members, couldn't enter the building until evening, and had to use a separate entrance when they did. She was the first woman ever to appear in the Calgary Petroleum Club at lunch hour. There was a furor about it across the country. A member named Bill Seibens led the way to keep women out. He took the view that it was a men's club, set up by men who wanted one place where there would be no women.

Pat made it very clear that she was coming in for lunch as the national energy minister, and as the energy minister she had every right to be in that club. On her first visit, there was a big turnout to witness her entrance. She gave a little speech, not about energy policy but about the fact that it was time to admit women to the Petroleum Club. After Pat Carney broke the glass ceiling, Bill Seibens didn't stand a chance. Soon women were admitted as members. I was on the executive committee of the Petroleum Club at the time and admired the way she handled that situation. It was not surprising that she came out on the winning side. She has usually been on the winning side throughout her career.

The process that brought the Alternative Energy Program into being began in October 1982. Pat Carney became the energy critic under Official Opposition Leader Joe Clark. She was the person we turned to because the Liberals had set the direction with the NEP and weren't willing to make serious changes. The CPA board members agreed that we had to come up with something to counter the NEP. It was beginning to be obvious that Trudeau was on his way out, and we knew we should prepare for the new government and a new energy minister. We agreed that there was a good chance that the new government would not be Liberal and therefore the person to deal with was Pat Carney, a potential Cabinet minister. She was extremely receptive to us. So we set out to put together an alternative to the NEP that would have CPA board approval, which meant unqualified industry support.

I led the task force that developed the policy and that quarterbacked it through the board, while Pat was Opposition energy critic and when she became energy minister following the 1984 election.

I set out to persuade the CPA board to put a high-level group together that would be capable of preparing an alternative policy. I wrote a confidential memo before our annual CPA retreat, to be discussed in the splendid solitude of the Banff Springs Hotel:

> At present the CPA has no comprehensive package of oil and gas policy, which could be offered as an alternative to the oil and gas policies of the NEP. Such a package is needed now as a focal point for CPA policy development in general and for presentational purposes in our public and government affairs programs. As the federal general election draws near [I was actually two years ahead of myself] and political parties begin to develop alternatives or "improvements" to the NEP, the need for such a document will become increasingly important.
>
> Development of an alternative oil and gas policy must take into account that the CPA has already acknowledged as valid the objectives of the NEP (security, opportunity and fairness). The alternative policy proposals can therefore only address the choice of means of achieving the objectives rather than arguing the objectives.
>
> The negative aspects of the NEP are primarily the Petroleum and Gas Resource Tax, PIP grants, discriminatory aspects, pricing regime, the retroactive 25% back-in and the complex and costly administrative burden. The work should begin as soon as possible on alternatives.

The board agreed, and the Imperial Oil representative, Don Lougheed, said, "Let's each of the big companies give Arne one man, a top technical person, and let him go to work on developing a policy that counteracts the NEP."

For the next year this became my full-time job, with the co-operation of Canadian Superior Oil and its president, Andy Janisch. My time was spent with the task force that studied, wrote, revised, rewrote and polished a comprehensive alternative policy. I worked with a blue-chip team of colleagues: Don Parkhill and Grant Gunderson of Canadian Superior; Don Bester and Laurie Martin of Mobil Oil Canada; Bernard Isautier from Canterra; Bill Loar of Suncor; Dick Haskayne of Home Oil; Ron Watkins, Jim Park and Randy Ottenbreit of Esso; Mike Ratuski of Gulf; Doug Stoneman from Shell; and Wally Muscony of Texaco. We were assisted by CPA staff members Hans Maciej and Jim Harrison.

We developed an alternative for every single item in the NEP. We said the objective of oil and gas policy should be the economic health of the nation: jobs and economic recovery. We established a policy that relied on the market, not government, to direct energy production and consumption. This would be the first time in Canada that market forces would prevail over government economic management. We said that the private sector should finance and operate future supply development. We said that the frontiers—the North and the offshore—should be developed. Much of what we proposed had previously not been thought of in government circles, much less proposed.

We asked for unrestricted access to export markets—no quotas, no export taxes. We asked for decontrol of oil and gas pricing, which would let Canadians buy and sell at prices the free market determined. And we asked for an overhaul of the entire federal and provincial royalty and tax system to encourage investment and ensure that governments got a reasonable share of oil and gas wealth; this would be consistent with the constitutional division of federal and provincial oil and gas ownership.

We completed the policy within a year. Drafting it took longer than we had expected, but because we took the time we needed to take, we had a quality product. I recall presenting the program in an earlier form, in a "dry run" to the board to make sure we were heading in the right direction. We decided we weren't ready, so we went back to work until we had a completed document that the CPA could recommend as the energy policy for Canada to whatever government would be in power.

When the policy was ready, I wrote a second confidential memo to the board that analyzed the way the federal government had "sold" the NEP in 1980, and I suggested that we steal their "playbook" to sell our policy. Then, we went to Ottawa to present it to Pat Carney, and she liked it. I recall how well informed she was on energy policy and how intelligently she dovetailed the Alternative Energy Program with the Conservative's bigger agenda. At the presentation and subsequently when we met with her about the alternative program, she grilled us on every aspect of the oil and gas policy in a way that showed she was the equal of any of us in her understanding of how the industry worked. Anyone who thinks she was in the back pocket of the oil industry certainly wasn't at those rough and tough interrogations.

I think we were in her back pocket by the end of the process.

After we presented the Alternative Energy Program to Pat, the CPA visited frequently with her and continued a favourable relationship with her. I spent most of my time with Pat during my second term as CPA chairman. Following the completion of the Alternative Energy Program, she was very receptive to any help we could give her.

When the election happened in 1984, the Liberals were thrown out of office and the new Conservative government was already up to speed on our alternative to the hated NEP. Brian Mulroney, the new prime minister, had a ready-made energy minister in Pat Carney. In turn, she had a ready-made oil and gas policy for the new energy era in Canada. Pat implemented the new policy carefully and in steps. For instance, she reduced the PGRT to 6 per cent before eliminating it completely. In the next eight years, the years of the Mulroney government, everything we recommended was incorporated in federal policy: market deregulation, the Atlantic and Western Accords, free trade, the overhaul of taxation and the obliteration of nearly all the measures of the NEP.

The Atlantic Accord, which was an agreement between the federal and Nova Scotia governments on royalties and regulation (Newfoundland signed later), applied to the East Coast offshore, and the Western Accord, also an agreement on royalties and regulation, applied to the Western Canadian Sedimentary Basin. Both of these agreements helped shape oil and gas policy and activity for the next several decades. I was given the opportunity to sign both accords on behalf of the Canadian Petroleum Association. The CPA's members—including Mobil Oil Canada—had been carrying out exploration programs offshore Nova Scotia and Newfoundland. The other signatories of the Atlantic Accord, in addition to the federal government and the governments of Nova Scotia, Newfoundland, New Brunswick and Prince Edward Island, included Amoco and Chevron. The Atlantic Accord signing took place in Halifax.

The Western Accord was signed in Calgary. The federal government and the provinces of British Columbia, Alberta and Saskatchewan signed the document. Again, I signed on behalf of the CPA, which represented the large producers, and Gwyn Morgan of Alberta Energy Company and the president of the Independent Petroleum Association of Canada signed on behalf of the small producers.

I truly felt a sense of accomplishment as I signed that accord on behalf of the CPA. I felt that many years of hard work and fighting had gone into that signature. When Pat Carney accepted the alternative oil and gas policy as a possibility when she was energy critic, and when she slowly put it into place as energy minister, I felt as if I had effected lasting change, change that would be good for the industry and good for Canada. I also knew I could return, whole-heartedly, to my work at Canadian Superior burdened with fewer politics—at least fewer federal politics!

24

The Homecoming

POLITICAL MATTERS CONTINUED to dog my steps in the 1980s, even after the Alternative Energy Program was implemented by the Canadian government. I was out of federal and provincial politics, but I was knee-deep in corporate politics. In the mid-1980s, Fred Ackman, my boss at Superior Oil, decided to make a number of big changes in Superior that resulted in a major schism on the Superior board, with half of the directors supporting his moves and the other half opposed. As a result, a decision was made to sell Superior Oil and Canadian Superior. My future suddenly became dubious. Where would I be working when this big sale was completed?

To execute the sale, a series of "show and tell" meetings was held in Houston and in Calgary for potential buyers. At these meetings, Superior and Canadian Superior showed all the details of the company's reserves and potential reserves. The "usual suspects"—Imperial, Chevron, Gulf, Shell and others—kicked the tires. One of the companies that made a strong approach to buy Canadian Superior was the Abu Dhabi National Energy Company, PJSC, also known as TAQA. Ironically, years later the same company purchased the assets of Shiningbank Energy Trust, of which I was the founding president.

Eventually Mobil Oil Corporation made an offer. On the weekend of March 10–11, 1984, Mobil and Superior agreed to the purchase and sale of 22 per cent of the Superior shares to Mobil (part of the Keck block), with an option to purchase the rest, if the minority shareholders agreed, for a total of $5.7 billion. It was a friendly deal and would be the third-largest sale of an oil company in American history, after the $13.2-billion acquisition of Gulf by Standard Oil of California and Texaco's $10.1-billion purchase of Getty Oil.

The deal set off great activity in Canadian Superior because the merger between Mobil and Superior Oil south of the border was being duplicated in Calgary where Mobil Oil Canada and Canadian Superior would be merged into a single company, with Mobil Canada being the survivor. Within a couple of weeks, a major meeting of Superior and Mobil executives was organized in Houston to discuss merger plans. I went to Houston as the sole executive from Canadian Superior. Mobil was represented by a number of top executives from New York and other Mobil affiliates in the United States. The top executive representing Mobil was Bill Tavoulareas.

When I was president of Mobil Oil Canada, Bill had visited Calgary on a number of occasions. On one of his trips I took him to the Calgary Stampede to see the chuckwagon races. We went on to Banff and Jasper and subsequently flew to Yellowknife in the Northwest Territories, where I had arranged a fishing trip for him and his wife. Bill had a very outgoing personality. It was a pleasure to be with him socially, and we had a good working relationship.

The Houston meeting was critical as it would determine my future. That week, an article by journalist Paul Taylor had appeared in the *Globe and Mail* with a headline speculating: "Mobil move may put Nielsen's job on the line." In the piece, Taylor quoted me saying, "I simply never expected this would happen." Taylor said that my "concern about the takeover is undoubtedly coloured by the fact that he used to work for Mobil and left on rather unpleasant terms to join Superior in 1978." Taylor recalled that, "Mr. Nielsen's dispute with Mobil dates back to 1977 when he decided to find a new job after working for the US oil company for 27 years. However Mobil did not take kindly to losing one of its top executives."

Taylor went on to write about the lawsuit. I wondered what would happen next.

On the third day of the Houston meeting, I received a telephone call requesting that I meet with Bill Tavoulareas in his hotel suite. I expected the worst, particularly considering the lawsuit between Mobil and me. I expected to be dismissed. When I arrived in his hotel room, I noticed Paul Taylor's article lying on the desk. Bill referred to the article and laughed. "Arne," he said, "not only will you have a job with us after the sale closes, but it will be a bigger one than you have had before. I want you to go back to Calgary and you will be responsible for running both companies, both Mobil Oil Canada and Canadian Superior. Don't worry about the lawsuit we had with you. We received very bad legal advice and shouldn't have done it. We regard you as a top administrator and oilman, with your knowledge of Canadian geology and the Canadian oil industry. You should be highly successful in this new enlarged position."

To say the least, I was flabbergasted. Bill advised that I would be reporting, not to Alex Massad, my old difficult boss, but to an engineer named Hank Holland. This was even better news. I first met Hank on my early assignments in Denver and Houston, and we had become good friends and successful colleagues. I left Bill's hotel room feeling very good. My future was now assured. Before I left Houston, I contacted Hank and we made the first plans for the merger of the two companies in Canada: obtaining formal corporate approvals, completing the complex legal paperwork and winding our way through the federal government's foreign investment review process.

Mobil Corporation wanted to buy Superior Oil for its assets south of the border, but the real gem they got was Canadian Superior: its land, production, cash and people—good people. Not to mention a great deal of cash. When Mobil acquired Canadian Superior, the cash we had in the bank in Canada went to the United States so fast you couldn't see it; I think that transfer took place with the "speed of light." They paid the 15 per cent withholding tax that the Kecks had begrudged the government. Mobil had big financial responsibilities worldwide, and here was all this money! They could hardly believe their good luck.

The merger felt like a homecoming to me.

I felt that the company and I were reconciled, with that foolish lawsuit put behind us. I was now fifty-nine, and it was apparent that I would reach Mobil's retirement age in this new position, which meant completing my career in Calgary. I had come home to stay. However, I faced a slight detour to Toronto. In my absence, Mobil Canada had moved its head office to Toronto, and I would have to move there for the time being, although I also had an office in Calgary.

By this time, I had married a wonderful woman named Valerie, in January 1982, and we had a son, Aksel. We found a delightful home in Toronto's lovely inner city neighbourhood of South Mills, which was reasonably close to my office. Our second son, Harry, was born in 1986, shortly after we moved to the city. Toronto is a terrific city for cultural events and social life, shopping and quick access to some nice holiday places. As the first family of a large and important oil company, Valerie and I received plenty of invitations. I am sure she

Valerie and me, with our son Aksel, at the Pembina discovery site, 1987.

would have been glad to stay in Toronto, and I could see the personal benefits, as well. My partisan feelings for Calgary aside, it quickly became apparent to me that Mobil Oil Canada headquarters did not belong in Toronto.

Mobil Oil Canada had moved its office from Calgary to Toronto for three reasons. The first was to gain proximity to New York. It was considered easier for the Canadians to go to New York for meetings than to have the Americans travel to Calgary. The second reason was Toronto's proximity to Ottawa and the perceived benefit of being close to the federal government with respect to political matters. The third reason was proximity to Halifax and the East Coast. Alex Massad had made the decision to move Mobil Oil Canada to Toronto, and the president of the day, Dorey Little, didn't object. He was an American with only loose ties to Calgary.

However, all the other major oil companies had their head offices in Calgary. And, companies that had located in Toronto because of central Canadian refining and retail marketing operations were also moving from Toronto to Calgary. In recent years, these had included Shell, Gulf and Texaco. The only exception to the migration west was Imperial Oil, whose executive felt that Imperial's head office belonged with its hundred-year history in central Canada. Nonetheless,

The Pembina discovery well, still producing twenty years after it came into production.

Imperial had exploration and production headquarters in Calgary and in due course moved its Canadian head office there, too.

Mobil had no connections to the financial markets of Bay Street and banked with oil and gas departments of the big Canadian banks in Calgary. We had no downstream refining and marketing operations in central Canada and Atlantic Canada. We did have newly discovered oil and gas reserves on the East Coast, but our partners in those discoveries were in Calgary. In Toronto we were too far from the centre of exploration and production activity, which left us not as well tuned into the industry as we needed to be. It wasn't just inconvenient, it was much less effective. We were like a fish out of water.

As soon as it was possible, I planned to bring Mobil's headquarters back to Calgary. The move required the approval of the corporate head office in New York and that meant the approval of Alex Massad, no friend of mine, and Bill Tavoulareas. However, in the meantime Tavoulareas had decided to take early retirement. His place was taken by a man on the corporate fast track named Dick Tucker.

Tucker did not like Alex Massad and knew that he was very unpopular in the exploration and producing segment of the corporation. He therefore shunted Massad from his position as president of exploration and production, and promoted a young executive named Paul Hoenmans into the job. Hoenmans was a Canadian petroleum engineer educated in western Canada who had cut his teeth in the Pembina oilfield. He had worked for me, and his wife had been my secretary. He knew the Canadian business to the core. He was an unusually bright guy and Mobil Corporation had put him on the fast track, transferring him to New York. He was also a very good friend of Dick Tucker.

When Hoenmans became my boss, there was no longer an impediment to moving the corporate office back to Calgary. I immediately made a trip to New York where Hoenmans, as I had expected, asked me how I liked Toronto. I said that I thought Toronto was a great city but that I strongly believed that Mobil Canada's head office belonged back in Calgary. My feeling was that the exploration and production sector of the Canadian oil business should be located in Calgary and that we were the only major company still headquartered in Toronto.

Hoenmans agreed and said we should soon be able to get the office back to Calgary. He cleared the move with the New York executive, and I assembled Mobil Oil Canada's Toronto-based staff for a meeting at which I stated we would be moving to Calgary within the next three months. Staff reaction was very positive except for the few Torontonians we had hired. Their reluctance to leave home was, of course, understandable.

Meanwhile, I had been executing the merger. As Mobil Oil Canada's operations staff and Canadian Superior occupied adjoining towers in Calgary Place Tower, the physical aspects of putting the companies together could be readily handled. I moved back to the twenty-fifth floor of Calgary Place and felt very much at home in the office that had been built for me when I leased the space for the company in 1973.

A new suite of vice-presidents, managers and other executives had to be selected from the two companies, with the best to be chosen at all levels. Obviously, there were redundancies, resulting in many early retirements and terminations. Many of my longtime friends were involved, but the chips were down and I was faced with making some difficult decisions. The complexity of getting the merger paperwork done was staggering; the deal was not formalized until January 1, 1986, nearly two years after I took my new job.

When the merger was complete, Mobil Oil Canada was one of the largest oil and gas producing entities in the country, ranking just behind Imperial Oil, Texaco and Chevron. The company's aggressiveness and competence had earned it a reputation matching the biggest players. Now it stood at the top based on the numbers, as well.

Now I entered into a very different period of my career. The Western Canadian Sedimentary Basin had matured as an oil province, and I had become an asset manager—and we had a very big asset worth several billion dollars.

My job was to get the most out of our people and the oil and gas reserves and resources that had already been discovered and, in some cases, were already well developed. These were peak years for the newly merged company. I was responsible for the care and feeding of very valuable assets.

With the merger complete and with federal and provincial politics behind me, I was now officially out of politics. The political environment in Canada was stable and favourable, probably never more so, with natural gas market deregulation progressing and free-trade agreements with the United States and Mexico coming into fruition. Commodity prices were recovering from the devastating lows of the early 1980s. The big public policy issues had been addressed and neither Mobil nor I saw the need for me to waste my time on these matters any longer. The Canadian Petroleum Association was disappearing in a "friendly" merger with the Independent Petroleum Association of Canada, to form the Canadian Association of Petroleum Producers (CAPP). It was time for new faces on the front line of government relations. I'll admit that leaving politics behind meant that my work wasn't as exciting as it was when we were waging the big political fights, but it was very satisfying.

Knowing how I felt about my relationship with Mobil by this point in my career might help you to understand how indignant I was when, ten years after my retirement, Mobil was acquired by Exxon Corporation in a friendly 1999 merger. All the Mobil annuitants were upset about it, even outraged. When I was growing up in Mobil it became a religion: "Beat Exxon. They are our biggest competitor." Here in Canada our rival was Exxon's subsidiary, Imperial Oil, and we fought tooth and nail to best them. Perhaps to outsiders this merger was like a David and Goliath match-up—with Exxon as the Goliath—but we always thought of ourselves as the bigger and stronger of the two. And now "we" were selling out to the other side. It was still "we," for me, even though I hadn't worked for the company for a decade.

Exxon wanted to grow. And there are two ways of growing for an oil and gas company. You can drill for reserves and production and grow gradually. Or you can buy somebody who has already done all the drilling and production. By 1989 it was pretty tough to grow the slow way. Exxon is a major exploration company worldwide. In almost every area where there is potential for oil and gas, you will find Exxon at work. But in a lot of these places, Mobil and Exxon were competitors. Meanwhile, Mobil had the same problem as Exxon—it also needed to grow.

The Mobil–Exxon transaction was an Exxon takeover because it ended up the survivor; even though the full formal name is ExxonMobil, the street name is still Exxon. We Mobil employees wanted to believe that Exxon had pulled a fast one, but before the deal happened, I was at a meeting in Phoenix and personally heard the head of Mobil Corporation clearly indicate that he would be in favour of Mobil merging with some other large company. At that time, Mobil had not reached the decision that it would be Exxon, but there was no question that Mobil was open to a merger. When the offer from Exxon came along, the Mobil board in New York said, "Yes," and approved it without complaint. It was a willing deal between two huge companies joining to form one because they were competitors in so many areas; combining forces enabled them to double their power in all the areas that were so important in oil and gas exploration. Competition is often a factor in major mergers.

The deal made sense, but we Mobil guys were very unhappy about it. Here was a company that we had been taught to "hate," and suddenly it was the other way around. So it was tough to take, but logical. And it worked. You see how successful the organization has become. It's the largest publicly traded company in the world, and every year it comes out with profit numbers that are higher than the year before.

The acquisition was historically significant because both companies had the same origin, Standard Oil Trust. In 1911 the United States Supreme Court had ordered that giant company to be dissolved under American anti-combines law. The two largest pieces after the break-up were Standard Oil of New Jersey—Exxon—and Standard Oil of New York—Mobil. Combined, those two entities represented, in 1911, 60 per cent of Standard Oil Trust. There were five other companies that came out of Standard Oil. These became Chevron, BP (America), Amoco, Conoco and Atlantic Richfield.

Exxon and Mobil were the largest survivors of Standard Oil of New Jersey and the largest again have combined.

25

New Frontiers

MY TWO TERMS as president of Mobil Oil Canada coincided with the exploration of what became known in the oil and gas industry as Canada's geological and engineering frontiers. The geological frontiers were the offshore waters of the Atlantic, Pacific and Arctic. The engineering frontier was Alberta's oil sands. Mobil's Sable Island natural gas discovery put us at the forefront of frontier exploration. However, the company abstained from involvement on the Pacific offshore and the Arctic Islands. It also waived investment in the oil sands and was only a passive partner in the western Arctic's Mackenzie Delta.

By 1985 the Nova Scotia offshore had turned into a "patient" investment. That year I spent a lot of time under the radar screen with federal and provincial politicians helping to seal the Atlantic Accord. The Progressive Conservatives were in power and I had a great relationship with Pat Carney.

It was obvious that there was a great deal of oil and gas to be produced. Mobil required some form of agreement to move things along. We did not want to take the chance and invest huge sums of money to develop and produce offshore areas unless we had a firm agreement, particularly on royalty rates and land tenure: How was the land to be disposed? What did they get? What did we get? Even the bad taste arising from the Petro-Canada back-in provisions of the National Energy Program was somewhat lessened. The Atlantic agreement came quite easily from my point of view. In due course, Cohasset was produced from floating tanker platforms beginning in 1992, and in 1999 gas flowed from Venture's wells.

On the Grand Banks of Newfoundland, Mobil was in the middle of things and I found myself as the chairman of the Hibernia oilfield partners group. Two major companies pioneered exploration on offshore Newfoundland: Mobil and Amoco. Amoco was the first to drill a shallow prospect, which resulted in nothing but eight or ten dry holes, so Amoco quit the hunt.

Mobil had a big spread of land in that offshore area that came with work commitments—spending requirements—enforced by the federal government. We had to do a lot of work to meet those requirements, and it cost a lot of money. We originally drilled four dry holes: the first three were totally dry with lots of good quality reservoir rock but absolutely no hydrocarbon. Then we drilled a well called Adolphus and found a bit of oil, not a commercial well, but enough to generate some interest. Adolphus gave us something to work with.

Meanwhile our results to date made New York a little upset. We needed a partner. The guys in New York said, "Come on now, you guys need to find a partner to give us some help with these commitments." So we did a deal with Gulf, swapping our interests in the East Coast offshore for theirs in the western Arctic. Now we had a 50/50 partner, but Gulf wasn't keen to spend a dime until we had a drilling target that looked better than Adolphus.

At this point, Gerry Henderson came into the picture. Gerry was the first Canadian-born president of Chevron Canada and a terrific geologist to boot. He had some good geologists working for him who saw something that we didn't see. Gerry pushed very hard with his boss in San Francisco, who controlled his purse strings, and got the okay to do a deal with Mobil. Chevron was just dying to get in and was very persistent, so Mobil did a deal for drilling Chevron's proposed well location. The working interests ended up being Chevron at approximately 50 per cent, Mobil at about 30 per cent, and Gulf with around 20 per cent. There was a minor partner, the US company Columbia Gas, with a 2.5 per cent interest. Chevron drilled a well not far from Adolphus on a good-looking structure that we had not elected to drill, and, in 1979, it made the Hibernia discovery—a huge find and a field worth talking about.

In all of Mobil's farm-out deals, we had a corporate requirement that if a discovery was made, Mobil had the right to take over operatorship. In most cases, it worked out fine. Mobil was a big and able company with lots of American help and expertise. Most companies accepted that. Not Chevron. They figured, "We're just as big as Mobil and we're just as good as Mobil, and we have made this discovery. We want to operate."

A big battle ensued. But the black and white of the agreement was that Mobil had the right to operate, and Chevron couldn't do a thing about that. So we became the operator at Hibernia and Chevron became a working interest partner. In spite of the disagreement, we got along extremely well with Chevron. It turned out to be a very good arrangement once Chevron got over the problem of not being able to operate something it had discovered.

I was at Canadian Superior when Hibernia was discovered, but I had rejoined Mobil by the time Mobil had to make a firm management arrangement with our partners. We set up a Hibernia development company, reflecting our various working interests, with Mobil people at the top in recognition of our operatorship. I chaired the working group. It became a good partnership arrangement between Mobil, Chevron and Gulf, and Columbia Gas exercised its sliver of the pie with magnanimity. Petro-Canada also exercised its back-in for 20 per cent, which was taken from all the partners proportionately.

The working partnership ended up working out well, but we did initially have some issues to iron out with the Newfoundland government on the arrangements for infrastructure, jobs and support services and how these would benefit the province. Premier Brian Peckford wanted more all the time. Eventually he came around. He saw the light; he knew that this was a big deal for Newfoundland, so we finally came to terms.

The agreement signing was a big event; it took place at a table with Premier Peckford and a deputy minister from the federal government. I was there representing Mobil and the partnership, and Columbia Gas was there, too. We signed the deal that turned out to be the accord that set the terms for us to operate off Newfoundland. I always liked Columbia Gas, and I made certain that on every issue their representative had his say. The company appreciated it and gave me a gavel when I retired, which was emblazoned with the words "small interest owner" because I made sure that this small interest company sitting with some of the world's biggest companies always had its chance to state a position on matters.

At the time Hibernia was discovered, it was thought to contain 300 million barrels of oil reserves. As more drilling was done, that estimate increased to 800 million, then 900 million and finally a billion barrels. Then another discovery was made nearby, Terra Nova, which added another 300 million barrels to the East Coast oil reserves.

The Hibernia discovery was followed closely by discoveries of the Hebron and Wild Rose fields by Chevron and Husky. Wild Rose looked like it was going to be a gas discovery with plenty of pay, but not commercial. With subsequent drilling, it emerged as a good oilfield that could be produced with semi-submersible rigs. Hebron was part of the same land deal with Mobil and was discovered by Chevron in the same time period as Hibernia, but it was too small at the time for commercial development. Hibernia looked big and very commercial, so Chevron, Mobil, Gulf, Petro-Canada and Columbia Gas decided jointly, "Let's develop Hibernia." Hebron had to wait. Within a short time from when it was discovered, Hibernia had an extension called Hibernia South. These fields, plus Hebron and White Rose, have resulted in a major oil and gas producing area.

Mobil was in a good position in the new frontier on the East Coast, but by the late 1980s, it had lost the opportunity to be a major player in the developing frontier of the oil sands in Western Canada. This was in spite of the fact that Mobil was one of the first companies to have been interested in the oil sands, way before my time. When the company first arrived in western Canada in 1943 as Socony-Vacuum, it had refining operations. Refining companies at that time did a lot of the early research on upgrading bitumen into light crude oil. Socony was operating its refining process prior to Karl Clark's success with catalyst-assisted hot water separation.

Clark was an engineering professor at the University of Alberta and, in association with the Alberta Research Council, worked for years on the development of the oil sands. He invented the process of heating a slurry of bitumen and hot water with chemical catalysts to separate the bitumen from the sand. His process, with certain modifications and updates, is the process that is used at oil sands plants today.

When I was the first district geologist for Mobil in Edmonton, a division of the company based in Dallas was investigating the oil sands. They did some shallow drilling in the oil sands in the Fort McMurray area, and then the cores were shipped to Dallas, where Mobil had a research facility. The cores were examined so we could discover whether or not oil could be produced from the deposit. My part in this story was very modest—I met the company airplane when it arrived from Fort McMurray and arranged to send the cores on to Dallas.

Socony took out some acreage that turned out to be the same acreage as was eventually developed by Sun Oil for the first commercial mine and upgrader called the Great Canadian Oil Sands project, now Suncor. Socony did some core-hole drilling to quantify the volume of bitumen. The program indicated that a thick body of oil sands was there. Then, the company tried different methods to extract the oil. They got some oil out with their techniques but not enough for commercial success.

They still held that land when I went to work for the company, and geologists were coming through Calgary to go up to Fort McMurray to do more investigative work. But, eventually, Socony abandoned the acreage. It realized that the oil sands had potential but the obstacle was commercial technology, and the company was numbered among the skeptics. Despite this culture of skepticism within Socony's ranks, a geologist named Dr. Cliff Corbett, who was for a time the president of the Socony Canadian subsidiary, developed one of the leading theories of oil sands formation. The oil sands have always been a puzzle for geologists. How did they form? Why are they so extensive, containing such a massive amount of oil? One of the obstacles to solving the problem is that the oil sands contain no fossil remains; they can't be given a precise geological date.

In 1955 Dr. Corbett published a paper in which he theorized that the oil in the sands was formed where it is now found in lower Cretaceous sands. He thought that the deposition of the sands and the formation of the oil took place within the same geological time frame. Other geologists believed the oil had migrated perhaps from lower Devonian beds, in the typical way most oil forms in a source rock then travels upward until it is trapped in a reservoir rock. Dr. Corbett believed that the sands were brought to a near-shore area of a shallow sea as sediments borne along in rivers. The sands were buried and sealed, and the organic material in them was turned into oil over geological time. Because this formation took place just below Earth's surface, there was not a great amount of geological heat or pressure, so the oil did not "mature" and break down into lighter crude oil and natural gas. Corbett described the bitumen as being petroleum in arrested development. He deserves to be remembered as Socony's contribution to the development of the Canadian oil sands in those early days.

When I was in Calgary as the staff geologist in 1956, Mobil asked me to identify oil sands leases that they could acquire to re-establish a position in the oil sands. It was very much like the decision to get into the East Coast and Canadian North. Someone in New York looked at a map of oil sands landholdings and said, "Where's the yellow (the colour used on Mobil's maps to designate its interests in a prospective area)?" There was also pressure from the Alberta government on oil companies to develop the oil sands. After a conference of oil sands experts at the University of Alberta in 1950, the government promoted development and persisted for several years in persuading good operating companies to get involved.

I researched all the information that was then available on the oil sands and selected three tracts of land, about 50,000 acres, which exhibited some potential. I selected the tracts based on maximum oil sand deposit and minimum overburden. The thickness of the sands indicated the volume of bitumen they contained. The thickness of overburden was a mining and cost problem. You wanted to have a deposit without much earth above it that would have to be removed before you could mine the bitumen. Mobil subsequently leased these tracts but did nothing with them until the 1970s, when the government started to push all the companies to do something with their lands. Then the activity resumed, and the company's interest perked up. Mobil then engaged in some work on the tracts I had selected. I had retired by this time.

Because Mobil was not more aggressively engaged in oil sands development, it lost an opportunity. That said, the company's was a forgivable mistake, given the obstacles to economic development at the time they were exploring the oil sands. There was little idea of the technology available today, and no thought of the scale of development that began in the 1990s, forty years after I selected those leases.

In 1974 I was asked by the provincial government to sit on the Alberta Oil Sands Technology Research Authority (AOSTRA), a Crown corporation established by the Lougheed government in 1974, which operated for more than fifteen years until disbanded by the Klein government in the early 1990s. The chairman was Bill Yurko, a politician; the rest of the board members were professionals, engineers, geologists and so forth. We had an advisory role. First, AOSTRA reviewed any scientific research and activity before it was approved by the provincial government. AOSTRA also did its own research, separate from the industry. The members of the authority were sharp people, the kind you wouldn't expect to find in a government organization.

The AOSTRA group was the first to use steam-assisted gravity drainage (SAG-D) technology in a pilot project designed to prove the technology's viability. This technology allows production of bitumen from oil sands too deep to mine. In the SAG-D process, two parallel horizontal well bores are drilled into the oil sands deposit. Steam is injected into the formation from the top well bore. The steam heats the oil and enables it to drain into the lower well bore. The lower well bore is lined with a steel pipe that has thousands of thin slits into which the heavy oil drains, with the assistance of pumps.

The pilot project at Fort McMurray at which AOSTRA tested the SAG-D process involved the construction of a shaft and tunnel below the oil sands. Our advisory committee went once to Fort McMurray to look at the SAG-D pilot project in action. We went down a short mining shaft into a longer tunnel. From the tunnel, pairs of pipes ran into the bitumen. The operators pumped steam into the top pipe, which heated the oil and made it more fluid so that it drained into the bottom pipe through tiny serrations in the well bore. There it was captured and pumped to the surface.

I don't think people realize that AOSTRA was a government project that worked very successfully. For the $70 or $80 million it invested in the authority and its research, the government may ultimately recover billions in royalties. In those days the Alberta government was willing to participate in what we called "pre-competitive research," research that can be made available to all companies, which then perfect technologies and exploit them competitively.

When Ralph Klein became the premier of Alberta, with a right-wing agenda, he said: "We don't need AOSTRA, private industry can do everything that AOSTRA can do...government has no business being in business." I remember the last meeting of AOSTRA. We had a dinner, and energy minister Pat Black said thank you and gave us a commemorative plaque.

It was an anti-climatic end to a venture that I had greatly enjoyed, and which had lasting significance and produced much more than Premier Klein was willing to credit. AOSTRA was one of the few government programs that worked well.

PART FOUR

Retirement and Beyond

26

With the Independents

I LOOKED WITH TREPIDATION upon retirement. I had been active in the oil and gas industry for forty years. However, at Mobil, retirement was mandatory. The company had specific rules about this matter, and my retirement would occur on December 31, 1989, the year of my sixty-fifth birthday. I come from a generation of oil and gas people in Canada, most of whom planned to spend their lives with a single company. When a geologist started his career, he thought long and hard about which company to join; it was a serious, long-term commitment on both sides. This is uncommon in today's industry, because of mergers and acquisitions and some companies enticing the best people in other companies to leave their job and "come over to our side."

The last week of December 1989 became a week of goodbyes. I went to New York at Mobil Oil Corporation's expense, where I was hosted at a party attended by all the senior executives. They presented me with a silver tray, which all of them had signed.

The Canadian Petroleum Association also had a function for me in Calgary and gave me a Mobil plaque, complete with the flying red horse logo. It was signed by all the CPA board members with whom I had worked for so long over the years. As well, there was a Mobil Oil Canada employees' office party, at which I was given another plaque, this one signed by all the employees.

A retirement plaque from the Canadian Petroleum Association signed by all the directors, 1989.

Finally, I attended Mobil Oil Canada's huge annual Christmas party, which took place between Christmas and New Year's at the Westin Hotel ballroom in Calgary. The ballroom was packed with seven hundred people. I got up in front of all of those people and gave my annual Christmas message, but this time it was a little different.

At the end of my remarks, I said, "I've chaired this Christmas party for many years but after tonight I won't be working for Mobil anymore." The words stuck in my throat, and I received a standing ovation that lasted for several minutes. Afterward, I went from table to table to extend my greetings and then I went out into the wintery night, and home.

I could see that the 1990s were shaping up to be a pretty exciting time for the oil and gas industry. Through hard work and creative enterprise, the industry had fully recovered from the devastation of the National Energy Program and the oil and gas price collapses of the 1980s. There was no way I intended to sit on a beach for the rest of my life and miss the opportunities that were emerging. I didn't want to "do retirement" that way. It was against my nature to simply stop working. I came from a generation of oilmen who frequently worked weekends. For many years, I skipped personal vacations in order that I could continue to work. I've always worked and I still want to, even today when I'm in my mid-eighties, and still go to the office most days.

I had my Mobil pension and my memories, but I wanted to continue to contribute to my industry, to my community and to my family; and I wanted to satisfy myself. The only way I could do that was to continue to work at whatever I could find. The opportunities that came my way came naturally, but not slowly. I went right back to work in January 1990. In addition to sitting as a director on several boards and after doing some consulting work, I became the president and CEO of four independent Canadian exploration and production companies—of course, at different times. The four companies I headed for various amounts of time were: Bowtex Petroleum, Poco Petroleums, Serenpet Energy and Shiningbank Energy. As things turned out, I would "retire" three more times during the next eighteen years.

Geology created the first "dynamic decade" in Alberta and western Canada through the discovery of large fields like Leduc and Pembina. As the companies of the day, led by the multinationals, created wealth from those discoveries, the rural agrarian economy of my youth in Standard was displaced by the modern oil and gas era. By the 1990s, the Western Canadian Sedimentary Basin was "mature." There were still large targets to be found, such as deep gas in the foothills and coalbed methane deposits on the plains, but they were technically more difficult and capital intensive to develop. They were as much engineering plays as they were geological.

The new generation of young entrepreneurs needed something to provide oil and gas reserves and production for their new companies. They found their new geological building blocks not by drilling but through deals. They bought their "discoveries." The established companies were disposing of oil and gas properties as they reassessed their options and reorganized their affairs in Canada and around the world. Everyone had a mergers and acquisitions department staffed by some of their best people.

There was also a seemingly endless stream of mergers and acquisitions, fuelled by the creativity of the equity markets. I was fascinated to watch as "old" reserves in the Pembina field changed hands to create new companies. The role of the geologist became a job of finding "upside" reserves on the properties that their companies purchased, and, often in collaboration with engineers, the job became one of finding what others had missed in the past.

These new companies were much different than Mobil and Canadian Superior, but the job of running them was basically the same so there was plenty of demand for executives with grey hair and experience. The energy and enthusiasm behind these companies was youthful, but their focus and stability owed a great deal to the senior members of the industry; executives like me, who had wisdom, patience and a few battle scars. There were companies that wanted me on their boards of directors, especially now that I was free of my obligations to Mobil and could participate in the affairs of other oil and gas exploration and production companies. The first opportunity that came along had its origin in a phone call I had received a dozen years previously.

In the late 1980s, the head executive at the Royal Trust Company was legendary Canadian banker Hartland MacDougall. Hart's career had included a stint at the top level of the Bank of Montreal, which had brought him to Calgary for major deals on more than one occasion. However, I met Hart in 1986 after the Mobil Oil–Superior Oil merger when I was president of Mobil Oil Canada headquartered in Toronto. At about that time, the Royal Trust Company in Toronto set up two income trusts entitled Royal Trust Energy 1 and Royal Trust Energy 2. Hart, who knew me well, asked me to become a director of these two trust companies. Subsequently, the trust companies were acquired by United States–based financial interests, and the names of the trust companies were changed to Westrock 1 and Westrock 2.

Well, the top men at Mobil in New York, Alex Massad and Bill Tavoulareas, said, "No." They said, "We want all of Arne's activities to be related to Mobil and not to be dissipated with some other company." I concurred with their viewpoint. I'd been with Mobil a long time, and I didn't want to be in trouble with them in the later years of my career. Hart McDougall bided his time.

Then, I retired from Mobil. I hadn't been retired any more than an hour when I got a call from Hart. "Arne," he said, "You're retired. Now you can join my boards." And so I did.

The head of these companies was a brilliant and pleasant individual named Marcel Tremblay, whom I was to know for a number of years. Marcel was a bilingual financial man whose origins were in Quebec. He became a shareholder and the president and CEO of the two trusts. Subsequently, another major ownership change occurred and the two trusts were combined to form the first major oil and gas trust company, Enerplus. Tremblay invited all of the directors of the Westrock companies to become directors of Enerplus, and most of them accepted, including me.

However, sitting on a board, no matter how dynamic the company, wasn't enough. I didn't just want to be the wise veteran at the board table, even though that was a lot of fun and very satisfying. I wanted to be in the thick of the action, creating things, working day to day with people as I had for forty years. I still wanted to drill wells, find oil and gas. My life of discovery wasn't over yet.

The first opportunity for me to get back into the action came straight away, when a very successful and well-known Calgary executive, Harold Milavsky, approached me shortly after I retired and asked me to run his company, Bowtex Petroleum. Harold was not an oilman but like many other wealthy Canadians had made a significant investment in oil because it had become a very attractive financial opportunity.

I first met Harold when he was head of Trizec, the billion-dollar real estate partnership owned by the Bronfman and Reichmann families, of which Peter Bronfman was the chairman. I was familiar with Trizec, its partners and Harold's great success at Trizec in my capacity as a director on the board of the Toronto Dominion Bank. Also, I had been head of Mobil Oil when its Calgary Place head-office building was constructed and I was dealing with real estate development matters as the prospective tenant of a new building. Harold's career started in the Mannix family's business empire, where he earned his sterling reputation as a business executive while he was the controller of Loram International, one of the Mannix core businesses. Then, he moved to Trizec and built it from a weakling of office development into a huge dollar success.

When he got in touch with me, Harold was a major shareholder and the chairman and director of Bowtex, which had a modest portfolio of producing properties concentrated on natural gas. His partner in the company was Edgar Bronfman. The Bronfman family—especially Peter and Edward—had included significant oil and gas assets in their financial empire over the years, including a major stake in the companies Ranger Oil and Westmin Resources.

Harold came to me and said, "Arne, you have all these years of experience, and I want you to be president of Bowtex." His offer was attractive. I had to go to Toronto for an interview with Edgar Bronfman. He was enthusiastic about me and the opportunities in western Canada. With Bronfman's endorsement, I found Harold's offer impossible to refuse and I became president of Bowtex.

I had a lot of flexibility in running the company. I could hire my own people, one of which was Grant Gunderson, an engineer and MBA. I appointed him the chief financial officer. Grant had worked closely with me at both Canadian Superior and Mobil and had played an important role on the alternative energy task force. I said, "Grant I need someone to help me." And he said "Sure." I very quickly gave him a lot of the responsibility for the development of the company. We concentrated on natural gas in a good time for markets and prices. For a small enterprise of about twenty employees, we did quite well.

Then, in 1993, I was approached by independent head hunters who represented Poco Petroleums. Its first president, Al Markin, had just left the company after a disagreement with the board. The head hunters said to me, "Bowtex is a just a little job; we've got a much better one for you." I had hired good people and Bowtex was ticking along. There was no doubt in my mind that Grant Gunderson could run the company if should I leave. The Poco offer was interesting.

Ed Galvin and Don Barkwell were the major founding shareholders of Poco Petroleums. I had known Ed for thirty years and had gotten along with him well. Earlier in his career, he founded a company called Canadian Industrial Gas and Oil Limited (CIGOL) with Manitoba executive Maurice Strong as partner. The company subsequently became Norcen Energy Resources, which became a very strong and influential presence in Alberta and western Canada. Galvin and Barkwell were its two senior executives, and I got to know them well through the CPA. I believed that we could work well together.

Poco was a full-fledged exploration and producing company. Originally, its properties were shallow gas fields in eastern Alberta that had turned out to be very successful. With the money from those early properties, Poco had the opportunity to became a big exploration and production company. It had acquired excellent properties in northern and western Alberta by the time I was approached by the headhunters.

When Galvin founded Poco, he had a major shareholder from the Toronto financial community, a gentleman by the name of Ned Goodman. I expressed an interest in the job and was asked to go to Toronto for an interview with him. Ned and I liked each other right away. He said, "I want you to have that job at Poco and I have a lot of strength on the board, so I will support you." I figured this was a "can't-miss" situation. However, Poco turned out to be the one big disappointment of my career. Within a few months of my arrival, Ed Galvin, Don Barkwell and I expressed differences over the future of the company. It wasn't a pleasant experience. Nonetheless, I should tell you a little about my three years at Poco because it was part of my life, and not everything in a career is smooth and easy.

At first, I was very much involved in moving Poco's activity from eastern Alberta into the foothills and near foothills, which represented a different kettle of fish from the shallow gas. It took a lot more capital and a lot more expertise to work in the foothills. We had some early success there, but we began having internal difficulties.

At issue was the timing of the Poco succession plan. When I was hired to run Poco as its chairman, president and chief executive officer, there was another candidate for the job who already worked for the company, an able young man named Craig Stewart. He was the protégé and had the backing of Ed Galvin. The board decided, at the behest of Ned, that Stewart was not yet ready to assume the position of president and CEO. Ned thought he was too young and did not have enough experience. I was the solution. The board decided, "Let Arne run the company for two or three years until Craig is ready."

The problem, however, was that Craig and I didn't get along. This was the first time and only time in my career that I came up against a guy in a company who worked for me with whom I couldn't get along. Just as Craig and I were finding out that our differences were not easy to mitigate, Ned decided to switch his investments from oil and gas to gold. In one fell swoop, he sold his 45 per cent ownership in Poco in a public offering. Then he left and had nothing more to do with the company. That was a difficult event from my personal perspective because my backer on the board was gone. Ed Galvin, who now had the power on the board to direct the company, clearly thought that Craig was ready and should succeed me sooner rather than later.

This became a tough situation. I was in trouble. I read the writing on the wall. I went back to the lawyer who had represented me in the Mobil lawsuit, Don Sabey, and got some good legal advice. He suggested that I make a deal with Poco that would "save face" for everyone concerned. I went to the board and negotiated a retirement date. I would continue as chairman, and Craig would become CEO.

A year prior to that date, we announced my retirement so that there would be no surprises for the shareholders and the markets. It was not an easy period because Craig was understandably impatient to take over the reins. But we saved the situation because I was able to leave under fairly normal circumstances.

Craig Stewart had the opportunity to get on with his career. In spite of our differences, I must say he did very well. I suppose in the end, it was what they call a win-win situation. In 2003 Poco was acquired in a very attractive deal by Burlington Resources, and that agreement demonstrated the talent of the people who ran Poco after I left, including Craig Stewart.

After I left Poco, I did considerable consulting. This was my Africa period—working in Senegal, Gambia and Morocco for the Canadian government. Canada had invested foreign aid funds in these countries and the Canadian International Development Agency (CIDA) sent me over to see how the money was being spent. One of my contacts in Ottawa was Joe Clark, who was the foreign affairs minister of the day. More than once I found myself bouncing around on the decrepit aircraft and battered buses of small regional air and bus lines in Africa, a passenger alongside the chickens and goats. Sometimes the destinations changed in mid-flight. Our arrivals were seldom on time. I was always thankful when the wheels touched down, and all I had suffered was a bit of inconvenience and the novelty that travel on that continent always brings.

After my Africa adventures, I accepted the opportunity to participate in one final enterprise: the creation of a new company from the raw material of an old one. The company I helped bring to life was Shiningbank Energy, an early energy income trust. It was a great success for me professionally and financially, and it brought me much career satisfaction.

27

Shiningbank and the Energy Trusts

IN ADDITION to my African consulting work, and being a director of the energy trusts that had been combined to form Enerplus, I was also chairman of the board of a conventional exploration and production company called Serenpet Energy.

Serenpet encountered financial problems with respect to debt it owed to the Royal Bank of Canada. The Serenpet board decided that these problems could be handled by converting a part of the company into an energy trust. We decided that Serenpet would sell assets to repay its debt. The properties would be sold to a newly formed energy income trust company. That would take some money, so the new energy trust would have to raise the initial capital, not just to buy properties but to hire staff, set up an office and commence operations.

I had theoretically "retired" again after I left Poco Petroleums, in order to have less work and to spend more time with my family. I had resigned as chairman of Serenpet but remained on its board. The new chairman of the board, Gerry Sutton, came to me and said, "Arne, we want you to run the new trust company that we plan to organize to solve Serenpet's financial problems."

At first, I said, "No. I just retired and you guys want to put me back to work again?" But Gerry replied, "Arne, without you as president, there's going to be no trust company; we won't be able to pay our debt and we'll go down the tube."

That put me in such a position that I had to say, "Yes." I couldn't refuse, even though when I accepted it, I was actually in retreat from the field of battle!

I agreed to be chairman of this new trust company that we were spinning out of Serenpet, but it was my requirement that I be joined by a younger person with both strong financial and operating experience. A number of individuals were very interested in the position, but the person elected by the board was David Fitzpatrick who, at the time, was executive vice-president and chief operating officer of Serenpet. After some consultations between us, he and I agreed we could work together to set up the trust. I would be chairman and chief executive officer, and he would be president and chief operating officer.

David was a young financial executive, and I was an old geologist, and we joined forces to set up an extremely successful company. In doing so, I gained the strongest and best working connection I've ever enjoyed with a colleague. In spite of the differences in our backgrounds and ages, we hit it off beautifully and continued working together seamlessly until the sale of Shiningbank to PrimeWest Energy in the summer of 2007.

The name, Shiningbank, came from an area where the company had properties, near a lake named Shiningbank located in northwestern Alberta, between Edson and Whitecourt, not far from the rugged and beautiful terrain where I'd surveyed and mapped the surface geology of the foothills as a summer student with the GSC many years previously.

David and I worked exceptionally well together because we could see eye-to-eye on major issues. For example, one of the first things we had to decide was how to differentiate ourselves from the other energy trusts being formed at the time—ARC, PrimeWest, Viking, Penn West and a few others. David and I agreed to become a natural gas–oriented trust. This was the first major decision that we made. We agreed on that policy, and we stuck to it.

Our gas-oriented mandate worked in the company's favour for half a dozen years. The benefit of the gas orientation eventually got lost in the shuffle, however, because with the rise of prices, conventional oil production came back into its own as an attractive investment choice.

We also agreed from the start that I would be the CEO and he would be the chief operating officer. Accordingly, we'd have different roles. We also agreed that, with me getting older, in due course, we would change roles, and I would become chairman and he would move into the CEO position. We picked the date for this change, and we stuck to it.

On that date, I went to the board and said, "I recommend that Dave become the CEO. He's now been tried and proven. He and I get along well; we'll continue to work jointly in the best interests of Shiningbank. He should now be CEO and the buck will stop at his desk and not at mine." After my little speech, David and I left the room. The board considered my recommendation, then we came back into the room and the board approved the changeover.

When the company was first formed, one of the things David and I had to agree on was the people we hired. We each interviewed potential key people at separate times. Then we compared notes and reached an agreement on which ones we could bring into the company. I believe his is the way in which top-level people should be hired. They should be interviewed separately by those involved in the process. Then the decision should be made jointly by all involved in the interviews.

We also had to agree on selecting a board, as well. I knew more about boards than Dave because of my extensive experience as a director; I'd been on many boards, from the biggest corporations to smallest ones, and I knew that a company like Shiningbank would be better off with a small board. We agreed to a small board of five directors, including Dave and me. Because I was the senior guy with knowledge on these kinds of things, I picked two of the directors, and Dave picked one. I picked Grant Gunderson, who'd been with me at Mobil, and Ted Best; both people I'd known for many years. Dave picked Warren Steckly, whom he'd known for several years. That board of five essentially did not change for ten years, we worked that well together. When we began getting big, we could see that five members were no longer enough. That's when we agreed to add Bob Hodgson, a corporate director who'd been a financial executive at TransCanada Pipelines.

Our first major effort together was to pay off the Royal Bank on behalf of Serenpet through the purchase and sale of properties. The capital raised would also allow us to establish enough funds to set up an operation. Dave and I took our first major fundraising trip together, covering all the major cities in Canada but concentrating on Toronto and Montreal. We were guided on this trip by Richardson Greenshields, an investment firm later purchased by RBC Dominion Securities. The trip was eminently successful and we raised over $50 million. We paid off the bank, hired key staff and got the trust under way.

Shiningbank prospered big time. We made some key acquisitions and hired an excellent staff. We were able to initiate distributions to our unit holders and gradually increase those over time. For ten years we had an average annual rate of return of 26 per cent, concentrating on gas rather than oil. (For most of its life, 75 per cent of the company's revenue was from natural gas.) However, the "trust" competition became stiff. In the same year that Shiningbank was formed in 1996, a number of other trusts also opened their doors. The two original trusts, Enerplus and Pengrowth, were also prospering.

During the early stages, I decided to resign from my position as a director of Enerplus in order to avoid conflicts of interest and to concentrate all of my attention on Shiningbank. When Dave Fitzpatrick took over as president and CEO and my title was changed to executive chairman, I dropped the "executive" in my title and remained as a "non-executive" chairman of Shiningbank for the duration of its existence. The term "executive chairman" suggests a little more hands-on power than "non-executive chairman" does. An executive chairman is involved to some degree in the executive management of the company, in conjunction with the CEO. For a while in the oil and gas business, we had quite a few companies in which the office of chairman and CEO were the same person. Changes in corporate governance and greater scrutiny of corporate affairs have brought that practice to an end.

A non-executive chairman's day-to-day influence is considerably less than an executive's. He operates at arms' length from the affairs of the company; for instance, he isn't likely to be keeping regular office hours at the company of which he's chairman. I was an exception to that rule because I continued to keep office hours after I gave up the "executive" chairman title. Due to the close working relationship between Dave and I, not all that much changed for me in terms of my participation at meetings and mentoring Dave, but he gained more authority and control in the business.

The board and I felt confident in Dave. I didn't feel I was really needed at all, except to do the jobs a chairman traditionally does: chairing meetings and dealing with the directors, reviewing documents and giving Dave advice when he wanted it.

Then, in spite of an election campaign promise on October 31, 2006, in the first budget of Stephen Harper's newly elected minority Conservative government, Minister of Finance Jim Flaherty announced a proposed change in the taxation of energy trusts. The companies had originally been set up on the basis of paying a minimum tax to the federal government. This enabled the trusts to maximize their distributions of company revenues to the unit holders. Flaherty announced a change that would result in the trusts being taxed at the same rate as other corporations, commencing in 2011. In other words, he wrote a "sunset" clause into the life of every income trust in Canada.

Flaherty's decision was a betrayal of the kind that encourages oil and gas companies to mistrust politicians of all stripes. He did not understand the income trusts and how they worked in the economy. He was concerned that the energy trusts avoided paying taxes by distributing profits to their owners who were mostly retired investors. His analysis completely ignored the taxes that the trust owners paid on the distributions.

After Flaherty's unexpected thunderbolt, the energy trusts—Shiningbank included—needed an exit strategy from the trust business model to an alternative that would, under extremely difficult circumstances, protect the interests of its unit holders and the long-term health of the oil and gas sector. Shiningbank's extraordinary success made it an irresistible takeover target.

Unfortunately, the federal government's precipitous action on income trusts speeded up the takeover process and took away some of our ability—as a board and executive management—to exert the appropriate level of control over the circumstances. In the spring of 2007, a larger trust, PrimeWest Energy, made a merger proposal to Shiningbank, which was accepted and subsequently consummated. The new company would be operating under the PrimeWest name and that company assumed control of the operations.

I had earlier decided to retire from Shiningbank and only stay on as chairman. However, the merger with PrimeWest, as lucrative as it turned out to be for me, resulted in separating me from anything connected with the energy trusts, the final executive job of my career. On three previous occasions, at Mobil, Poco and Serenpet, my retirements had proved to be phantoms. This time, my retirement from Shiningbank, coming as it did close to my eighty-second birthday, looked like the real thing. This retirement enabled me to spend my working hours solely on matters related to other corporate directorships and to devote more personal time to my family and my wife's cats.

Through all the decisions Dave and I made together, we always found it relatively easy to reach agreement because we developed a relationship of trust and respect, and the relationship remained exactly the same until the day PrimeWest acquired the assets of Shiningbank and took over the company. The two of us could agree on everything of significance, and it didn't take us much time to make the big decisions.

We never had a harsh word, and it is pretty unusual that two people who are so different can set up an organization and get along so well. We were both good at our different disciplines. He was an intense person; I was more laid-back, and that worked well, too. While I was writing this book, I had lunch with him regularly and he had become one of my very best friends. I've written about the people who influenced my life. I hope I'm someone he'll look back on some day; maybe he'll add Arne Nielsen to the list of people who influenced his life.

I got a letter from David shortly after the merger of Shiningbank and PrimeWest in which he wrote about how he appreciated the way we worked together, concluding by saying how fortunate he was to have met me. I've never received a letter like that before, and I didn't expect it. It wasn't necessary, but that letter exemplifies the relationship we had. That relationship was a major reason why Shiningbank was so successful.

During the Shiningbank years, I received the greatest honour of my life when, in 2000, the University of Alberta awarded me with an honorary doctorate. It is the top recognition that a university can give, and I recognized it as the ultimate honour because my life's work had reflected very positively on my alma mater. I am particularly proud of this award because five of my eight children—Allan, Brian, Dianne, Robin, Garry and Paul—are graduates of the University of Alberta, and Brian was a professor of physical education there until his recent retirement.

Shiningbank was my last full-time job, but I maintain an office in downtown Calgary. I have gone to work in the corporate world every day for sixty years and plan to continue to do so for a while yet. I don't want you to say, "He had a good, full career," because it isn't over just yet. I no longer need a corner office, but I enjoy a place to work for a few hours every week day, to keep in touch with the industry that has been my way of life as well as my career. It's also a place where people can look for me because, one never knows, there may be one more job with one more retirement waiting out there.

28

Lessons Learned

NEAR STANDARD, Alberta, where I grew up, there was a little town called Chancellor. It has all but disappeared now. When I was a youth, you could tell the size and importance of a town by the number of grain elevators along its railway track. Standard had six elevators and Chancellor had two, which eventually became none. Even then, Chancellor wasn't much.

When I was a young man, fresh out of university, I was sent by Socony to my old home town to find oil. There was a man at Chancellor who ran a grocery store, a well-liked person. He made a trip to Texas and when he came back he had a black box. He said that he could find oil using this box. We've all heard and laughed about "black boxes," those devices that promise to find oil with no scientific basis for the claim. I saw the grocer's black box myself. One thing was true about it, it was black. The people of Chancellor believed in him, totally. They said: "This guy has a box that came up from Texas, and they know how to find oil in Texas, so why shouldn't it work in Chancellor?"

The people looked at me, educated at the University of Alberta as a geologist, and at my father, a reputable local farmer. But they said, "What do we need Nielsen for? This guy can do it with a black box and he has no education at all." It didn't help the Nielsen side of the argument that Socony sent me to the area to be the well-site geologist on a dry hole. So, for a while, it looked like the black box was going to win.

However, eventually people used their heads. I found some gas nearby in a second well Socony drilled. And the grocer's black box resulted in nothing. He talked the farmers into putting money into that black box, and they actually drilled two or three wells. And they were dry. Needless to say, that was a big "loss of face" for the black box, and pretty soon no one talked any more about black boxes.

Versions of this story have played out in many places over the years. Somebody comes up with a wand, and they dowse for oil as they walk through the field. Someone else comes up with a black box.

One lesson I have learned in my life is that, with intelligence and persistence and with the right tools (not black boxes), things have a tendency to work out one way or another. When something isn't going to work out, if you use your head, you usually know that in advance and the smart person admits it and gets on with life. Success doesn't come easily, and you don't find it with a black box.

My career, as geologist, executive and "politician," took place in the golden age of petroleum geologists in North America. When I came into the business, there was very little oil and gas production in western Canada but great potential. The US companies had come in droves with large amounts of capital to invest after Leduc. They came to find reserves and establish production here. The time was right, and we were ready for it. I was a member of the first generation of Canadians trained professionally in Canadian universities to find and produce oil and gas. My generation of Canadian geologists and geophysicists discovered an immense amount of oil and gas within our national boundaries. Even when we were funded by foreign companies, the brains were Canadian.

The timing of my coming into the industry and the half-century I have been in it were also the best years for the owners and managers of oil corporations from the largest multinational to the smallest junior oil company. These corporations created enormous personal and public wealth, and the economic benefits they generated spread across the nation. They were also the best years politically, even if you factor in the infamous National Energy Program. I enjoyed working with several energy ministers no matter what party they belonged to: Joe Greene, Donald Macdonald, Marc Lalonde, Jean Chrétien and Pat Carney.

Throughout my time in the industry, we had good government in Alberta, where we found 85 per cent of our present oil and gas reserves. Alberta has dealt fairly and squarely with the industry. From Ernest Manning and Peter Lougheed, to Don Getty and Ralph Klein—the government moved in the correct vein. It treated industry fairly and it worked for the public interest at the same time.

Has this wisdom and fairness ended? The jury is out. Many believe that Premier Ed Stelmach, Ralph Klein's successor, changed the game. Did his review of oil and gas royalties signal a less hospitable environment for the industry? Did the untimely changes he made to royalty rates, just as oil and gas prices encountered one of their regular down-cycles, mean that he didn't care if he killed the "golden goose" of the Alberta economy? Premier Alison Redford has the opportunity to fix things. Will she? Only time will tell.

At the end of a career that spans six full decades, you will understand my temptation to muse about two fundamental questions that have occupied a good deal of my time and attention: What are the attributes of a great CEO? What makes a great oil and gas company?

I think there are four attributes of a great oil and gas industry leader. Skill in communications is the first of those attributes. There are lots of would-be leaders out there, but if they can't communicate, they can't make a valid point. As a CEO, you must have the ability to get up, talk and make your point and persuade people to agree with you. I think it's best if you have the ability to get up on your feet and do it off the top of your head. Of course, you need to have mastered your responsibilities to do this.

Another required skill is the leaders' ability to relate successfully to the people with whom they must deal. You have to be able to work with all others in the company, and at all levels: above you on your board, parallel with you and below you.

A great CEO must also be a good judge of character. She or he must recognize the kind of people who should be working for the company, and the kind that shouldn't. Even when people are knowledgeable, they may not be suitable. You've got to have people who can work together with a team. Mavericks who won't work in a team won't help the company.

The fourth attribute of a great CEO is knowledge of the business: operational knowledge and technical knowledge, a good combination of both. In the early days, the top man was nearly always a geologist because to be successful you had to have oil and gas, and it was the geologists who found it. In time, engineers also became presidents. Once a discovery has been made, geologists don't know what to do with it. At that stage, you must have good engineers to develop and bring the production on stream. A geologist can't do that.

In the end, a good CEO needs to understand something of all the professions employed by his company, but he must also be a member of one of those professions. As an aside, geologists need good geophysicists. There was a time when geologists and geophysicists didn't get along. It was just ridiculous. They finally smartened up and realized they'd have to work together to be successful.

A great company depends on the quality of the people who work for it, which depends on how they are recruited, what tasks they are given to do, how well they perform those tasks, and how much further training and development they are willing to engage in. At Mobil, we were hand-picked at the moment of being hired, and then for every promotion and transfer that followed. The objective was always to give us the opportunity to realize our potential, and in return, eventually, the company had the best people in the right jobs.

For very big companies to succeed, patience and discipline are required. In a fast-moving business, where wealth is often built quickly and a company's fortunes can turn on a dime due to a big discovery or bad political decision, paradoxically, a fundamental characteristic of success is patience. There is no better illustration of that than Mobil's involvement on the East Coast of Canada, and in the offshore plays of Sable Island and Hibernia. Socony-Vacuum, as Mobil was then named, drilled the company's first dry hole offshore Prince Edward Island in 1943. Mobil acquired its first Sable Island permits offshore Nova Scotia in 1959. We drilled our first stratigraphic test on Sable Island in 1966–67. We made the first Sable Island discovery, the E-48, in 1971. We found the Cohasset oilfield in 1973, but didn't produce it for another nineteen years. We found the Venture gas field in 1979, but didn't produce it for market until 1999, twenty years later. In all, Mobil sank $5.2 billion into offshore Nova Scotia, and it took some time to recover that investment. Patience is a virtue.

Big companies need time to do big things. Success is a matter of detail and internal process, which requires discipline. Minimizing risk is a part of the discipline—for example, in geology and government relations. As a big company, Mobil had plenty of capital. One of the great arguments for defending foreign investment in Canadian oil was: "Who do you want to develop your resource but capable companies with large amounts of capital to invest?"

Most major accomplishments are achieved by a group and not by one person. At every stage of my life and career, I have worked as a member of a group. As a kid playing baseball, I learned the value of a team in which everyone plays his position well. In the Canadian Tank Corps, the command structure was clear, and the corps' success depended on the entire crew. On the Barren Lands, our Geological Survey of Canada exploration crews depended for survival and comfort on co-operation within the crews and on the reliability of unseen people—pilots and party chiefs, for example. As an exploration geologist, I depended on the work of other geologists, geophysicists, engineers and the seismic and drilling crews. When I made the Pembina discovery, I relied on the advice, in-sights and skills of many other people. The higher I climbed up the corporate ladder in Mobil Oil, the more I observed the absolute importance of working in a company where everyone carried a part of the load.

—⌇—

Looking into the future, there are two great questions facing the oil and gas industry that revolve around two geological questions. Are we running out of oil and natural gas? And is our consumption of fossil fuels changing Earth's climate to a degree that threatens the future of livable conditions on the planet? Geologists understand climate change and the exhaustion of petroleum differently than other scientists and environmentalists. We see both issues as part of the history of Earth, in terms of geological changes that take place over billions of years.

One of the lessons that I brought home with me from China in 1973, when I was among the first Western oilmen to be shown the progress of the Chinese petroleum industry, is that we have no final idea, yet, of just how much oil remains to be discovered on Earth. The future of fossil fuel isn't a question of whether we will run out, but whether it can be produced economically and in an environmentally sound way, or whether a better source of energy will be discovered.

Once, coal replaced wood as the primary fuel for the human race. As I was beginning my career, oil replaced coal. Later, natural gas became as important as oil. Sheik Zaki Yamani, the famous Saudi oil minister and chairman of OPEC, gave a speech in Calgary in 1977, and I'll never forget one of his lines: "The Stone Age didn't end because we ran out of stones and the Oil Age won't end because we run out of oil."

Earth's climate has been changing for 4.5 billion years without human intervention or influence. And hydrocarbons—coal, natural gas, crude oil—are among the most common natural compounds found on Earth, and across our solar system for that matter. We geologists know that there have been major climate changes many times throughout Earth's life. We can go back to the end of the Cambrian, we can go back to the end of almost all the geological periods—Cambrian, Ordovician, Silurian, Devonian, the two Mississippian,

upper and lower and on to the Cenozoic, Triassic, Jurassic and Cretaceous—
on many occasions, during those hundreds of millions of years, there were
big-time changes in Earth's climate.

We all learned in school about the ice ages. Glaciers came from the North
and moved down across North America and covered much of it several times.
And every time there was an ice age, it ended, and big lakes formed in front of
the glaciers as they retreated, huge bodies of water that supported their own
flora and fauna. This isn't a matter of guesswork; it is a matter of knowledge
based on fossil evidence.

The most recent ice age ended ten thousand years ago. And geologic history
shows that if you go back more that 60 million years to the Upper Cretaceous
period, there was an ocean that extended from what is now the Beaufort Sea
to the Gulf of Mexico, continuous all the way. That was a natural inundation
that subsequently retreated. Such changes happened on six or seven different
occasions, when the ocean moved back and forth across North America. During
those inundations and recessions, the climate changed. It also changed when
the ice ages and the glaciers came and went.

Geologists recognize natural forces accounted for the change, not people
with their cars or campfires. Popular opinion now holds that climate is changing again, and that it's the 6 or 7 billion people on Earth who are changing it.

The American Association of Petroleum Geologists has published a statement on behalf of all their members that presents geological thinking and
attitudes on current climate and geologic history. Here is a summary of the
AAPG position:

Geologists study the history of the earth and realize climate has changed
often in the past due to natural causes. The Earth's climate naturally
varies constantly, in both directions, at varying rates and on many scales.
In recent decades, global temperatures have risen. Yet our planet has
been far warmer and cooler than today many times in the geologic past,
including the past 10,000 years.

Certain climate simulation models predict that the warming trends
will continue however to be predictive, any model of future climate
should also accurately model known climate and greenhouse gas
variations recorded in the geologic history of the past 200,000 years.

AAPG supports expanding scientific climate research into the
basic controls on climate, specifically including the geological, solar
and astronomic aspects of climate change. Research should include

understanding causes of past climate change and the potential effects of both increasing and decreasing temperatures in the futures.

AAPG supports research to narrow probabilistic ranges on the effect of anthropogenic CO_2 on global climate.

AAPG supports reducing emissions from fossil fuel as a worthy goal. However, emissions reduction has an economic cost, which must be compared to the potential environmental gain.

My views on climate change are somewhat different than those of the AAPG. I am convinced, scientifically, that it is erroneous to blame climate change exclusively on fossil fuel use and other human activity that generates greenhouse gases. In geological terms, human-generated greenhouse gases are a small piece of a much bigger climate-change puzzle. This is not to say that we should not look for cleaner ways to use fossil fuels and alternatives to coal, oil and natural gas in the future. Pollution from fossil fuel consumption makes life in the world's major cities unhealthy and unpleasant, and for the first time in human history, as the third millennium begins, more than half the people of the world live in cities. By the middle of this, the twenty-first century, more than 8 billion people will share the globe. They all deserve a better life.

I know that I will not be here to see it, but I believe that the same ingenuity and spirit that brought my father and mother to Canada to build new lives for their children, and the same ingenuity and spirit with which my generation changed the world by ushering in the modern oil age during the six decades of my career, will be employed by present and future generations of geologists, engineers, politicians and visionaries in business and the wider community, living tens of thousands of "lives of discovery" to find new fuels, and new ways to use old fuels, which will make Earth more habitable and create the opportunity for good and productive lives for all people.

29

Allies and Advocates

ONE OF THE REASONS I am a reluctant memoirist is that I don't like to toot my own horn. I am reluctant to make claims on my own behalf. I owe far too much to too many people to boast. I enjoy reading history and biographies about the lives of great people, but such books are usually inaccurate because they don't say enough about the people around the great politician, king, general or scientist: the people who participated in the success of the hero or heroine of the story.

Scarcely a month passes without my reading the obituary of someone I worked with and respected. Already the twentieth century is slipping away from memory and with it the colleagues and friends of a lifetime in oil and gas exploration during its golden decades. There are nine people who stand out for me. They immensely influenced my life and contributed to the degree of success I have achieved.

The first and greatest influence was my father, Aksel Nielsen. He was a quiet, simple, humble man, deeply religious and deeply devoted to his family. He immigrated to North America because it had the one thing he could not find in his native Denmark: opportunity. His family fulfilled that objective. He dominated and directed my early life. He insisted I go to university. He infected me with his curiosity about geology. I inherited his commitment to a high standard of ethical personal conduct. He died in 1971 at the age of eighty-two, and I have now lived longer than he. Among his personal effects when he passed away were one or two news clippings and magazine articles about my accomplishments; I trust that he recognized that his efforts made on my behalf paid off.

Next to my father, my elder brother, Gerhardt Nielsen, was the member of my family who most influenced my life. He was as good and helpful a brother as anyone would wish for. For many years, we had a typical big brother–little brother relationship. From an early age, I found myself following in Gerhardt's footsteps. We played a lot of baseball together. We worked together in our father's fields with such interesting projects as poisoning gophers, picking weeds, pitching hay, shovelling wheat and setting stooks. Gerhardt was a perfectionist and frequently was very critical of my performance. I had to work hard at all of these farm activities to match my brother's performance levels.

Over the years, Gerhardt gave me very sound brotherly advice on nearly all matters. On the other side of the coin, I helped him with much of his homework. It was shocking when Gerhardt was diagnosed with Parkinson's disease and his death was inevitable. When he passed on, I lost my best friend and counsellor. I gave his eulogy at his funeral and it was the most difficult speech I have ever had to give.

When I started university in 1946 with the objective of becoming a geologist, the first professional geologist with whom I became involved was Dr. Robert (Bob) Folinsbee. He was a "hard-rock" geologist, and he spent his summers leading Geological Survey of Canada field parties in northern Canada. I was fortunate he selected me to be a summer student on his geological party in the Barren Lands between Yellowknife and Hudson Bay. From him I learned more basic geology than I had been taught in the university classroom. I also learned behaviours that would contribute to my character, such as extremely hard work, not giving up, and completing every day the mapping objectives that we had planned in the morning. Dr. Folinsbee was my first mentor and, during the following years, I sought his advice on many occasions. Sadly, Dr. Folinsbee died of cancer while I was writing this book.

Dr. Charles (Charlie) Stelck was another geology professor at the University of Alberta. At the time of this writing, he is a Professor Emeritus. Charlie Stelck did more for his students, including me, both professionally and personally than any other professor who ever taught at that university. He was extremely articulate and had a great sense of humour, which made his classes extremely interesting. His major attribute was his personal relationships with each student. Charlie knew the personal circumstances of everyone in his class and provided maximum assistance to students with problems.

I found that I had an affinity for the geological science of palaeontology. Although I could have done postgraduate work at the University of Alberta, there were American universities more distinguished in this field. One of these was Stanford, from which Dr. Stelck had obtained his doctorate, and another one was Northwestern in Chicago. With Charlie's help, I was able to gain a scholarship at Northwestern and was scheduled to go there in the fall of 1948, and bring my family as well. Then one of my sons became very ill with a longer term problem that required both parents' attention. My attendance at Northwestern was postponed and subsequently cancelled. However, Charlie Stelck arranged for me to carry out a study of the Cretaceous-era Foraminfera fossils at the University of Alberta for my MSC.

When I went to work for Socony-Vacuum, my first boss was Dr. Joe Spivak. When I first met him, I knew that he was the type of executive with whom I could relate. The first job he gave me was on a wildcat well which was being drilled near Standard, a mile-and-a-half from my home. A number of other more senior geologists were available but Dr. Spivak, knowing my family connection, selected me. My great respect for him was never misplaced. For thirty-five years, he was a mentor without parallel. Among many other things, I learned from him how to manage large groups of people in a quiet but efficient manner.

As my career advanced, I dealt with many complex managerial and technical problems, and on numerous occasions, I went to Dr. Spivak for his advice. When I moved from Mobil to Canadian Superior, I had a long discussion with him. I remember his final advice on the subject. He said, "Arne, I have known you for a long time and have seen you make many decisions. Although I hate to see you leave Mobil, if you think that it is the right decision, I know that it is the correct one." Joe unfortunately passed away prematurely from cancer. For the rest of my career, when faced with major decisions, I frequently ask myself, "What would Joe do?"

In 1959 Mobil had a major reorganization, and I was transferred from my position as chief geologist in Calgary to exploration manager of the new Denver Division. My boss became Jim Watts, an engineer from Los Angeles. For the next few years, I reported to him on Mobil's exploration in thirty-six states. I gained a huge respect for him in a very short period of time. He gave me complete freedom on all exploration matters. He took the position that I had proven myself in Canada, otherwise I would not have been appointed to my position.

Jim was one of the strongest technical executives with whom I have ever worked. He knew the oil business from top to bottom. In addition to his strong technical and managerial ability, Jim was a personable and caring individual. When one of my sons was critically ill and required full-time attendance by a family member, Jim and his wife helped my wife and me, frequently sitting all night at the bedside of my son. I have never known his equal in combining executive strength with personal care and attention. He taught me that personal interest in an employee's family was just as important as the professional connections.

Don Sabey was a litigator with the eminent law firm Bennett Jones when my job change from Mobil to Canadian Superior brought about the famous lawsuit against me by Mobil. For two years, I spent approximately half my time with Don Sabey, and I came to know him extremely well. I gained a tremendous respect for him. He was personable and very sensitive to any problems that surfaced within my family. In the courthouse, Don showed all the characteristics of a top-notch litigation lawyer. I subsequently called on Don's services again for other legal matters. He became a good friend, as well as a strong legal counsel during one of the most difficult events of my career. I still see him on occasion, and his son, Alex, worked for Canadian Superior.

When I was still a young executive with Mobil here in Calgary, I had a financial crisis. I needed some help from my bank, the Toronto Dominion. I sat down with a loans officer. He absolutely refused to offer any realistic help. I was taken aback because I had a good job. But this young banker was adamant, and we were at an impasse. So the bank brought in a second person named Bill Dingee. Bill was completely different in his attitude. He wanted to help and had confidence in me. He and I worked out a solution that included some of his personal money, which he quietly loaned to me privately. His boss got wind of this and called us in together. In that meeting he hammered Bill big time and threatened to fire him, all in the presence of the client Bill was helping—me. I straightened out my affairs, and paid back Bill's loan to me and to the bank. Bill Dingee has remained my banker for over thirty years. I can call on him when I need advice on all business and personal matters.

Toward the later part of my career at Mobil, the company hired one of western Canada's accomplished geophysicists, Valerie Thomas. Her achievements had been recognized by her peers, who elected her to the executive of the Canadian Society of Exploration Geophysicists, and ultimately its first woman president.

She joined Mobil Oil Canada not long after Evelyn passed away, and I met her first during the customary interview that I did with each new employee. We became good friends and she helped me through one of the most difficult periods of my life. Without her strength and support, the years during which I was alone would have been almost intolerable to bear.

Valerie and I had many things in common, such as our exploration professions, our strong interest in the oil and gas business (and business generally), enjoyment of travel and an active social life. As I progressed up the corporate ladder, Valerie provided invaluable advice and strong support during business and personal crises, which I would have found difficult to handle by myself.

When we first met at Mobil, Alex Massad advised me that company policy would not permit us to continue seeing each other while working for Mobil and that "one of us would have to go." I decided not to mention this to Valerie, although she knew Massad had concerns about us. Valerie decided to resign from Mobil and, without telling me, made her first visit to New York to meet with Massad. He was not expecting her. She thought that personalizing the issue could be helpful. At the time of her resignation, she had obtained a position with Gulf Oil Canada as a project manager of Beaufort Sea exploration and subsequently as a business development executive. When I learned of their meeting, I admired her courage. Her visit to Massad and her decision to leave Mobil in order that our relationship could continue further cemented our bond, and we were married on January 16, 1981.

We have two sons, Aksel named for my father, and Harry. Valerie is a very committed mother and puts a great deal of time into her relationship with the boys.

Valerie's professional life has followed a fascinating direction. She was elected to the board of Alberta Energy Company then was appointed by the prime minister as a director of the Bank of Canada. After Alberta Energy's merger with PanCanadian Petroleum to form EnCana, Valerie became chair of the board's environmental committee. EnCana became widely recognized for its efforts in responsible environmental management during her tenure. Subsequently, she joined the board of Cenovus, the oil sands company created by EnCana. In addition, Valerie was elected and continues to sit on the board of Wajax, a national distributor of heavy equipment, diesel engines and industrial components, headquartered in Ontario. She was also elected the president of the Calgary Chamber of Commerce—the first woman in the city's history to have that position. Valerie developed the idea of my writing this memoir. Although I was at first reluctant, she persisted, and I finally agreed.

What I remember most fondly about the corporate competition are my peers in the big companies, especially the Canadians. Their accomplishments put mine in an important context: I wasn't the only Canadian executive

Our sons Aksel and Harry, 2001.

doing big and interesting things during the best years of oil exploration in this country.

At Chevron, Gerry Henderson was, for a time, the only other Canadian besides me to run a multinational oil company. Gerry was a tremendous exploration geologist. He led the discovery of oil at Hibernia and the West Pembina pinnacle reef discovery, the last of the conventional crude oil elephant discoveries in western Canada. Gerry was one of the most admirable men in the oil industry in his time and a huge contributor to the success of the over-all industry.

Another Canadian who led a multinational oil company, Bill Gatenby of Texaco Canada, was a farmboy like me, only he grew up in Saskatchewan. Like me, he loved baseball, but he was really good at it, a great player. That got him a scholarship to the University of Oklahoma where he studied engineering.

Valerie and me, 2001.

Another great Canadian was Jack Macleod at Shell Canada. Although he came from Nova Scotia, Jack became a Calgarian to the bone. He was a super guy, a great guy to deal with and died of cancer at far too young an age, but not before he brought a lot of honour to Shell and to the industry in general.

Imperial Oil always had one top executive in Toronto and one in Calgary. The person in Toronto was the boss. The man in Calgary ran the exploration and production operation. Bill Twaits was in Toronto during my years, and he was followed by Jack Armstrong. Bob Petersen was the man in Calgary for most of my career. He was with the company a very long time, and I know him well. More recently, Esso was run by Doug Baldwin who is now chairman of Talisman Energy. If you knew these leaders, you also knew why Imperial was such a successful enterprise.

BP had some good people in Canada, too. Among them, Ted Best and Fred McKinnon both had huge impacts on our industry. I also had great admiration for another Canadian, David Mitchell, who was a member of the National Advisory Committee on Petroleum when he was at BP. He became the founding president of Alberta Energy Company and when AEC merged with PanCanadian to become EnCana, David, who was retired, continued to play an advisory role with the company as its "Dean."

James Buckee, the chairman of Talisman, was the number-two guy with BP when BP decided to withdraw to England. Buckee stayed here and set up Talisman. He has a "good old British" background, and he hired a lot of "good old British" staff. Talisman has proved to be successful in Canada and internationally. The other notable Englishman who had a top executive position in western Canada was Charles Lee. He ran a storied independent company called Western Decalta Petroleum. He was a thoughtful man who was one of the spokespeople for the industry in the 1960s and 1970s. His partner, Al Ross, was a member of NACOP with me.

Three men at Gulf are lodged in my memory for their excellence as leaders: Stan Pearson, Oscar Erdman and Harry Carlyle. Carlyle and I made the deal that gave Gulf an interest in all of Mobil's East Coast holdings and Mobil a piece of their Canadian Arctic plays, including the Mackenzie Valley.

Finally, there was my neighbour on Britannia Drive, Jack Gallagher. He loved to jog and one day he knocked on my door in his jogging clothes, came in and proposed a deal with Canadian Superior involving our joint major properties in the Beaufort Sea. We made a deal that day in my living room. Gallagher also tried to persuade me to become the president of PanArctic Oils. He was an excellent geologist and executive, and the combination contributed to Dome's success as an exploration company in western Canada and the Arctic. He found a lot of oil and gas, and he hired good people who found even more. And he had a great knack for raising money. One of the people he hired was a Manitoba lawyer named Bill Richards. Gallagher and Richards ran Dome together. It was a real disappointment when the company got into financial trouble and Jack and Bill had a falling out. Jack fought against the Amoco takeover of Dome. He wanted Dome back and to have a second chance at running it. He had political connections and wanted to be appointed to the Senate of Canada. However, he died prematurely of cancer.

At my age, one is surrounded by the ghosts of family, friends and colleagues. My ghosts rank with the best of human beings, the most successful and, at times, the most tragic. The best people I knew in the oil business were all honourable. They had proven technical and professional abilities and they were leaders, top-notch communicators with superior human relations abilities. Certainly, we did well for ourselves and we had political power—often, when society looks at the oil industry, it can't see past those two things—but we also created lasting value for others, substantial wealth for our shareholders, our country and our age.

This is our real legacy.

Epilogue

IN THE SPRING of 2008, my boyhood home was moved from the farm my parents settled before the Great War and where I grew up to the Danish Canadian National Museum and Gardens in Dickson, Alberta. All the children but my brother, Gerhardt, moved away from the small wood-frame house—twenty-eight feet by thirty-two feet with four rooms. After my mother died, it remained father's residence and he stayed there until his death. Gerhardt lived with him and they farmed the land together. After my father died, Gerhardt married and his wife, Mavis, didn't wish to live there, so the farm passed out of family hands.

Dickson is located in west-central Alberta where the rolling parklands rise up to the foothills. It was another Danish community, founded prior to Standard. My father and his group from Iowa had briefly considered settling there when they first came to Canada but rejected that idea in favour of accepting the CPR's offer at Standard. Much later, my preacher brother, Ejvind, was the pastor of the Danish Lutheran Church there for a number of years.

Now, the Nielsen house will be restored and refurbished and be open for the visitors who will come there to learn, not just the history of the Danish people in Alberta, but of the hardships and rewards of the development of rural Alberta in the province's first decades. In future years, thousands of visitors will cross the first threshold of my life and tread on the same floors that I crawled on as an infant.

It's quite a privilege to become part of history while still alive.

Index